WHY
BUILDINGS
FALL DOWN

WHY BUILDINGS FALL DOWN,

How Structures Fail

MATTHYS LEVY
and
MARIO SALVADORI

Illustrations by
KEVIN WOEST

W · W · NORTON & COMPANY
New York   London

The text of this book is composed in Aster
with the display set in Avant Garde Gothic
Manufacturing by The Maple-Vail Book Manufacturing Group.
Book design by Jacques Chazaud

Library of Congress Cataloging-in-Publication Data
Levy, Matthys.
    Why buildings fall down: how structures fail / Matthys Levy and
Mario Salvadori.
        p.   cm.
    Includes index.
        1. Building failures.   2. Structural failures.   I. Levy, Matthys, 1929–
Salvadori, Mario George, 1907–   II. Title.
    TH441.L48   1992
    690'.21—dc20   91–34954

ISBN 0-393-03356-2

W.W. Norton & Company, Inc., 500 Fifth Avenue, New York, N.Y. 10110
W.W. Norton & Company Ltd., 10 Coptic Street, London WCIA 1PU

1 2 3 4 5 6 7 8 9 0

To the memory of my mother-in-law, Judith Book-
man, who, upon receiving on her ninety-second
birthday the first copy of *Why Buildings Stand Up*,
said matter-of-factly: "This is nice, but I would be
much more interested in reading why they fall
down."

MARIO G. SALVADORI

To the children yet unborn
For whom discovering the past
Will open the door to the future.

MATTHYS P. LEVY

Contents

Preface

It seemed almost unavoidable that having written a book entitled *Why Buildings Stand Up*, I should be pushed by my friends (and my wonderfully friendly editor, Edwin Barber) to write another called—what else?—*Why Buildings Fall Down*.

I have at long last given in to the temptation of explaining structural failures in lay language, a simple but exciting task, but only because the coauthor of another of my books, Matthys Levy, a master of structural design, has enthusiastically accepted to write it with me.

He and I can apply eighty-five years of design and teaching experience, and sixty of investigations into structural failures, to the job of helping us relieve the fears of the uninitiated, while taking the reader on an interesting and, we hope, entertaining trip that will make the reader see buildings as never before: with a clear understanding of why they stand up and why, yes, but once in a blue moon, they fall down.

Mario Salvadori

Acknowledgments

Besides those we might have unjustly forgotten, we thank the following friends who helped us bring this book into print and do this in an alphabetical order that is not to be interpreted as a hierarchy of gratitude:

Edwin F. Barber, our patient, friendly, encouraging, and skillful master editor

Mindy Hepner, our word-processing expert who almost allowed us to meet our schedule

Julie Hubley Levy, understanding critic, enthusiastic and loving supporter

Landon Prieur, the Weidlinger Associates librarian, who ferreted out valuable hidden sources of information

Carol B. Salvadori, private editor and copy reader to one of us, who translated into correct English all the Italianate chapters of this book

Erica Vogt and Midge Esterman, our extraordinary secretaries at Weidlinger Associates, who, unbelievably, succeeded in putting this book together.

Introduction

Once upon a time there were Seven Wonders of the World. Now only one survives: the mountainlike Pyramid of Khufu in the Egyptian desert near Cairo.

The other six have fallen down.

It is the destiny of the man-made environment to vanish, but we, short-lived men and women, look at our buildings so convinced they will stand forever that when some do collapse, we are surprised and concerned.

Our surprise may be partly due to the fact that most of us judge buildings by their facades: They look beautiful when very old and ugly when very young, the opposite of human faces. But this kind of judgment is superficial and misleading; a much better metaphor for a building is the human body.

A building is conceived when designed, born when built, alive while standing, dead from old age or an unexpected accident. It breathes through the mouth of its windows and the lungs of its air-conditioning system. It circulates fluids through the veins and arteries of its pipes and sends messages to all parts of its body through the nervous system of its electric wires. A building reacts to changes in its outer or inner conditions through its brain of feed-back systems, is protected by the skin of its facade, supported by the skeleton of its columns, beams, and slabs, and rests on the feet of its foundations. Like most human bodies, most buildings have full lives, and then they die.

The accidental death of a building is always due to the failure of its skeleton, the *structure*. Since the readers of this book are interested in learning why buildings fall down, they expect from us an explanation of structural failures. But just as medical doctors consider health to be the norm and disease the exception, and gain most of their knowledge from illness, so engineers consider standing buildings the norm and structural failures the exception, although they learn a lot from failures. Our readers then should know why almost all buildings stand up. This may appear a difficult task. Buildings serve so many purposes and come in so many shapes. They consist of so many materials meant to resist so many kinds of loads and forces. How can a mere layperson understand how structures work?

Luckily one need not be an expert. Structural behavior can be understood by the uninitiated on the basis of physical intuition and without appeal to physics or mathematics simply because whatever the structural system—the steel frame of an office building or the dome of a church—whatever the materials used in construction—steel, wood, reinforced concrete, or stone—and whatever the forces acting on it—caused by gravity, wind, earthquake, temperature changes, or uneven settlements of the soil—the elements of a structure can react to these forces only by being *pulled* or *pushed*.

Come along with us then on this voyage of discovery. Once you appreciate how structures behave, you will also learn that as if they had a social duty toward us, structures always do their very best *not to fall down*.

The readers eager to acquire a better understanding of why almost all buildings stand up may refer to the appendices of this book, where the basic behavior of structures is explained in simple terms and without any appeal to notions of mathematics or physics.

WHY
BUILDINGS
FALL DOWN

1

The First Structural Failure

If you wish to control the future, study the past.

Confucius

According to the Old Testament, the early inhabitants of the earth, the ancient Babylonians, were "of one language, and of one speech." Linguists, with the help of archaeologists, paleontologists, and geneticists, have been able to reconstruct between 150 and 200 words of this Babylonian-claimed *proto-world* language, the earliest we know of in humanity's one hundred thousand years. It is a magnificent thought: one people, one language. But our earliest forefathers were not content. So ambitious were they that they determined to build a city with a tower reaching heaven, and God, offended by their pride, broke their single speech into so many different languages that the Babylonians, unable to understand one another, were stymied in their plan, and their tower collapsed. The God offenders were scattered over the face of the earth: "Therefore is the name of it called Babel [from the Hebrew *balal* (to mix up)]; because the Lord did there confound the language of all the earth."

Thus was the first structural collapse attributed to the Almighty, an excuse denied to today's engineers, despite events known in the trade as "acts of God." In their hearts, engineers know that a simpler explanation can be found for the collapse of the Tower of Babel. Even the toughest stone would eventually crack under the weight of more and more stones piled up on it, and even if the mythical tower had not reached such a height, an earthquake would have brought it down because the earthquake forces grow in proportion to the weight of a building and the square of the height.

Of the Seven Wonders of the World, only one stands today: Khufu's pyramid in Egypt. What happened to the other six? Several, like the Hanging Gardens of Babylon, probably were abandoned and died. The Pharos (lighthouse) of Alexandria in Egypt, completed by Sostratus Cnidus in the reign of Ptolemy II, c. 280 B.C., which is estimated to have been an incredible 350 ft. (105 m) high, was demolished by an earthquake in the thirteenth century. The Greek Mausoleum of Halicarnassus of c. 352 B.C., built in today's Turkey in memory of Mausolus of Caria, was also demolished by an earthquake in the fourteenth century and became a quarry supplying stone to the Knights of St. John as they built their castle. Some of its sculpture was recovered in 1856 by Sir Charles Newton, who shipped it from Halicarnassus to the British Museum in London. The Temple of Artemis, at Ephesus in Greece (now Turkey), built c. 550 B.C., burned down in the fourth century B.C., was rebuilt in the third, and was destroyed by the Goths when they sacked Ephesus A.D. 362. The Colossus of Rhodes in Greece and the Olympian Statue of Zeus in Athens, the work of the greatest sculptor of antiquity, Phidias, in 435 B.C., were probably vandalized by later invaders or dismantled to recover the golden decoration of Zeus' image. Only Egypt's pyramids remain standing after almost five thousand years, *but not all of them:* The Pyramid at Meidum has shed 250,000 tons of limestone outer casings, and what remains of it is a three-step structure emerging from a sea of sand and stone blocks (Fig. 1.1).

The Egyptian pyramids were built to solve four problems, all essential to that first of all centralized states, but each of a basically different nature: the solution of the mystery of death, a spir-

itual problem; the assertion of the divine power of the pharaohs, a
political problem; the employment of the peasant masses during
the Nile's floodtime that made the valley fertile but deprived them
of work, a social problem; and the need of an observatory for the
study of the heavens, a scientific problem.

The shape of these man-made mountains is the most logical for
monuments of great height (up to 481 ft. [144 m]) to be erected in
a country where the only available structural material was stone:
the local stone along the northern banks of the Nile used to build
the central mound and the white limestone of the southern Tura
quarries for the finished outer casings. The Egyptians did not know
the block and tackle, did not use the wheel for transportation of
heavy loads, and knew no metal harder than copper. It is amazing,
therefore, to realize that they cut, transported, and erected pyramid blocks weighing from 2.5 tons (2.3 million of them for the Great
Pyramid at Gizeh) to 20 tons (for the roof of the king's chamber
there).

1.1 Pyramid of Meidum

In the belief that the dead had to be surrounded by all the conveniences of life in order to be happy, the all-powerful Egyptian priests filled the pyramid chambers around the king's sarcophagus with his most precious possessions and closed them with ingenious stone doors to prevent thievery. Then, as now, the thieves were smarter than the police, and the treasures were looted throughout thirty Egyptian dynasties.

Aware that the top stones of a pyramid had to support only their own weight, while the bottom blocks supported the weight of *all* the stones above them—6.5 million tons in the Great Pyramid at Gizeh—they adopted for the sloping faces of all of them, except two, a angle of 52°, which gives a height of 2 / π or about two-thirds of the side of the square base.* Thus the increasing weight supported from the top down burdened a larger and larger number of blocks, and the pyramids had a geometrical shape similar to that of most mountains. This is the natural shape caused by gravity, since the main forces *usually* acting on both pyramids and mountains are due to their own weight, the so-called *dead load*.

We can now ask: Was the Meidum Pyramid so poorly built that it could not even support its own weight? Historians have explained the Meidum disaster as caused by the theft of pyramidal blocks to place in other monuments and temples. The trouble with this hypothesis is that there are no temples or cities in the neighborhood at Meidum. Most of its two-ton blocks lie around its base. It is now believed that the casings' blocks collapsed as a consequence of an earthquake. But it may be objected: How come this happened at Meidum and at no other pyramid? Here is where engineering design explains the reason of this exception, together with the story told by the other two pyramids at Meidum.

Learning the lesson of the Meidum Pyramid, the designers of the next pyramid, the Bent Pyramid at Dahshur (Fig. 1.2), which

---

* Since it is believed that the Egyptians measured distances by counting the number of turns of a circular wheel, their use of the ratio 2 / π does not prove that they knew the exact value of π (the ratio between the circumference and the diameter of a circle), since this value disappears in the *ratio* of two lengths both measured in terms of π. In fact, they gave π the biblical value 3. It is more likely that the ratio was derived as $\sqrt{\emptyset/2}$ where $\emptyset = 1.618$ is the golden number which is defined as the ratio of the major to the minor segment of a line, equal to the ratio of the whole line to the major segment. The greeks, the Romans, and the Egyptians imbued the golden section with magical aesthetic properties.

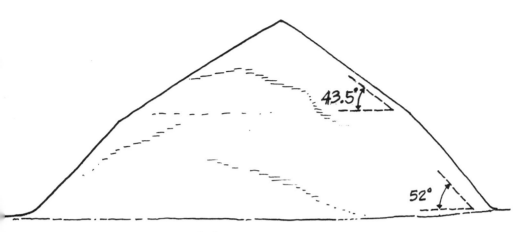

1.2 Bent Pyramid at Dahshur

had been started with a slope of 52°, continued it, from about two-thirds of the way up, at the safer angle of 43.5°. That angle gives a ratio of height to side of only 1.5 / π or about one-half rather than two-thirds of the side. The next pyramid, the Red Pyramid at Dahshur, was erected from day one at the safe angle of 43.5°, but from then on all the pyramids standing today used the classical slope of 52°.

A careful inspection of the Meidum Pyramid reveals two significant features that explain both its collapse and the more daring angle of its successors. The bottom casings, still intact, show that the pyramid was started at the 52° angle but that the foundation under these casings rests directly on desert sand rather than, as usual, on rock and that the casings blocks are set in *horizontal* layers and not *inclined inward,* as in all other pyramids (Fig. 1.3). Thus two relatively *minor* design decisions were responsible for the catastrophe, since a sandy soil magnifies the earthquake forces and setting the casings horizontally made it easier for them to slide out and fall to the ground.

1.3a   Meidum Pyramid Foundation

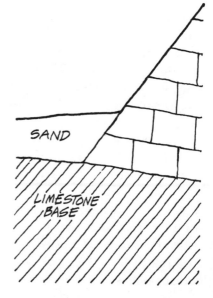

1.3b   Standard Pyramid Foundation

This lesson was not lost on Imhotep, the greatest mathematician and engineer in Egyptian history, whose design of the Great Pyramid at Gizeh in the Fourth Dynasty was imitated in all technical details in all later pyramids. Imhotep was made a god and venerated by the Egyptians for three thousand years. We cannot help remembering that poor Filippo Brunelleschi (1377–1446), a devout Catholic, was not even beatified although he built *without a scaffold* the magnificent dome of the Florence cathedral, Santa Maria del Fiore, which could well be considered a miracle.*

---

* Unfortunately two miracles are required to be made a blessed and four for sainthood.

2.1 Empire State Building

2

Miracle on Thirty-fourth Street

A Throw of the Dice Will Never Eliminate Chance.

Stéphane Mallarmé

King Kong, the hyperthyroid gorilla from the classic 1933 Hollywood movie, climbs up the limestone face of New York's Empire State Building to escape his captors. From his lofty perch, holding on to the spire with one hand, he swats attacking planes with the other. For the world's largest gorilla, no other image but the world's tallest building could set the stage for such a mortal combat. Far above the landscape of other New York skyscrapers, the Empire State Building (Fig. 2.1) rises majestically, 1,250 ft. (381 m) into the sky, its top often shrouded in low-hanging clouds.

On July 28, 1945, nearly three months after the defeat of the Nazi government and the end of the war in Europe, on the very

day the U.S. Senate ratified the United Nations Charter, Lieutenant Colonel W. F. Smith, Jr., took off at 8:55 A.M. from Bedford,
Massachusetts, in a B-25 bomber for a flight to Newark, New Jersey. With two other occupants, the plane flew on the gray morning
at an estimated 250 mph (400 km/h) arriving in the New York
area less than an hour later. Lieutenant Colonel Smith was advised
by the control tower at La Guardia Airport that the ceiling, the
distance from the ground to the clouds, was less than 1,000 ft. (300
m). This implied that clouds and fog would have obscured the tops
of New York's skyscrapers, especially the then tallest, the Empire
State Building.

The pilot, flying under visual rules, was required to maintain 3
mi (5 km) forward visibility. If unable to do so between La Guardia
and Newark airports, he was required to land at La Guardia. Smith
ignored that requirement. Continuing toward Newark, he was seen
heading in a southwesterly direction, weaving through the maze
of skyscrapers over Manhattan and crossing low-hanging clouds.
Heading toward Forty-second Street, the plane flew down out of a
cloud at no more than 400 ft. (120 m) above the ground, at which
point it started climbing in a right turn. In an effort to slow the

POINT OF
COLLISION

2.2   Seventy-ninth Floor: Collision Area

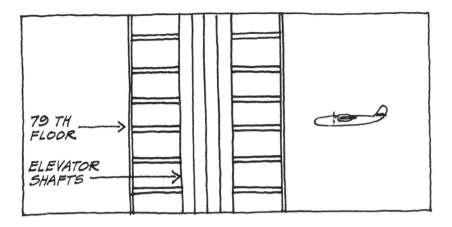

2.3a B-25 Just before Impact

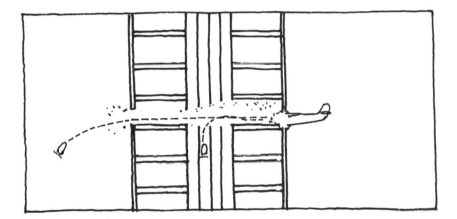

2.3b Impact and Path of Motors

plane, the wheels were lowered moments before the plane struck the Empire State Building on the north face of the seventy-ninth floor, 913 ft. (278 m) above the ground, ripping a hole 18 ft. (5.5 m) wide and 20 ft. (6 m) high in the outer wall of the building (Fig. 2.2). The force of the impact sheared off the wings of the plane and propelled one of the two motors across the width of the building, through the opposite wall, and down through the twelfth-story roof of a building across Thirty-third Street, starting a destructive fire that demolished the studio of Henry Hering, a noted sculptor of the time (Fig. 2.3). The other motor and part of the landing gear crashed into an elevator shaft and fell all the way down to the subcellar onto the top of an unoccupied elevator. Two women in another elevator fell seventy-five stories when the cable holding their cab snapped, cut by flying shrapnel. Miraculously they escaped with their lives, although they were seriously injured, when automatic devices sufficiently slowed the free fall of the cab. Flames from the burning gasoline killed most of the thirteen victims, including the crew of the plane.

"I couldn't believe my own eyes," said a witness, looking out from the 103d-story observatory, "when I saw the plane come out of the overcast. Then it struck the building with a force that sent a tremor through the whole structure." The crash spilled gasoline from the ruptured tanks, which immediately ignited, illuminating the tower of the building for a brief instant before it disappeared again in the mist and the smoke from the burning plane. As the spilled gasoline burned, flaming debris rained down the face of the building. The ebullient mayor of the city, Fiorello La Guardia, arriving, as usual right behind his fire fighters, on the scene of the inferno at the seventy-ninth floor, was seen shaking his fist and muttering: "I told them not to fly over the city."

The center of impact aligned almost exactly with a column on the face of the tower. The right motor passed on one side of the column and the left motor on the opposite side (Fig. 2.4). The column itself was barely damaged, although a steel beam supporting

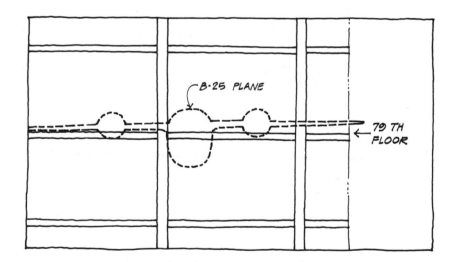

2.4   B-25 Straddling Column

the masonry wall struck by the right motor was torn out, and a second beam supporting the floor slab was bent back 18 in. (450 mm). The plane apparently struck the seventy-ninth floor dead-on, which explains the lack of damage to the column. Had the plane been just a bit higher or lower, it might have struck and bent the column, and then . . .

What happened in 1945 was a consequence of the *redundancy* inherent in a frame structure (see p. 55 and Chapter 5). A frame structure is one in which beams and columns are rigidly connected, either welded or bolted together. The connections in the frame of the Empire State Building were executed with rivets, as was customary at the time of its construction in 1932. The building, with columns spaced about 19 ft. (5.8 m) on center in both directions, was like a centipede that can compensate for the loss of a leg by redistributing its weight to the remaining legs. This is redundancy, an essential and common characteristic of structures that survive accidental damage or partial failure. (Every instance of collapse described in this book may be attributed to lack of redundancy.)

In quantitative terms, the impact of the ten-ton plane smashing into the extremely stiff eighty-thousand-ton building is close to trying to move the proverbial immovable object. The Empire State Building was designed to resist a wind load momentum two hundred times the momentum of the B-25. Lieutenant Colonel Smith's plane dealt a great whack, but even the reported mild shaking reported by witnesses is consistent with the plane's small weight compared with the building's mass. The same witnesses described the movement as a "double (back and forth) movement" and then a "settling." Unlike a guitar string which vibrates back and forth for a long time, the tower finds its movements arrested as if by a brake, a characteristic called *damping*. Older heavy masonry-clad towers exhibit strong damping because of friction between the elements of its structure and those of its walls, while modern lighter skyscrapers sometimes vibrate in long, wide undulations sufficient to cause seasickness to the occupants. Some poorly damped tall buildings have to be evacuated when wind velocities reach critical values, and on such occasions the patrons of a well-known rooftop café in New York are given the option of a rain check or a free drink when the chandelier starts swinging back and forth.

The dramatic impact of the bomber with the Empire State Building raises the question of the probability of such a catastrophe. Occasionally, nowadays, an aircraft will crash into a building near an airport during landing or takeoff. But no plane has hit a skyscraper since the Empire State catastrophe. The accident closest to such an event occurred when a helicopter's landing gear crumpled as it set down on the rooftop landing pad on the fiftieth floor of New York's Pan Am Building on May 16, 1977. The craft tipped over, snapping off one of its rotor blades, which flew off like a boomerang, killing four people on the roof and a walker-by on the street below when the blade spiraled down from the roof. "There was nothing but screaming metal and glass flying," said one witness as the runaway blade smashed into the ground. After an investigation the landing pad was permanently closed in recognition of its potentially dangerous central city location. With the increasingly sophisticated instrumentation of modern airplanes, the likelihood of such an event's happening again is ever smaller—a real blessing if we consider the increasing air traffic around the world's cities.

3

Will the Pantheon Stand Up Forever?

> Not all that shines is gold.
>
> British proverb

The pyramids of Egypt, all but one, have laughed at gravity, heat, wind, rain, lightning, and earthquake for almost five thousand years. They even survived with equanimity the guns of the Ottomans, which turned on them, seeking to blast their way into the treasures of the pharaohs.

But we, children of a different era, do not want our lives to be enclosed, to be shielded from the mystery. We are eager to participate in it, to gather with our brothers and sisters in a community of thought that will lift us above the mundane. We need to be together in sorrow and in joy. Thus we rarely build monolithic monuments. Instead, we build domes.

The dome, equally curved in all directions, is a Platonic shape of ideal perfection, a man-made sky apparently unbound and yet

3.1   Pantheon: Interior View

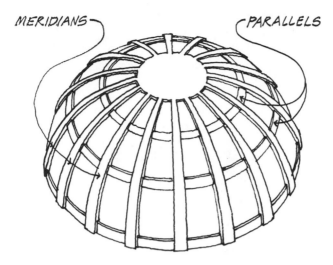

MERIDIANS

PARALLELS

3.2 Meridians and Parallels of a Dome

protective, a beacon from afar and a refuge from within, inexplicably beautiful and miraculously strong. The large dome had its humble origins in the small domed rooms of the Assyrians thirty-three hundred years ago or so. By A.D. 200 dome technology had produced the majestic and massive Pantheon, the Roman temple to all the gods (Fig. 3.1), and it goes on to even greater glory: in the light masonry roof of Hagia Sophia in Constantinople, floating over the light of its windows since A.D. 537; in the roof of Santa Maria del Fiore, erected without a scaffold above the tile roofs of Florence by Brunelleschi in 1420; and in the double dome completed in Rome by Giacomo della Porta in 1590 over St. Peter's, the architectural masterpiece of Michelangelo and the largest church in Christendom. Having lasted longer than most man-built structures, will these domes ever collapse? How were they given such amazing stability?

Domes are the most impressive members of a family of structures, called *form-resistant* by the great Italian structuralist Pier Luigi Nervi because they owe their stability to their curved, continuous shape. A dome may be naïvely thought to be a series of vertical arches (its meridians) rotated around a vertical axis and sharing a common keystone, and in fact, a dome does carry to earth its own weight and the additional weights on it by such a mechanism. But these imaginary arches are not independent of each other; they are, so to say, glued together and, hence, *work together* (Fig. 3.2). While an arch needs massive outside buttresses to prevent its

3.3 Hagia Sophia, Istanbul, Turkey

opening up and collapsing, the ideal vertical arches of a dome cannot open up under load and do not need buttresses, because their parallels, the ideal horizontal circles of its surface, act like the hoops of a barrel that keep the staves together. (Of course, in order to act like hoops, the parallels must be capable of developing a relatively small amount of tension, at least in the lower part of the dome [see p. 297, Fig. D17]). Thus, because of the interaction of the meridians and the parallels, domes are not only exceptionally strong against gravity loads but extremely rigid.

It is this rigidity that makes domes sensitive to soil differential settlements and earthquakes and causes them to collapse. The dome of Hagia Sophia partially collapsed in 553 and 557 and again in 989 and 1436, always because of earthquakes (Fig. 3.3). Its architects, Anthemius of Tralles and Isodorus of Miletus, probably knew that a dome of a material weak in tension should be buttressed uniformly all around its base. Unfortunately the requirements of the new Christian liturgy demanded a church in the shape of a cross with unequal arms, unable to provide uniform buttressing. The Byzantines hadn't had such a problem; they had built their churches until then with four equal arms. The dome of Hagia Sophia was not finally stabilized until 1847–49 by the Swiss architects Gaspar and Giuseppe Fossati, who circled the base with iron chains. Similar remedies had been implemented a few centuries earlier to stabilize the domes of Santa Maria del Fiore in Florence and of St. Peter's in Rome (Figs. 3.4 and 3.5).

Oddly, our oldest domes, so girt by chains, may have a better chance of surviving than many recent ones. Scientific knowledge of structural materials and systems was not at all sophisticated until the beginning of the nineteenth century, and being aware of their ignorance, architects-engineers opted to choose conservative structures, often heavier (although not necessarily stronger) than necessary. Moreover, ancient domes, always held in such awe by succeeding generations of worshipers, are monitored uninterrupt-edly and carefully maintained. How could a Roman citizenry allow the collapse of the dome of St. Peter's or, for that matter, how can

3.4 Santa Maria del Fiore, Florence, Italy

3.5 St. Peter's, Rome, Italy

any American allow the collapse of the Washington Capitol? And yet our tendency to build ever more daring structures with ever-decreasing amounts of new materials can lead to unexpected failures, and domes are not excepted.

Blown-up Domes

The people of Florence were not surprised when, in 1417, a forty-year-old member of the goldsmiths' guild, by the name of Filippo Brunelleschi, won the competition for the completion of their cathedral, interrupted for almost two centuries by the financial needs of warfare (Fig. 3.4). The task was to build a dome. All the other architects had presented design proposals requiring the dome to be supported by costly wooden scaffolds during construction, but Brunelleschi had convinced the committee in charge of the bids that his design could be erected *without* a scaffold! Since no mathematical calculations were available at the time to prove Brunelleschi's brash assumption, he obtained the job by illustrating his proposed procedure for the erection of a double dome by means of a brick model. No more convincing proof could be offered today, when formwork costs as much as the concrete domes poured on them. The committee was convinced and appointed him but put Lorenzo Ghiberti in over him. A fellow guild member and sculptor, although a year younger than Brunelleschi, Ghiberti was already famous for his design of the bronze portals of the Florence baptistery, so incredibly beautiful they were nicknamed the Gates of Paradise. Brunelleschi had lost the competition for the design of the gates and was resentful of this appointment. He became suddenly ill and took to bed but recovered miraculously only two months later upon hearing that the construction of his dome had been stymied and Ghiberti fired. He began then to raise the dome in 1420 and died in 1446, just before the lantern he had designed was ready to be lifted to the top of the dome. He is buried in the cathedral next to a plaque expressing the admiration of the Florentines for their great son.

From the mid-nineteenth century on dome technology advanced rapidly. The invention of reinforced concrete in the 1850s, the mathematical proof of the amazing structural properties of curved surfaces in the 1890s, the greatly reduced labor involved in pouring a concrete dome compared with the demands of a masonry or tile dome, and finally their greatly reduced thickness and weight of reinforced concrete domes made them popular in the first half of the twentieth century as the cover for all kinds of large halls. The interior dome of Brunelleschi's masterpiece had weighed 350 psf or pounds per square foot (17.5 kN/m² or kilo Newtons per square meter), while a concrete dome spanning the same diameter (147 ft. [44 m]) with a thickness of only 8 in. (200 mm) weighs 100 psf (5 kN/m²). If we consider that an eggshell is nothing but two domes of minimal thickness that are glued together but that cannot be squashed by the pressure of our hands and realize that the ratio of span to thickness in an eggshell is about 30 while that in a conservatively designed concrete dome may be 300, we will appreciate that a concrete dome is ten times thinner than an eggshell but just as strong. No wonder modern domes are called *thin-shell domes*.

Thin concrete domes can be built on lighter scaffolds, but labor costs make curved formwork expensive to erect, and a number of procedures have been invented to reduce their cost. In 1940 the concept of a form made out of an inflatable balloon was proposed and used by the California architect Wallace Neff for a dome spanning 100 ft. (30 m). Neff's procedure consisted in inflating a balloon of sailcloth made airtight by wetting, then laying on it the flexible reinforcing steel bars and spraying on it increasing thicknesses of concrete using a concrete gun. A number of such bubble houses were built in Florida using Neff's system.

A more ingenious and economical procedure based on the balloon concept was introduced in the 1960s by the Italian architect Dante Bini. Bini used a spherical balloon of plastic fabric, laying the reinforcing bars *and* pouring the concrete on it *before* it was inflated, then lifting the wet concrete *and* its reinforcing by pumping air in the balloon. Two days later the balloon was deflated, openings (for the door and windows) were cut in the concrete with a rotary saw, and the balloon was pulled out, ready to be reused. Dante Bini is without a doubt the builder of the largest number of domes in history, more than fifteen hundred of them, 25 to 300 ft. (7.5–90 m) in span, in twenty-three countries, from Italy to Australia and from Japan to Israel, but *none* in the United States.

The Binishell operation is simple but delicate. It requires the experience of a well-trained crew. It is also important to realize that the final shape of the dome, structurally essential to its resistance, depends on four factors: (1) the air pressure in the balloon; (2) the tension developed in the spiral springs used to keep in place the reinforcing bars and the wet concrete; (3) the weight and distribution of the concrete; and (4) the (variable) air temperature during the time it takes the dome concrete to set (Fig. 3.6). To balance these four factors, the pressure in the balloon must be carefully monitored, automatically or by hand. Too high a pressure lifts the top of the dome and modifies its shape; too low a pressure dangerously flattens the top of the dome, depriving it of its curvature and transforming it into a weak, thin, flat slab. The influence of these factors explains the collapse of two Binishells in Australia, the only ones ever to collapse of the many built, singly or in a variety of combinations, for schools, gymnasiums, tennis field roofs, one-family houses, and grain and chemical storage.

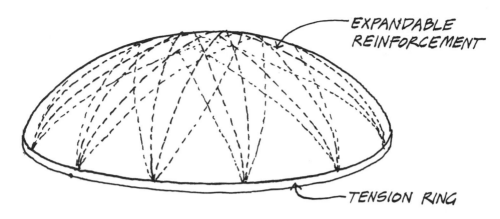

EXPANDABLE
REINFORCEMENT

TENSION RING

3.6 Partially Inflated Binishell

The first Binishell collapse occurred two days after the erection of a 120 ft. (36 m) diameter dome housing a rural school. The shell had been erected during an exceptionally hot spell followed by a sudden thunderstorm that lowered the air temperature by 50°F (28°C). The reduction in the balloon pressure responding to this thermal change flattened the dome so dramatically over a circular area of 40 ft. (12 m) diameter that the operator immediately activated the fans but, because of his inexperience, did not stop them in time so that the flat section was raised above the design level. In trying to correct this overpressure, the operator kept raising and lowering the pressure in the balloon, flattening and raising the top of the shell and developing in it a crack along the 40 ft. (12 m) diameter circle (Fig. 3.7). Upon deflation of the balloon this portion of the shell first developed an inverted shape and then collapsed entirely, while the remaining part of the shell stood up.

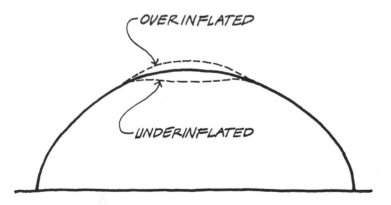

OVERINFLATED

UNDERINFLATED

3.7   Binishell Collapse—the Result of Over- / Underinflation

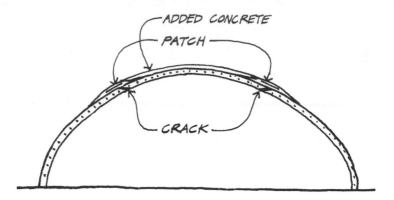

3.8   Binishell Collapse—the Result of Added Weight of Concrete

A second Australian school dome developed an identical circular crack that was immediately noticed by the engineer on the site. Remedial action was taken without delay. It consisted of adding meridional steel bars in the area of the crack and pouring concrete over them and then pouring more concrete over the area of the shell above the crack (Fig. 3.8). This additional concrete did not become monolithic, did not, in fact, blend with the hardened shell concrete, and the original dome was thus weighed down by a considerable added dead load. When concrete is loaded above its allowable stress, it slowly "creeps"—that is, gives in under load in the overstressed areas. The original dome, because of its small thickness, could not support the added load and slowly flattened. Ten years after erection it became inverted and collapsed, luckily without human loss. We believe that these two exceptional failures show the exacting requirements of the Binishell technology. On the other hand, the successful experience with similar construction in underdeveloped countries indicates that it may be safely adopted even where technology is not advanced.

Why hasn't the Bini technology invaded the United States so far? A careful study of the U.S. development of buildings for other than religious purposes shows that with a few minor exceptions, no proposed designs in a *round* configuration have been successful, whatever the materials or the technology involved. The United States is a country of highly standardized equipment and materials. Eighty percent of one-family housing in the United States is built by the owners, who are not professional builders. Most of those houses come to the site completely finished on a trailer or are prefabricated in a factory and assembled on-site in a few days. In this environment, buildings with a circular plan present difficulties for the insertion of standard windows and doors as well as for placement of furniture conceived for rooms with a rectangular plan. One may even speculate that interesting and even economical as they may be, curved spaces are alien to our culture for historical reasons that have produced inherited psychological prejudices. This prejudice may be quite old. Although the nomadic American Indians lived in round tepees, the Anasazi of the Chaco Canyon in northwestern New Mexico lived in stone houses on rectangular bases up to five stories high. They limited the use of curved

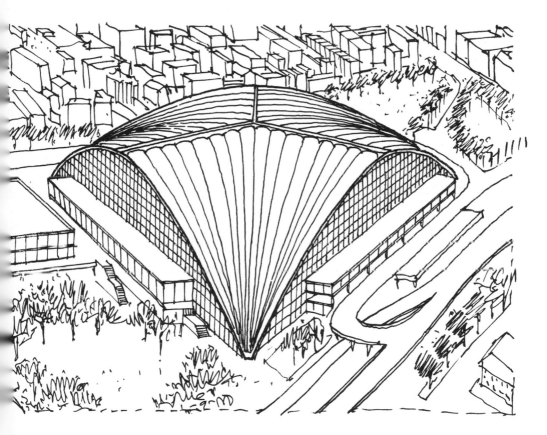

3.9 Centre National des Industries et Techniques (CNIT) Dome, Paris, France

walls to buildings with religious and social purposes. Moreover, since we are mostly the descendants of recent European pioneers, whose ancestors (with rare exceptions) lived in rectangular buildings for over twenty-five hundred years, we may conjecture that an ingrained mental objection to curved buildings may by now be congenital in us.

The largest dome ever built, the concrete, triangular double dome of the CNIT (Centre National des Industries et des Techniques), in Paris, 720 ft. (216 m) on a side, was originally dedicated to technological exhibits. At present it covers a deluxe hotel and a mall of chic stores (Fig. 3.9). Hagia Sophia in Constantinople, first a Christian church and then a Muslim mosque for centuries, is now a museum (Fig. 3.3). The aborigines of Tierra del Fuego may have erected stone domes, but they limited their use to religious purposes and lived in the open air, exposed to the glacial winds eternally blowing from the South Pole. If we add to all the other probable causes of our dislike of round spaces our newly developed skills in the construction of large, *flat* roofs, we may surmise that the kingdom of the dome may be near an end. Some of us are nostalgic about it, but progress cannot be stopped. Moreover, we know that each historical period must create its own monuments, and we are building ours according to our aesthetic feelings and our new technologies. Let the domes be.

The C. W. Post Dome Collapse

In 1970 C. W. Post College, part of Long Island University, built an elegant theater center seating thirty-five hundred spectators on its lovely 360 acre (146 ha) campus at Brookville, Long Island, New York. Known locally as the Dome Auditorium, the dome was supported on a circle of steel columns, connected at the top to a horizontal canopy that rested on an external brick wall. The 170 ft. (51 m) shallow dome carried its weight and the superimposed loads of snow, ice, and wind to the circle of columns by means of forty meridional trusses of steel pipes (Fig. 3.10). The trusses were hooped by horizontal steel parallels in the shape of a channel ([), creating a hybrid structure that imitated in part the large steel section American domes and in part the lighter European steel pipe domes. The top of the dome was strengthened by a steel compression ring, and the bottom by the circular canopy acting as a tension ring. The

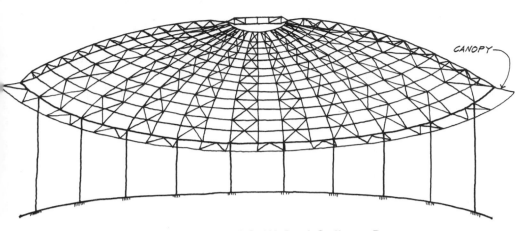

3.10 Diagrammatic Layout of C. W. Post College Dome Structure

rectangular meshes of the reticulated structural network were cross-braced by two diagonal steel pipes at *alternate* sectors between adjacent trusses. The dome roof surface consisted of plywood panels covered by a thermal insulating material, called Tectum, and a coating of a plastic, called Hypalon, for waterproofing.

The C. W. Post dome had little, if anything, in common with the classical domes of masonry or concrete. Its shallow profile had a ratio of rise to span of only 1 to 7, as against that of 1 to 2 of the Pantheon in Rome or the 1 to 1.35 of Brunelleschi's dome, *a quinto acuto** (Fig. 3.11), in Florence. Its structure was reticulated rather than continuous. Its weight of steel was less than 10 psf (0.5 kN/m²), compared with the hundreds of pounds of masonry or concrete in domes of similar span. The Dome Auditorium was considered a significant, daring building symbolic of our technological era. It had been honored with numerous architectural awards.

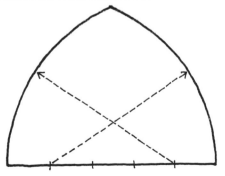

3.11 Arch *A Quinto Acuto*

* An arch in which a radius four units long springs from a base five units long.

The Butler Manufacturing Company of Grandview, Missouri, specialists in the construction of hangars for small planes, had designed, manufactured, and erected the dome using the patented Triodetic design, invented in Germany in the 1940s and used in the United States since 1965. It was designed in accordance with a classical simplified structural theory, usually applied to concrete thin-shell domes and known as the *membrane theory*. Its stability had been checked by a very recent theory proposed by James O. Crooker of the Butler Manufacturing Company and Kenneth P. Buchert, a professor at the University of Missouri, supported by the results of numerous tests on the difficult-to-analyze connections of the crimped-end pipes. The chief structural engineer of the Butler company stated in writing that "when properly erected on an adequate foundation, the triodetic dome would carry the prescribed loads of wind, snow and ice, and the structural dead load, as required by the governing codes." The auditorium had been last inspected in the fall of 1977—seven years after completion—by an inspector of the Brookville building department and found satisfactory. Permit of Occupancy No. 995 had been issued. On the back of the permit, handwritten unsigned notes stated that the drawings had been checked by the New York State Code Bureau. The dome had stood up proudly and safely for seven years under winter snows and island winds. Designers, manufacturers, erectors, and users, as well as the college administration, acting as general contractor and owner, could not have been more conservative, cautious, and satisfied. Or could they?

Between 2:00 and 3:00 A.M. on Saturday, January 21, 1978, the center dome suddenly caved in under mounds of snow and ice. "It looks like a giant cracked eggshell," commented Officer Stephen Chand of the Old Brookville Police Department (Fig. 3.12). Only four days earlier the 360 by 300 ft. (110 × 90 m) *flat* steel roof of the Hartford Civic Center Arena had collapsed under similar conditions (see p. 68), and one could have heard then the "amateur structuralists" comment on the traditional strength of the dome, the prototypical "form-resistant" structure: "They should have used a dome instead of a flat roof. It would have been stronger and cheaper!" But now. . . ?

Police, college officials, the press, and the representatives of the Insurance Company of North America, carrier for the university, rushed to the site. "We are thankful nobody was hurt," said Edward J. Cook, the president of the fifty-four-year-old institution, whose

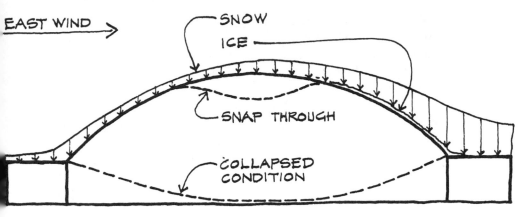

3.12 Stages of Collapse of C. W. Post Dome

fourteen thousand students were away on Christmas vacation. But the two-million-dollar auditorium had been destroyed, and *nobody* could or would say whether by the forces of nature or by structural mistakes in design or construction.

The experts were called in.

Three days later Nicholas W. Koziakin, a structural engineer with the renowned New York City office of Mueser, Rutledge, Johnston and DeSimone, inspected the site and, after numerous additional visits, presented on May 10 his thorough but qualitative report. He concluded mainly that the dome had been underdesigned by a simplified theory *inapplicable* to the reticulated dome structure, based on the assumption of *uniform* dead and live loads, and that the nonuniform snow blown on the dome by the wind, and the ice found under the snow the day of his first visit, may well have stressed the structure above allowable limits (Fig. 3.12). He advised that a more realistic model of the reticulated dome should be analyzed by a rigorous theory to check the design. Weidlinger Associates was entrusted with this analysis, and its report of May 1979 proved Mr. Koziakin's conclusions to have been entirely correct. As in some other structures, for the reticulated dome of the C. W. Post center "less was more." A snow load of only *one-fourth* the load required by the code but concentrated over a sector *one-third* of its surface was bound to collapse the dome! Indeed, that had been the story on the night of January 21, 1978, when a load of snow blown by an east wind had lodged onto the *leeward* side of the dome.

This interesting but somewhat puzzling result can easily be explained by the elementary *membrane theory* assumptions made in the design. This extremely simple theory was derived (toward the end of the last century) to evaluate the structural behavior of *perfectly* spherical or rotational dome shapes, which are made out of materials with *identical* properties at each point of, *and* in any direction on the dome surface (they are called *isotropic*), under gravity loads *perfectly* symmetrical about the vertical axis of the dome or, in case of winds, under horizontal loads equally *pushing* on the wind side and *pulling* on the leeward side of the dome. (The last assumption is contrary to the action of wind on actual domes and to test results on dome models in a wind tunnel. It was used before the advent of the computer and is now abandoned. Wind actually exerts *suction* over most of the surface of a shallow dome.)

Under these conditions the theory proves that symmetrical gravity loads per unit of dome surface (or, as assumed for the snow load, per unit of floor area covered by the dome) are carried to the dome circular support by the meridians stressed in compression and the parallels acting as hoops, *provided* the support forces, or reactions, act in a direction tangential to the dome surface. For example, they should act vertically upward on a dome in the shape of a half sphere (Fig. 3.13a) and in an inclined direction on a *shallow* dome (Fig. 3.13b). The membrane theory also shows that the hoop parallels *above* an opening angle of 52° are compressed and those *below* 52° are in tension (see p. 305, Fig. D27). In other words, in a shallow dome with an opening angle of less than 52° both meridians and parallels act in compression. Tests show that thin spherical domes of steel or concrete behave exactly as predicted by membrane theory *if* the conditions of the theory are strictly satisfied.

**3.13a Dome Reactions
—Half Sphere**

**3.13b Dome Reactions
—Shallow Sphere**

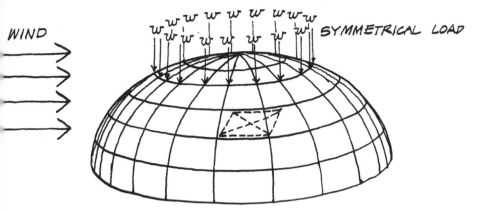

WIND

SYMMETRICAL LOAD

3.14 Skewing of Radial Ribs Caused by Wind

The application of membrane theory to reticulated domes is based on a clever but incorrect assumption: that they behave *as if* they were continuous and with a thickness obtained by spreading *uniformly* the weight of their framework over the surface of the dome. (Since reticulated domes weigh 5 to 10 psf [0.25–0.50 kN/m²] for spans of the order of 100 to 200 ft. [30–60 m], and steel weighs 490 lb. cu. ft. or pounds per cubic foot [80 kN/m³], the "equivalent membrane thickness" of steel domes varies between ⅙ and ⅓ in. [4 and 8 mm]!) It is fairly obvious that a reticulated dome does not have the same structural properties at every point and in all directions (it doesn't even exist at points *inside* its meshes); it is nonisotropic or *anisotropic*.

But perhaps the most dangerous consequence of using membrane theory in the design of shallow reticulated domes is that under symmetrical gravity loads its meshes *shrink* (slightly) on all four sides, *remaining square*, while under wind loads they become skewed (Fig. 3.14) and require diagonals to be stable. Finally, since most of the bars of the mesh are compressed, reticulated domes must be checked against the dangerous phenomenon of *instability in buckling as a whole*, which causes the dome to invert or *snap through*. (You may easily check instability in buckling by pushing down on a thin metal or plastic ruler that will bend out at right angles to its thin surface and lose all capacity to resist compression higher than a small push [p. 289, Fig. D4].) Rather unwisely the

C. W. Post dome had been designed with diagonal cross bracing between meridional trusses in every alternate sector, and additionally, the bracing was not designed to take substantial compressive forces but only to prevent the trusses from twisting, according to a code requirement that was incorrectly applied to the design.

Weidlinger Associates checked by computer these theoretical conclusions on a realistic model of the reticulated structure, and its results were validated by the ripping off of the roofing materials and inspection of the uncovered roof structure. All the compressed diagonals, inclined in the direction of the wind, were buckled, and those tensed were overstressed; the upper compressed ring was bent and twisted. For lack of an adequate stabilizing system the dome collapsed like a pack of cards. A variety of minor miscalculations was also noted in the design: The equivalent membrane thickness was taken half as thick as that obtained by spreading evenly the structural steel; the dead load of the structure had been undervalued by 17 percent; the compressive force in the meridional trusses had been allotted equally to their upper and lower chords, despite the fact that the trusses also bend. But the most significant error had been made in the evaluation of the dome's stability against *snap-through* (the phenomenon that collapsed the two Binishells discussed earlier in this chapter), leading to a coefficient of safety of 8.51 that gave false confidence in the dome's capacity against this dangerous phenomenon. Behind this statement lies an interesting story.

The theoretical buckling load for an isotropic sphere under uniform pressure was derived at the beginning of the century by the great Russian structuralist Stephen Timoshenko. He proved that it was proportional to the thickness of the shell and to the elastic modulus of the material (a coefficient measuring its strain under stress [see p. 279]) and inversely proportional to its radius. His formula for a steel sphere carries a coefficient $c = 0.6$ in front of it. Theodor von Karman, in collaboration with Hsue Shen Tsien, refined his derivation in the thirties and changed the value of c to 0.366, the value used in the Butler design. A search of the literature on the subject showed Mario Salvadori that the experimental value of c was at most 0.20. A safety factor of 3 is usually adopted against the danger of dome snap-through, reducing the design value of the coefficient c to 0.07 and leading to an *unsafe* value for the coefficient of safety equal to less than one-tenth the value of 8.51 used in the Butler design.

As shown in the following section, the failure of the C. W. Post dome was not unique. If there is a moral to the story of the Dome Auditorium collapse, it is simply that each new design must be analyzed by the results of the latest theories *and* experimental investigations and that a knowledge of elementary structural theory should not be trusted whenever one moves beyond the limits of traditional structures proved safe by their age. Approximate methods of design had to be used sometimes, even in our recent past, for lack of available theoretical knowledge or computing facilities, but designers aware of their limitations then used higher coefficients of safety. The structural engineer must be grateful for the incredibly swift progress achieved in computing during the last few decades that allows the routine solution today of problems that even master designers were unable to analyze only a few years ago.

Daring and prudence, when used together, lead to new *and* safe structures. Today we can be more confident than ever of our designs and hence more innovative, but if wise, we are also perpetually vigilant. This is why almost all our structures stand up.

The Puzzling Failure of the Bucharest Dome

In 1960 the municipality of Bucharest, Romania, decided to erect a large multipurpose hall to be used for exhibitions, public performances, and meetings. Designed by Dr. Engineer Ferdinand Lederer and fabricated in Brno, Czechoslovakia, the hall was inaugurated in August 1962. It was an imposing and elegant structure, consisting of a cylindrical base of reinforced concrete with glass walls, covered by a 307 ft. (93.5 m) diameter dome of steel pipes, with a rise of 1 to 5. A 57 ft. (16.8 m) diameter lantern, 10 ft. (3 m) high, covered its central area (Fig. 3.15).

The reticulated, steel pipe structure was visible from the interior of the hall in all its geometrical elegance. It consisted of three layers of pipes: the intermediate oriented along the parallels (or hoops) of the dome, the upper and lower along lines inclined at opposite angles to the meridians, together creating a mesh of almost equilateral triangles (Fig. 3.16a). At the points of intersection of the three layers the pipes were tied by *bridles*, strips of metal tightened

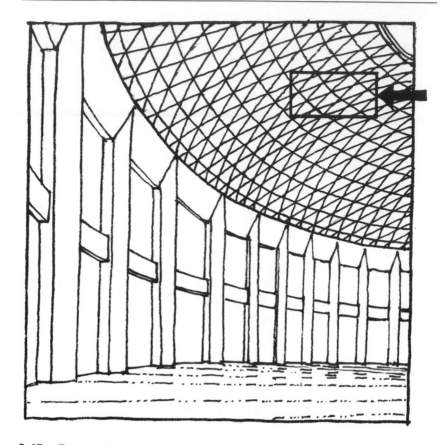

3.15 Dome in Bucharest, Romania

to prevent their sliding (Fig. 3.16b). The pipes had outer diameters varying from 1.5 in. (3 cm) to 4 in. (10 cm) and looked like thin pencil lines against the background of the roof deck of the dome. The weight (or dead load) of the roof—consisting of the pipe structure, the roof deck, and the outer aluminum panels—was 11.3 psf (55 kg/m²). The weight of the pipe structure was amazingly low, only 6.7 psf (33 kg/m²).

The fairly new structure of the dome was conservatively designed in accordance with the best engineering practice of the time. Besides its own weight, it was assumed to carry the concentrated loads of lights, scoreboards, and catwalks and a snow load uniformly distributed per unit of floor area of the hall or a nonuniform (antisymmetric) snow load with a maximum value twice that of the uniform load. The maximum wind pressure and suction were assumed equal, and the horizontal earthquake forces to be one-tenth of the dome's permanent load. All the values used for these forces would be considered acceptable today, although those depending on local conditions (wind, snow, and earthquakes) would probably be checked experimentally.

The European tendency to design very light dome structures stemmed from the designers' virtuosity and competitiveness but, more important, from economic considerations deriving from the high cost of materials and the relatively low cost of labor. In the Bucharest dome these suggested the adoption of the pipe structure

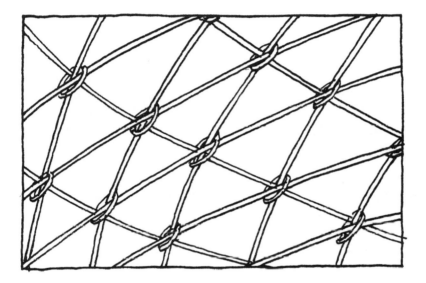

3.16a   Bar Arrangement in Bucharest Dome

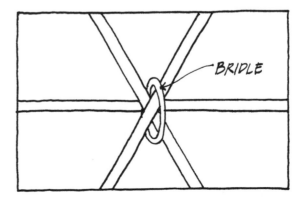

**3.16b
Detail of Bridle**

and, particularly, that of the bridle connections at the joints, which minimized the cost of one of the most expensive structural items in any reticulated dome, in terms both of materials and of labor. The dome in the Romanian capital looked like a triumph of high technology over the forces of nature and of economics. Its structural scheme had been successfully employed in Eastern Europe before, giving additional reassurance of its safety.

Unfortunately, as the saying goes, "All that glitters is not gold." On the evening of January 30, 1963, only seventeen months after its erection, the dome collapsed after a modest snow load, less than one-third the snow load it had been designed to support, had accumulated on it. Interestingly enough, the pipe structure was not torn apart; it just snapped through, hanging, almost undamaged in the shape of a dish, above the floor from the robust concrete ring at its base.

We have seen in the previous section that reticulated domes are often designed as if they were thin continuous shells, by uniformly spreading the material of the bars or pipes over their surface and estimating the thickness of the "equivalent" thin shell. This approach had been used by Lederer in designing the Bucharest dome, but without the help of the fundamental studies of D. T. Wright on the thickness of the equivalent shell (that were published only in 1965) and without a realistic assessment of the two most essential structural characteristics of a reticulated dome: its *local* and *overall* buckling capacities. The reader may remember the discussion in the previous section concerning the value of the overall buckling capacity of a thin-shell dome, which is expressed in terms of the value of a so-called *buckling coefficient*, whose safe value is assumed in good engineering practice to be ten times smaller than the value derived by purely theoretical considerations. In the design of the Bucharest dome the buckling coefficient was chosen twice as large as the safe value, leading us to believe that the Achilles' heel of the dome lay in a buckling weakness. Yet the collapse puzzle is not solved by this realization. Even if the buckling coefficient was *doubled* in the design, the snow load at the time of collapse was less than *one-third* of the design load and should not have buckled the dome. We owe the solution of this mystery to the investigation of the collapse by A. A. Beles and M. A. Soare, both of the University of Bucharest.

As emphasized in Appendix D, the unusual strength exhibited by a thin-shell dome stems from its monolithicity, which allows the shell to work as a series of arches along the meridians restrained by a series of hoops along the parallels. An inspection of the collapsed, inverted Bucharest dome showed the investigators that the snow had accumulated along five radial lines, with a weight almost twice that of the maximum nonuniform design load. This concentrated load had buckled the parallel pipes *locally* along five radial lines and developed radial valleys at right angles to the parallels (Fig. 3.17). Thus bent into a wavy shape, the hoops were unable to develop the compression needed to restrain the meridians, and as the dome started inverting, their wavy deflections increased in amplitude, further reducing their strength. Rather than behave as stiff rings around the surface of the dome, the hoops became flexible, and the dome lost the capacity to support its own weight and the (small) weight of accumulated snow.

Soare also remarked later that the bridle node connections had been entirely unable to prevent the relative sliding of the pipes meeting at the nodes. Rigid connections at the nodes of a reticulated dome are essential to maintain unchanged the geometry of the dome and to prevent bending deformations at the joints; no

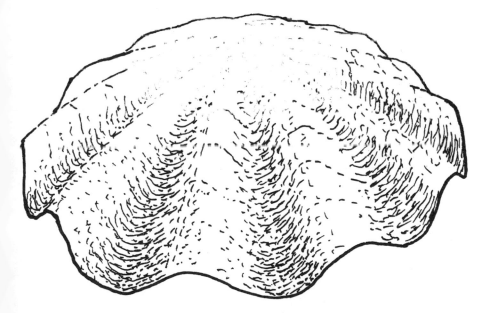

3.17 Local Radial Buckling of a Dome

light reticulated dome can be self-supporting without the satisfaction of these two conditions. Thus a probably minor saving in the cost of the connections may well have been a major contributory cause of the collapse.

Luckily nobody was killed or hurt in the collapse of the Bucharest dome. It was redesigned as a steel dome of standard sections (steel angles and wide-flange beams) and stands majestically again in the center of the Romanian capital, but with a structure *five times* heavier than that of the original dome. It would be interesting to speculate why the Bucharest dome stood up for seventeen months, going unscathed through a first winter, or why other domes, supported by structures identical to that of the Bucharest dome, are still standing in other parts of Eastern Europe. But these would probably be stultifying efforts since local conditions vary dramatically from site to site, and as we have just seen, a minor neglected factor may be the cause of a total collapse.

4

For Lack of Redundancy

For winter's rains and ruins are over,
And all the season of snows and sins. . . .

Algernon Charles Swinburne

Redundancy is a needed property of all languages. It is a safeguard that permits us to understand a sentence even if we miss some of the words. The degree of redundancy varies with the language: Russian does not have the article "the" but declines nouns; Italian has two forms of "the," one for masculine and one for feminine nouns, but does not decline nouns; Latin and German have masculine, feminine, *and* neutral nouns, pronouns, and adjectives *and* declines them all; Greek has singular, *dual*, and plural forms for verbs; but English does not decline and considers all these other redundancies to be unnecessary complications. On the other hand, ancient Hebrew lacked the verb "to be," without which we certainly would be unable to express our-

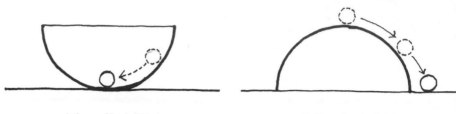

4.1a   Stability   **4.1b   Instability**

selves. The safeguard of a language to prevent total failure in communication, even when partial failure occurs, is perfectly analogous to the amount of redundancy the designer puts into a structure to avoid total failure in case of local failures and varies with the type of structure (see Appendix D). Structural redundancy essentially allows the loads to be carried in more than one way—i.e., through more than one path through the structure—and must be considered a needed characteristic in any large structure or any structure whose failure may cause extensive damage or loss of life.

The following two cases of catastrophic collapse are representative of the consequences of lack of redundancy in the main carrying mechanisms of large structures. In practice, *all* structural failures may be considered due to a lack of redundancy, but the two cases we illustrate here have in common one more interesting feature: Their *chain reaction* or *progressive* collapses were the consequence of local *elastic instabilities*. The simplest example of the difference between a stable and an unstable mechanical situation is demonstrated by a marble resting at the bottom of a bowl as against one balanced at the top of the same bowl turned upside down (Fig. 4.1). If the marble is displaced from its bottom position in the bowl, it tends to return to it and *stay there;* the marble is in a *stable* position. If the bowl is turned upside down and the marble is balanced at its top, even a small displacement of the marble tends to move it *away* from its original position—that is, to increase *irreversibly* its displacement. In this case the marble situation is *unstable*. In cases of *elastic instability* the characteristics of the structure are such that if either the *load* reaches a so-called *critical value* or its *stiffness* is *lower* than a critical value, a progressive increase in stress occurs in the first case, and a progressive increase in deflection occurs in the second. Since, moreover, such increases are irreversible, they lead to the failure of the structure in either case.

The Sudden Failure
of the Kemper Arena Roof

Kansas City, Kansas, and Kansas City, Missouri, the twin cities
across the confluence of the Ohio and the Kansas rivers, grew out
of historical settlements on the main trails followed by the pioneers
going west. Kansas City, Kansas, was incorporated first, in 1850,
and reached a population of 168,000 in 1970. Kansas City, Missouri, was incorporated in 1859 but soon overcame its twin sister
and by 1970 was a metropolis of more than 500,000 people, proud
of its Nelson Gallery, its museum of the arts, its symphony orches-
tra, and its university. Culture and wealth were popular in Kansas
City, and so were sports. In 1973 the Kansas City Royals, the local
baseball team, built themselves an open-air stadium seating 47,000
fans, and the Kansas City Kings, the local basketball team, a 17,000-
seat covered arena on the old site of the Royals Horse and Cattle
Fair. Named after R. Crosby Kemper, one of the city's founding
fathers, the Kemper Memorial Arena, also known as the Royals
Arena from its location, hosted the Kings' games before the team
was sold to Sacramento. Rodeos, ice shows, collegiate basketball
games, and the games of the Kansas City Comets, the local soccer
team, as well as crowds of large conventions, often filled its great
hall.

This superb arena was of such architectural significance that
the American Institute of Architects honored it in 1976 with one of
its prestigious awards and confirmed its importance as a monu-

4.2   Kemper Arena: Side View

ment by holding in it its 1979 national convention. The Kemper
Arena, designed by Helmuth Jahn of the renowned office of C. F.
Murphy, stood on a high, isolated site at the outskirts of the city,
its 4 acre (1.6 ha) roof and the upper part of its walls hanging from
three majestic portals of steel tubing and its self-supporting walls
enclosing the brightly illuminated interior space, 360 ft. (108 m)
long, 324 ft. (97 m) wide, and 60 ft. (18 m) high (Figure 4.2). Structurally elegant, functionally practical, and aesthetically pleasing,
the arena was a covered stadium to make Kansas City proud. It
cost the city $23.2 million, and all visitors to the growing metrop-
olis—whether fans, conventioneers, or just vacationers—considered it worth a side trip. Why was its glory marred after only
six years?

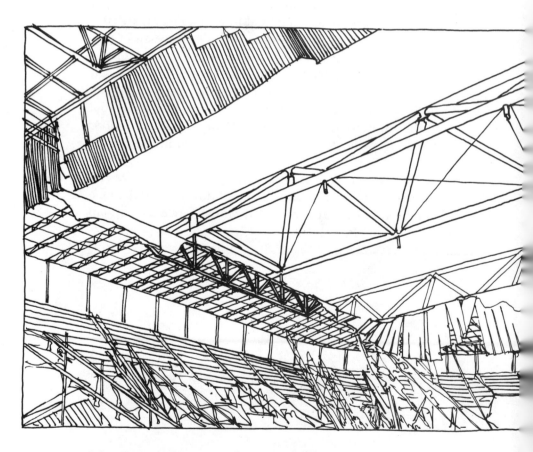

4.3   Kemper Arena: after the Collapse

On June 4, 1979, at about 6:45 P.M. a downpour of 4.25 in. (11 mm) of water per hour began falling on the Kansas City area, accompanied by a north wind gusting to 70 mph (112 km/hr). Twenty-five minutes later Arthur LaMuster, an arena employee and the sole person in it at the time, heard strange noises emanating from the great hall and went into it to ascertain their origin. When the noises suddenly became explosive, he barely had time to run out of the building before the central portion of the hanging roof, a 1 acre (0.4 ha) area, 200 by 215 ft. (60 × 65m), rapidly collapsed and, acting like a giant piston, raised the interior pressure in the hall that blew out some of the walls of the arena without damaging the portals. The floor, where thousands attending the American Institute of Architects Convention had been sitting only twenty-four hours before, became encumbered by twisted steel joists and trusses mixed with chunks of concrete from the roof deck (Fig. 4.3). Kansas City was stunned.

It took four years for the city's case against the members of the construction team to reach the court, while experts for all parties vied to determine the causes of the failure. These were apparently numerous, complex, debatable, and hard to prove, since no single cause could explain the collapse of such a modern, supposedly well-designed structure. Yet, to the surprise of the citizenry, the case was settled on the second day in court, obviously because all parties had agreed to avoid long, expensive litigation. The city recovered some, but not all, of the damages from its own insurance carrier on the arena and from the insurers of the construction team. As the Kansas City citizens asked to know how this disaster could have happened, the press reported an avalanche of witness and expert opinions, each having a different view of the collapse but all agreeing that rain and wind had a lot to do with it. On the other hand, everybody knew that during the six years the arena had stood it had survived, without apparent damage, more severe downpours and higher winds than those of June 4, 1979. Even a layperson understood that additional causes *must* have contributed to the failure.

Retained by one of the subcontractors of the arena structure to investigate the collapse, Weidlinger Associates was able to obtain all the documents pertaining to its design and construction and to reach a clear picture of this initially puzzling failure. To illustrate them, a not particularly difficult task, it will be necessary first to describe the unusual but brilliantly conceived structure of the arena.

The arena's structural system consisted of a reinforced concrete roof supported by steel trusses hanging from three enormous portals (Fig. 4.4). This schematic description of the structural system, unfortunately, is insufficient to explain the complex causes of the collapse and requires of the interested reader a more detailed understanding of how the roof was designed.

The basic structural elements supporting the loads of the roof itself and those acting on it, as well as the weight of the upper part of the walls of the arena, were three external space frames spaced at 153 ft. (46 m) in the north-south direction in the shape of rectangular portals, 360 ft. (108m) long in the east-west direction, and 81 ft. (24 m) high (Fig. 4.4). The horizontal element, or beam, of the portals consisted of a *space frame* of steel tubes with an equilateral

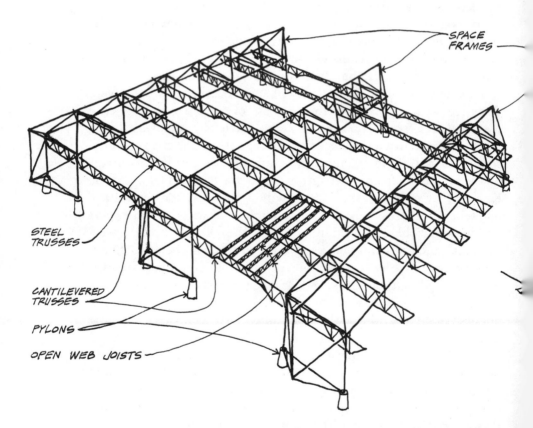

SPACE FRAMES

STEEL TRUSSES

CANTILEVERED TRUSSES

PYLONS

OPEN WEB JOISTS

4.4 Diagrammatic Layout of Structure of the Kemper Arena

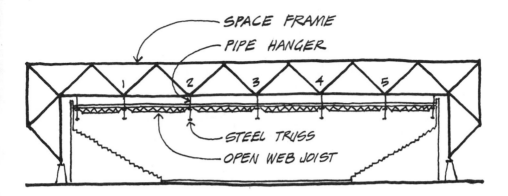

4.5 Cross Section of the Kemper Arena

triangular cross section, whose three sides were laced by zigzag-ging *diagonals,* connecting the two *lower chords* to the single *upper chord* of the beam (Fig. 4.5). The three sides of the triangular cross section were 54 ft. (16 m) wide. The vertical sides, or columns, of the portals were also triangular in cross section and were sup-ported by two reinforced concrete *conical footings,* 54 ft. (16 m) apart in the north-south direction, resting on underground piles (Fig. 4.4).

The roof structure consisted of concrete reinforced by a corru-gated steel deck (Figs. 4.4 and 4.5), supported on light steel *open web joists,* light trusses with steel angle chords and bent rod diag-onals, 54 ft. (16 m) long and spaced 9 ft. (2.7 m) in the north-south direction. The joists rested on the north-south system of trusses, each consisting of two trusses 99 ft. (30 m) long (referred to by the experts as the *drop trusses*), supported at their ends on three deeper 54 ft. (16 m) long trusses (referred to as the *cantilever trusses*). Finally, the truss system was hung from the lower chords of the three por-tals by forty-two *connectors* or *hanger assemblies* (seven in the east-west direction by six in the north-south direction) on a square grid 54 ft. (16 m) on a side.

The hanger assembly, because of its two essential functions, does not consist of a simple rod as the word "hanger" may have implied to the reader (Fig. 4.6). Since the weight of the roof itself is 26 psf (1.3 kN/m²), or about 1,500 tons, and since the roof was designed to carry 25 psf (1.25 kN/m²) of additional load caused by rain, the load of the mechanical systems, and other hanging loads (or about

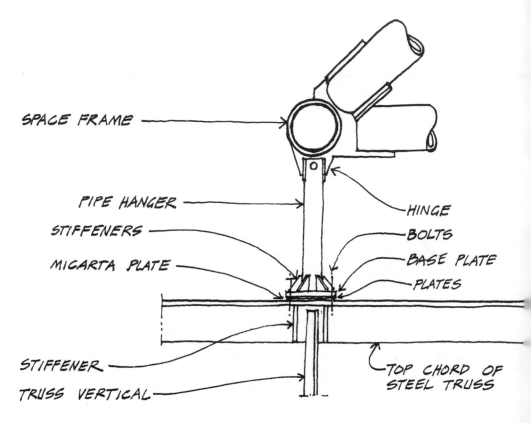

SPACE FRAME

PIPE HANGER

STIFFENERS

MICARTA PLATE

HINGE

BOLTS

BASE PLATE

PLATES

STIFFENER

TRUSS VERTICAL

TOP CHORD OF
STEEL TRUSS

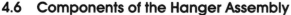

4.6 Components of the Hanger Assembly

another 1,500 tons), then each of the forty-two hangers was to support in *tension* 140,000 lb. (622 kN). Moreover, they had to resist the horizontal, variable wind forces (exerted on the roof and on the upper part of the walls hanging from it), which tended to move the roof horizontally as a gigantic pendulum. For this purpose six of the hangers were hinged both at their top and about halfway down their length, while the remaining thirty-six were hinged only at the top and connected (almost) rigidly to the top chord of the large trusses. While the two-hinge hangers allowed the roof to move as a pendulum, the single-hinge hangers limited the horizontal roof motions to the *bending* deflections of these hangers (Fig. 4.7).

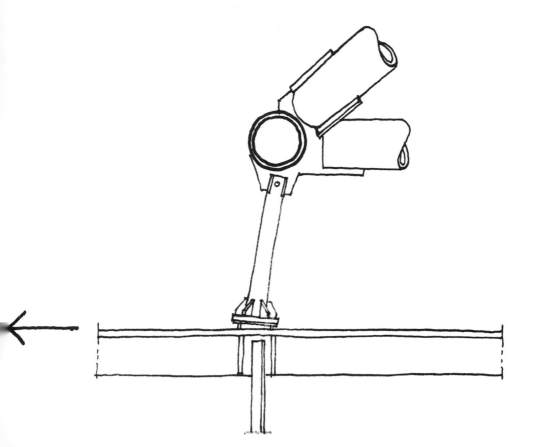

4.7 Hanger Assembly: bent by Lateral Force

   The connection between the bottom of the hangers and the bottom chords of the trusses consisted of a steel base plate with four vertical stiffeners and four holes through which four high-strength steel bolts were tightened (Fig. 4.6). To guarantee good contact between the base plate and the trusses' top chord, a thin plate of a plastic composite, called Textolite, was sandwiched between these two elements so that this connection was not entirely rigid. It has been estimated that during the six years preceding the failure these connections were subjected to at least twenty-four thousand oscillations, which in turn introduced oscillating variations in the initial tension of the bolts. As explained in Chapter 8, steel subjected to stress oscillations suffers from *fatigue* and fails at lower load values than under steady loads. Because of the type of steel used in the high-strength bolts (called *A490*), steel codes warn against their use under variable loads, something that may not have been taken into account in the arena design, possibly because the coefficient of safety of the bolts *under design loads* appeared to be sufficiently high. By now it must be obvious to the reader that the minute details of the design of the hanger assemblies have been so carefully described because they may have had an important role in the failure of the arena roof.

In rapidly growing towns with temporarily overloaded sewer systems, it is not unusual for roof drainage systems to be designed not to dispose immediately of sudden downpours of rain but to use roofs as temporary reservoirs and to limit the flow rate of the roof drains. The 129,000 sq. ft. (12000 m²) roof of the arena had been provided with only eight 5 in. (130 mm) diameter drains deliberately prevented from discharging more than at a modest rate (one-tenth of a cubic foot of water per second [0.0015 m³/sec]) when the water on the roof reached 2 in. (5 mm) of depth. (For a maximum downpour with a chance of occurring once in ten years the Kansas City code requires one such drain every 200 sq. ft. (19 m²) of roof, or 55 drains.) The drains allowed substantial water accumulation on the roof, limited only by scuppers (openings) along the perimeter of the roof, through which the rainwater could fall directly to the ground in an emergency. These were set 2 in. (5 mm) above the roof level and enabled the roof to store, as in a pool, at least that much water on the periphery and more in the interior of the roof, where the roof deflection would result in a greater depth of water.

The water accumulation on the roof was aggravated by two wind actions: the 70 mph (112 km/hr) gusts that pushed (by horizontal friction) the accumulated water from the north to the south portion of the roof and the upward suction, decreasing from north to south, created by the wind in turning from a vertical direction along the north wall to a horizontal direction on the roof, a phenomenon known as the *Bernoulli effect*. The Bernoulli suction also propelled the water from the north to the south portion of the roof.

As if all the causes we have mentioned so far were not sufficient to produce a dangerous accumulation of water on the southern portion of the roof, a purely structural phenomenon must be added to the list. When water accumulates over a stiff horizontal structure, its elastic deflections are small enough to allow us to neglect the small amount of added water in the shallow, barely curved structure (Fig. 4.8). On the contrary, when a horizontal roof structure is flexible, the amount of water gathering on its downward bent shape increases its deflection, which in turn allows more water to gather on it, which induces greater deflection, in a vicious circle of increasing loads and deflection making the roof structure *unstable*. This so-called *ponding* of a horizontal roof depends on the stiffness of the structure and on the unit weight g of the liquid accumulating on it. For a given structure, if the *critical g* producing ponding is greater than the unit weight of water (usually taken as one), the roof is stable; if g is smaller than one, the roof is unstable.

For a common structure, consisting of a rectangular grid of main and secondary beams (a two-degree system), ponding formulas have been derived and adopted in all structural codes. In the case of the arena roof, if only the contributions of the joists and the trusses were taken into account in computing the roof stiffness, the roof would have most probably appeared to be stiff enough to be stable. But when the ponding formulas were extended to a four-degree system, including the deformations of the deck, the joists, the trusses, *and* the long span portals, the critical value of g was found to be only 0.627. The Kemper Arena roof was unstable and allowed an increasing amount of water to accumulate up to a depth of 9 in. (229 mm) at the drains.

Numerous experts inspecting the fallen sections of the roof all agreed that the first bolts to fail were those of hangers No. 1 in Fig. 4.5, followed by those of hangers 3, 2, and 4 in the same figure, all

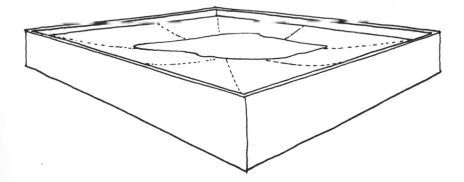

4.8 Ponding of a Flat Roof

of them in the south half of the roof. A simple calculation then proved that if a *single* hanger failed because of bolt fatigue, the adjoining hangers, unable to carry the additional pull from the failed hanger, would rapidly fail in a chain reaction as the result of *lack of redundancy*. (The explosive sounds reported by Arthur LaMuster were most probably those of snapping hangers.)

It is thus seen that the collapse of the Kemper Arena could not be explained by a single cause and that intensity of rain downpour, drain deficiencies, wind effects, fatigue of bolts, and lack of redun-

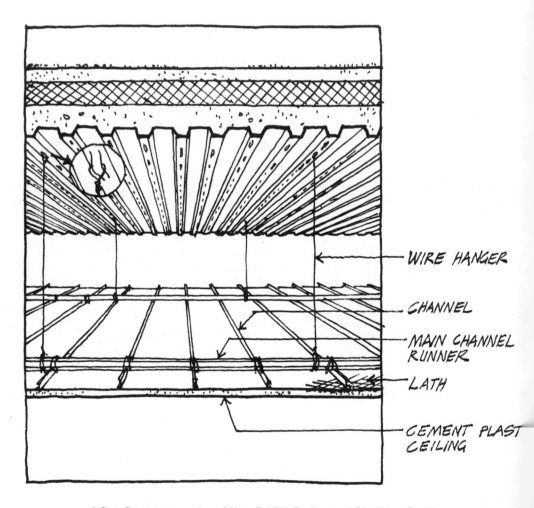

4.9   Components of the PATH Railroad Station Ceiling

dancy all contributed to the catastrophe. Some press reports at the time attributed the failure to the bolts, thus making the collapse more easily understood and more dramatic (SINGLE BOLT COLLAPSES ARENA!), but technologists know that rare are the cases in which one can clearly attribute a structural failure to a single, undebatable cause. Engineering reality is usually complex and subtle.

The Kemper Arena looks today again exactly as it did before the collapse, but . . . the center of the roof has been raised by 30 in. (760 mm) and now slopes down toward the perimeter, fourteen drains have been added at the roof perimeter, the hangers have been modified and welded to the trusses, the trusses have been strengthened, and the joists made deeper, all at the cost of $5.2 million. By September 1979 the reconstruction was in full swing, and by 1981 the "new" arena was triumphantly inaugurated, just as another tragedy struck Kansas City (see Chapter 15). When in 1983 the collapse case reached the court and was settled in two days, the disaster had been practically forgotten, a rare example of structural and administrative wisdom.

In a final remark, we must point out that the quick resolution of the case of the Kemper Arena collapse may have been due in large measure to the fact that the catastrophe did not involve casualties, a rare occurrence in the failure of a large structure. But casualties may occur even in minor failures. In the failure of a hung precast concrete ceiling at the train station of the PATH system in Jersey City, New Jersey, in 1983, the damage involved was small in comparison with that of the Kemper Arena and due to a single cause: the lack of redundancy in the simple wire hanger system from which the ceiling hung inside the station (Fig. 4.9). As a worker was checking the wire connections between the ceiling and the roof deck, one of the metal attachments connecting the wire to the deck above failed, and the remaining wires snapped in a rapid chain reaction, killing two pedestrians instantly when the fifty-ton ceiling fell on them.

It must not be thought that the size of a failing structure is in any way related to the damage it may do. The following story of the dramatic collapse of the roof of the Hartford Arena is a good demonstration that pure luck is an important component in human affairs, even when they involve technology.

Hartford Arena Roof Collapse

On the evening of January 17, 1978, Horace Becker was staying at the Hartford, Connecticut, Sheraton Hotel in a room facing the Civic Center Arena. As he retired, he looked out the window and saw snow falling heavily for the second time that week. In the middle of the night (it was actually 4:15 A.M.) he was awakened by what sounded like a "loud cracking noise," which continued for some time. Startled into a fully awakened state, he looked out the window again and saw, diagonally across the street from the hotel, the northwest corner of the arena roof rise and the center sink with a whooshing sound. Within seconds the windows of his room had started to shake, and thinking that a plane had crashed on the building, Mr. Becker dropped to the floor. When the noise stopped,

4.10   Hartford Center Roof: after the Collapse

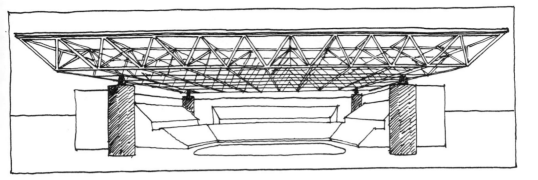

4.11 Hartford Center Space Frame Diagram

he looked out again and saw the other three corners of the arena also pointing skyward. Like a four-cornered hat, the 2.4 acre (9.7 ha) roof of the arena had settled down in the center, throwing up a cloud of debris in the air and tossing pieces of roof insulation down on the parking deck immediately below Mr. Becker's room (Fig. 4.10).

That same night roofs fell in two other Connecticut towns. Three days later, after a third heavy snowfall, the roof of the auditorium at C. W. Post College on Long Island collapsed (see p. 42). In fact, throughout that winter hundreds of roofs fell under the weight of unusually heavy snowfalls, but none was as dramatic as the Hartford collapse. Had the roof fallen six hours earlier, many of the five thousand fans watching a basketball game might have been killed or injured. Luckily, the fourteen hundred tons of twisted steel, gypsum roofing panels, and insulation fell on ten thousand empty seats.

The arena roof (Fig. 4.11) measured 300 by 360 ft. (91 × 110 m) and was constructed as a *space frame*, 21 ft. (6.4 m) deep, a structure consisting of top and bottom square grids of horizontal steel bars with joints, or *nodes*, 30 ft. (9 m) on center connected by diagonal bars between the horizontally staggered nodes of the upper and lower grids. The resulting space frame looked like a series of linked pyramidal trusses. The 30 ft. (9 m) long top horizontals were braced by intermediate diagonals, and the main diagonals were braced at their midpoints by an intermediate layer of horizontal bars.

The top horizontal bars of most space frames perform a double function: They support the roofing panels, and they act as upper structural members of the space frame. In the Hartford roof, however, the roofing panels were supported on short vertical posts above

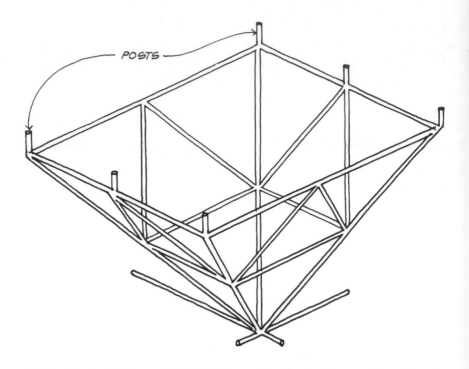

POSTS

4.12   Typical Pyramid Module with Posts Supporting Roof Panels

the top nodes of the space frame (Fig. 4.12). The designers claimed two advantages for this scheme: (1) If the height of the posts was varied, the roof could be sloped to provide positive drainage independently of the original level and the deflections of the top bars of the space frame, and (2) the top bars of the frame would not be subjected to bending stresses from roof loads.

Additionally, three unusual concepts characterized the design of the Hartford roof: (1) The frame's top horizontal bars were configured in the shape of a cross built up of four steel angles (Fig. 4.13). (Unfortunately the cross is not a particularly efficient section for a compression element because it bends and twists under relatively small stresses and hence *buckles* more easily than if the same amount of material were used in a tube or an I bar shape.) (2) A truss *node* is usually the theoretical point where the center lines of all the bars connected at the node intersect, but in the Hartford frame the top horizontal bars intersected at one point, and the diagonal bars at another, somewhat below the first. Thus the forces transmitted between diagonal and horizontal bars caused bending stresses in these bars (Fig. 4.13). (3) The overall space frame roof was supported on four enormous pylon legs located 45 ft. (13.7 m) *inboard* of the four edges of the space frame, rather than on boundary columns or walls (Fig. 4.11).

In spite of the unusual aspects of its design the frame appeared to be sturdy. For five years, it withstood the harsh Hartford weather before suddenly failing on that winter night although it gave many hints of impending danger, surprisingly ignored by architects, engineers, builders, and inspectors.

Vincent Kling, a well-known Philadelphia architect, was engaged in 1970 as architect of the proposed Civic Center, and he hired the Hartford office of Fraoli, Blum & Yesselman, Engineers to design the structure of the arena. Early in the design phase the engineers proposed a unique roof structure that they thought would save half a million dollars in construction cost but that required a complex computer analysis to check its safety. The city gladly granted the additional fee for this money-saving analysis, which proved to everybody's satisfaction the innovative structural scheme was safe.

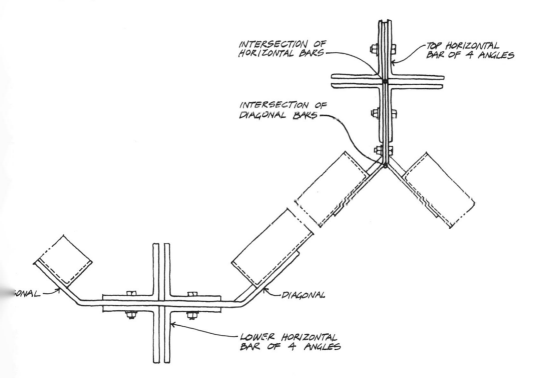

4.13 Diagonals Eccentrically Connected to Cross-Shaped Chords

A year later the construction documents were completed, the project was put out to public bid, and the construction of the roof structure was awarded to the Bethlehem Steel Company of Bethlehem, Pennsylvania. Gulick-Henderson, an inspection and testing agency, was engaged to ensure correct execution of the design.

A unique aspect of the construction procedure concerned the method of erection. Instead of the frame's being assembled in place almost 100 ft. (30 m) above the ground, a costly, time-consuming, and somewhat dangerous procedure, it was completely assembled on the ground. Not only was the structure bolted together, but the heating and ventilation ducts, the drain pipes, and the electrical conduits, as well as the service catwalks, were assembled while the structure sat on the ground. Only a badly timed painter's strike prevented the structure from receiving its final coat of light gray paint before erection. Assembly of the roof frame, begun on the floor of the arena in February 1972, was completed by July of that year. *It was during this short assembly time that the engineers were notified by the inspection agency of a suspicious and excessive deflection of some nodes, but soon the roof was ready to be lifted, and it began to move up slowly.*

The lifting process was completed in two weeks by means of hydraulic jacks fixed to the top of the four pylons. It was an impressive and awe-inspiring sight to see a roof the size of a football field rising slowly upward, day after day, in preestablished steps. *A concerned citizen who witnessed the operation questioned the capacity of such an immense structure to withstand the forces of wind and snow but was reassured by the engineers that he had no reason to worry.*

In January 1973 the roof, in its final position but not yet burdened by the weight of the roof deck, was measured to have a deflection at the center *twice* that predicted by the computer analysis. When notified of this condition, *the engineers expressed no concern, explaining that such discrepancies had to be expected in view of the simplifying assumptions of the theoretical calculations.* The contractor installing the fascia panels covering the space frame at the top of the four facades claimed that the actual boundary deflections of the structure were so random that when he tried to mate the prepunched holes in the two pieces of steel of the space frame and the facade panels and to insert bolts, he encountered such difficulties (because the holes did not line up) that he had to weld rather than bolt the joint.

By mid-1974, after the roof was completed, another technically minded citizen expressed concern about the large dip he had noticed in the roof that he believed might indicate an unsafe structure. *Once again the engineer, this time joined by the contractor, assured the city that there was no reason for concern.* Finally, in January 1975, a few days before the official opening of the center, a councilwoman made it public that a construction worker had told her the actual deflection of the roof was almost twice the predicted value. In light of the earlier assurances, this "political" concern was not even referred to the engineers, but independent measurements taken three months later by the city confirmed the anomalous deflections. By this time such statements were probably treated as rumors based on earlier allegations.

Five years later the roof collapsed.

Within days of the collapse experts had been retained by the city to address the issue of the responsibility and possibly the culpability of contractors, architects, and engineers (who engaged their own experts to protect their respective interests). This army of experts crawled like ants over the wreckage for weeks, looking for clues to the cause of the disaster, while the city announced: "We'll build a new structure. . . . It will be bigger and better, and it will have a different kind of roof."

The first question explored by the experts concerned the weight of snow and ice that had accumulated on the roof the night of January 17. Accurate measurements showed that the actual weight (the live load) of the accumulated snow from the two storms preceding the collapse was about half the live load specified by the code; the weight of the roof (the dead load), was also checked and turned out to be 25 percent greater than that assumed in the design. However, the sum of the dead and live loads was less than the total load assumed in the design. In any case, the *code safety factor* should have easily taken care of even such an accidental overload.

Attention was then directed to the configuration of the actual structure in comparison with the mathematical model postulated by the designers. The structural model had assumed that *all* the top chord bars were braced laterally by the *inclined* secondary diagonals, and this was the case in the interior of the space frame where diagonals form a pyramid (Fig. 4.12). But along the frame edges, the diagonals and top bars were *in the same inclined plane;* hence buckling out of this plane was not prevented. The top bars were free to bend outward, or *buckle,* in a direction perpendicular

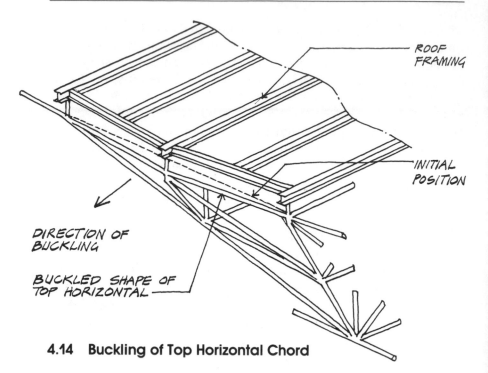

ROOF
FRAMING

INITIAL
POSITION

DIRECTION OF
BUCKLING

BUCKLED SHAPE OF
TOP HORIZONTAL

4.14   Buckling of Top Horizontal Chord

to that plane (Fig. 4.14). Prevention of buckling would have required the *outer top horizontals* to be four times stiffer than the typical *interior* top horizontals because the outer horizontals had *twice* the unbraced length. Since the top horizontals were the same size as the interior horizontals, they were doomed to buckle.

The question remained: Why did the roof survive for five years?

To answer this puzzling question, a study was made of the *progressive* failure of the roof. A computer model of the roof structure with correct buckling lengths and stiffnesses of *all* bars was "loaded" in steps, searching for the value of the load at which the *first* bar would buckle. This load was conservatively evaluated (by ignoring the springlike restraint offered by the actual connections) to be 13 percent *below* the total load actually on the roof on the day of failure. Loading of the model was increased further to explore what happened *after* the first bar buckled. When a member of a frame buckles, it transfers its load to adjacent bars that most of the time cannot carry the extra load and then also buckle. The failure of additional bars transfers their load *progressively* to new bars until the roof cannot carry any greater load and begins to collapse. This collapse live load was found to be only 20 percent above the actual measured snow and ice load and to cause a progressive inward folding pattern of the roof similar to that observed after the failure. Since no real structure is quite as perfect as the equivalent computer model, the actual failure of the Hartford Civil Center roof must have taken place at a load somewhat above that causing the buckling of the first bar and below that calculated as the ultimate collapse load. Progressive collapse can start as the result of even a minor deficiency unless *redundancy* is introduced as a matter of structural insurance, and it is sad to note that the addition of less than fifty bars to brace the top outer horizontals to a frame consisting of almost five thousand bars would have made the Hartford roof safe by preventing bar buckling.

Once the wreckage was cleared away, the firm of Ellerbe Architects of Minnesota began planning for a new arena. True to the promise of the city fathers, it was bigger, seating four thousand more spectators than the old one. Its roof was simpler, with two ordinary parallel vertical trusses sitting on the same four pylons raised up 12 ft. (3.6 m) to fit the grander facility (Fig. 4.15). Secondary trusses were framed into these primary trusses at six locations, and tertiary trusses framed into the secondary ones, resulting in a grid of trusses bearing a family resemblance to the original roof. The revamped coliseum began to take shape sixteen months after the collapse and by the spring of 1980 was ready to receive its first guests, the fans of a local hockey team that had been homeless for over two years.

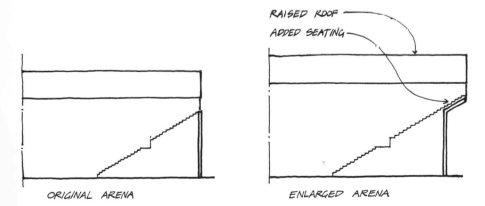

4.15   **Section through Original and Enlarged Arena**

5

Big Bangs

> The only stable thing is movement.
>
> Jean Tinguely

The Infernal Tower

In the early-morning hours of May 16, 1968, Ivy Hodge awoke in her flat on the eighteenth floor of Ronan Point Tower. She had moved into the newly constructed block of apartments in Canning Town, east of London, almost a month to the day earlier. She put on her slippers and dressing gown and went to the kitchen. Her apartment in the southeast corner of the tower consisted of a living room, a bedroom, a kitchen, and a bath, in a compact layout typical of postwar construction. She filled the kettle with water, placed it on the stove and, at exactly five forty-five, lit a match to light the burner. . . . She knew that when the gas pressure dropped, as it often did in those years, the pilot light would go out and gas would escape into the room from the unattended stove when the

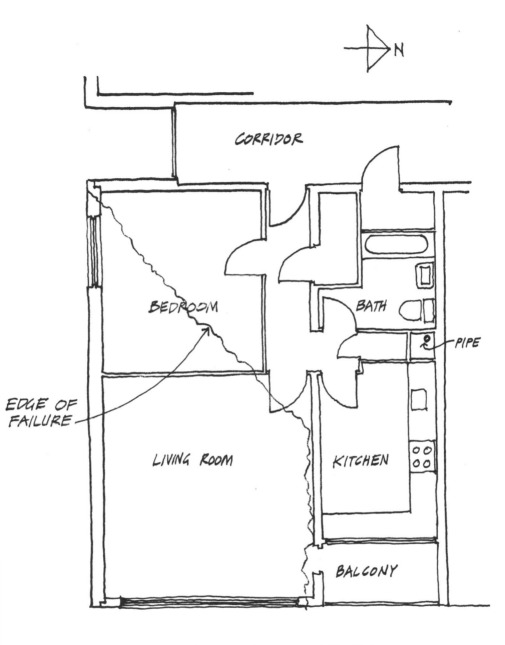

LAYOUT OF FLAT 90

5.1   Ivy Hodge's Apartment at Ronan Point

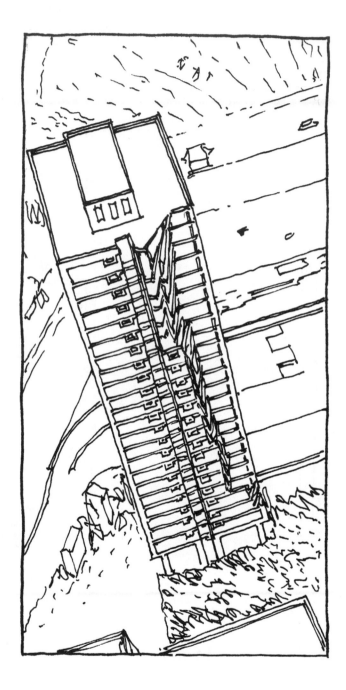

5.2   Ronan Point Collapse

pressure came back. Therefore, she had disconnected the pilot light some weeks earlier for fear of explosion and had not smelled gas either then or three hours earlier when she had gone to the bathroom.

One witness described a blue flash; another, a vivid red flame. The explosion blew out the window wall of the kitchen and the south load-bearing wall of the living room. Floor by floor, in a domino fashion, the entire corner of the tower collapsed. Miss Hodge was lying, dazed, in a pool of water spilled from the overturned kettle, looking out at the morning sky all around her. The living room of her flat and half her bedroom had vanished (Fig. 5.1). She suffered second-degree burns on her face and arms but was otherwise unhurt. Four sleeping residents died on the lower floors, crushed in their bedrooms when the giant concrete panels making up the structure of the building came tumbling down, raising clouds of gray dust (Fig. 5.2).

The twenty-two-story tower destroyed by the explosion was the second of a planned nine identical building complex to be built on the site by the Larsen-Nielsen prefabrication system. This construction system, which used room-size panels of reinforced concrete for load-bearing walls and floors, stacked them like a house of cards to create housing units and was one of many similar systems brought forth after the end of World War II. A severe housing shortage had been brought about throughout Europe by the extensive destruction caused by the war (over one-quarter of the dwellings in the neighborhood of Ronan Point had been demolished by enemy action), which led to the welcome introduction of many large concrete panel prefabrication systems. The increased productivity obtained by shifting a substantial part of the building process from the site to the factory meant savings in cost, reduction of manpower, and shortening of construction time, desirable goals at any time but particularly after the war. Although differing in details, all these systems involved floor panels sitting on wall panels. The joints between these two types of panels were usually filled with *grout*, a cement-sand and water mixture, and sometimes strengthened by reinforcing steel so placed as to lock the panels together, providing continuity and mutual interaction (Fig. 5.3). The Larsen-Nielsen system had joints with grout between tooth-edged floor panels, but no steel reinforcing to provide a sound connection between these panels and the wall panels above and below. Thus a sufficient horizontal force, like that of an explosion, could easily push a wall panel off the floor. Since the explosion in Miss Hodge's apartment did not damage her eardrums, it was deemed to have caused a pressure against the wall panels of less than 10 psi (0.07 N/mm²). Yet tests showed that this pressure, equivalent to that felt when one swims under only 10 ft. (3 m) of water, was high enough to cause the failure of a reinforced concrete wall either by bending it or by overcoming the friction resulting from the gravity loads and kicking it out. Tests conducted by experts from the tribunal established by the government to determine the cause of the collapse showed that the wall panel would slide out against the floor panel at a pressure of 2.8 psi (0.02 N/mm²), less than one-third that of the explosion. A witness in a nearby factory reported seeing the wall of Miss Hodge's living room "come out as if pushed sideways and then fall," which is consistent with the fact that the strength of the wall panel in bending was greater than the resistance of the joint in friction. Had the explosion occurred on a lower floor, the loads compressing the wall panels and the resulting friction might have been large enough to have prevented a failure of the wall by sliding.

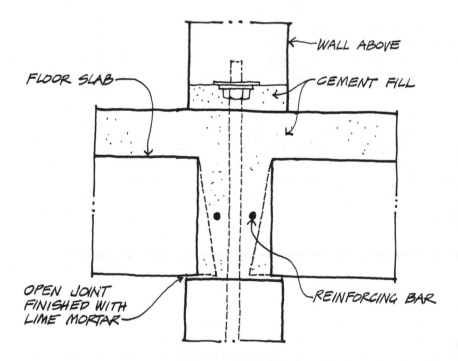

5.3   Joint between Interior Wall and Floor Slabs

Once one wall panel blew out, the wall panels above it were left unsupported and fell. The floor panels that were consequently left virtually unsupported then crashed down on the floor below, overloading it and causing a *progressive collapse* of all the walls and floors below. This highly unusual mode of failure led to a reevaluation of building regulations around the world, in terms both of safety and of unusual loads. The importance of *continuity* in joints of buildings and of *redundancy* in structures was awakened in the profession. Redundancy implies that a structure can carry loads by more than one mechanism—that is, that the forces on it can follow alternate paths to the ground. It guarantees that if one mechanism fails, loads can still be carried by other mechanisms (see p. 55). Consider, for example, a tower firmly supported on four legs. The failure of one leg will severely cripple the tower, but the tower may still survive, although the remaining three legs are overloaded, because the rest of the structure will adapt itself to carrying the load by *redistributing* it to the remaining legs.

An explosion is such a rare event that codes do not make it the basis for design, except for certain military buildings, but as a consequence of the Ronan Point catastrophe, a design philosophy became accepted that considers the possibility of an explosion capable of destroying its immediate vicinity without causing substantial damage elsewhere in the structure. This approach guarantees that a building will not fail in a progressive manner even if some structural elements are severely strained, and building codes have been modified throughout the world accordingly, making us all even safer from unusual dangerous events.

But what was the real cause of the explosion at Ronan Point? It was uncovered by the tribunal only after interviewing dozens of witnesses. Some weeks before the disaster a friend of Miss Hodge, Charley Pike, had offered to install the stove in her kitchen. Since he was not a professional plumber, he did not pay particular attention to the fittings required to make the connection between the pipe behind the stove and the gas riser that distributed gas throughout the building. A brass nut connecting the two pipes (later found to be below the standards set by the British Gas Board) could have been easily fractured when overtightened by a wrench and have caused a slow leak of gas. In fact, this is exactly what happened, although Miss Hodge did not smell the gas, possibly because of her half-awake state when she lit the match. The immediate consequence of the Ronan Point disaster was to cause the discontinuance of gas service to all similarly designed large concrete panel structures, of which there were more than six hundred throughout Great Britain.

The need to strengthen Ronan Point was obvious, but discussions about what to do and who should pay for the remedial work moved the matter into the sociopolitical arena. Within a year of the disaster the debris was cleared away, and the wing rebuilt with a *blast angle,* a reinforced joint detail preventing the separation of the wall from the floor. The tower was reoccupied; but in 1984 cracks began appearing in other walls, and the entire tower was evacuated. Eventually, in May 1986, the building, which the press had dubbed the "Infernal Tower," was swathed in a coat of reinforced polystyrene to contain the dust of demolition, and the tower was demolished, floor by floor, in a procedure that reversed that used in construction. Forty-one weeks later only the foundations remained, a monument to a failed dream of industrialized construction gone only eighteen years after its erection. Since it would have cost six times more to strengthen the tower in accordance

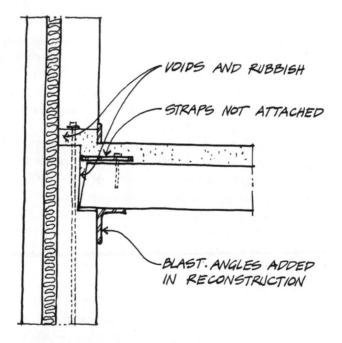

5.4 Joint between Floor Slab and Outside Wall—Reinforced after the Blast

with the new building regulations spawned by the disaster than to demolish it, the only cause of the final disappearance of the Ronan Point tower was money.

In a startling afterword to the disaster, evidence of incredibly shoddy workmanship was revealed as the tower was demolished. The tower had been dismantled rather than blown up as a result of the pressure brought to bear on the government by an architect, Sam Webb, who suspected poor construction. And right he was: The joints between the walls and slab, supposedly packed with mortar, were discovered to be full of voids and rubbish (Fig. 5.4). Upon this revelation, *hundreds* of similarly built apartment towers were deemed unsafe and also demolished. As late as 1991 six were blown up simultaneously in Salford, England, closing a sad chapter unjustly blamed on the lack of conscience of the sixties.

The Big Bang
on Forty-fifth Street

Cartoonist Rube Goldberg drew phantasmagorical machines that Jean Tinguely, a Swiss kinetic sculptor popular in the 1960s, brought to life. A machine designed by Tinguely to destroy itself, entitled *Homage to New York*, sat for a while in the garden of the Museum of Modern Art in New York until a time mechanism set it in motion, and indeed, it broke apart. The following story will show the reader that Goldberg-Tinguely assemblages do exist in real life and not only in the fantasy world of modern sculpture.

New York City morning newspapers of April 23, 1974, featured the usual number of disasters, among them the crash of a Pan Am 707 jet on Bali (the fourth Pan Am 707 to crash in nine months) and a powerful explosion in New York that, at 6:57 A.M. of the previous day, had torn through a twenty-four-story office building near the United Nations headquarters.

The explosion had knocked down a 50 ft. (16 m) wide section of the building, blown out windows, and collapsed ceilings in neighboring apartment buildings. Miraculously no one was killed, undoubtedly because the blast occurred in the early morning, when only a few tenants were already at work. Since the building housed the UN missions of Indonesia and Burundi, some of the first officers to arrive at the scene were special agents of the Federal Bureau of Investigation. Both they and the New York Police Department's bomb section quickly ruled out the possibility of terrorism as the cause of the blast. Mayor Abraham Beame promptly established a board of inquiry to determine the cause of the explosion and establish possible violations of city ordinances.

What had happened? The answer to the question is a story of convoluted coincidences and outright negligence, as well as a dramatic illustration of the role of chance in human affairs.

In 1929, at the dawn of the Great Depression, a twenty-four-story apartment building, typical of the middle-income housing of the time, had been erected across a lot facing south on Forty-fifth Street and north on Forty-sixth Street near Second Avenue. As the neighborhood declined in attractiveness, the owner of the building rented space in its lower floors to commercial businesses and, eventually, the entire sixth floor to a photographic processing lab. In 1971, with the approval and the financial support of the owner, the lab installed in the basement one hydropneumatic tank system, a tank, and a pressuring pump of the kind commonly found in the basement of one- and two-family houses to bring water to the floors above. These glass-lined tanks consist of a vertical steel cylinder up to 6 ft. (1.8 m) high, with walls less than 0.1 in. (2.5 mm) thick, closed at top and bottom by domed shaped steel *heads* (Fig. 5.5). They are called *hydropneumatic* (a combined word from the Greek *hydro* for "water" and *pneuma* for "air") because the top of the tank contains a pocket of air pressurized by a rotary pump that pushes down on the water below.

The New York City Building Code specifies that these systems must be designed and fabricated in accordance with the Code for Unfired Pressure Vessels of the American Society of Mechanical Engineers, a strict code demanding pressure relief valves, pressure reading gauges and other safety devices and that all work on these systems be done by licensed plumbers. The system installed in the building had been approved by the Department of Buildings of the Housing and Development Administration of the City of New York.

In 1973 the photo lab augmented the system by the addition of four new tanks, but it doesn't appear that this modification was approved by the responsible city department. Then, on April 20, 1974 (two days before the explosion), a partial modification was introduced in the system by two *unlicensed* plumbers, who replaced the impellers (the turbine wheels that pressurize the air and water in the tanks) of two pumps and added one *automatic* pressure-regulating valve to the system. They did not entirely complete their job, intending to come back a few days later to check the system and add other required pressure relief devices, which should have been installed on the same day.

Very early on the morning of the blast an employee of the photo lab went to the basement and closed the safety switch on Tank No. 2, instantly starting the pump, but when he returned to the lab on the sixth floor, he noticed that the pressure gauge there showed almost no pressure in the system. He went right back to the basement to check the problem and found Tank No. 2 lying on its side on the floor and water flooding the area from a broken pipe that had been connected to the tank. He also smelled gas. He left immediately to call for help, but before he could reach the lobby, a powerful explosion engulfed him in dust and flying debris.

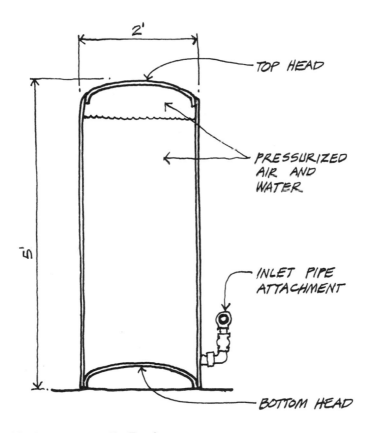

5.5 Hydropneumatic Tank

Consolidated Edison, the gas company, closed the gas main and reported that no gas leaks had been found outside the building, although several tenants claimed to have smelled gas during the weekend that had just ended. Immediate inspection of the building's basement was prevented by the floodwater but was urgently needed since the blast appeared to have originated there before traveling up the building in the elevator shafts and a stair, both located against the blown-out west wall of the building. As soon as the flooding was stopped and the gas main closed, the inspection by the New York Fire Department revealed an incredible series of events.

The act of closing the safety switch to start the No. 2 pump had caused the pressure-limiting safety device, an essential part of the control system, to be overridden. But this particular tank did not have a pressure relief valve that would automatically open at a value of the pressure usually below the design pressure of the tank. Therefore, the pump kept operating, trying to pressurize the tanks to its (the pump's) limit, which was more than twice the value for which the tanks were designed. The tanks were shaped like cylindrical rockets, with domed top and domed bottom heads, and when the pressure reached the heads' ultimate capacity, first the bottom dome of Tank No. 2 buckled and *inverted* (snapped through), and then, as the pump kept increasing the pressure, the weld connecting the bottom dome to the cylinder ruptured. The compressed air pocket at the top of the tank, suddenly free to expand, pushed the water out of the bottom of the tank and fired the tank upward like a rocket that struck, at a tremendous velocity, an overhead 6 in. (150 mm) gas line hanging from the ceiling *directly* above the five gas tanks (Fig. 5.6).

Under normal circumstances, the consequences of the tank's hitting the pipe, even at an impact velocity estimated at 60 to 100 mph (100–160 km/hr), would have been a bent pipe. Unfortunately, because of shoddy workmanship, this pipe was joined (about 6 to 10 ft. [2–3 m] from the point of impact) to another length of pipe with a coupling that had been only *partially* screwed together on one side when first installed (Fig. 5.6). The defective coupling fractured, allowing gas to start leaking (shades of Ronan Point!). Then the elevators, taking early-morning employees to their floors, sucked up the leaking gas from the basement and diffused it throughout the *entire* building. Finally, at 6:57 A.M., a spark from either a relay switch or a switch in one of the elevator cabs or, possibly, from a match struck to light a cigarette, ignited the explosive mixture of air and gas and detonated the fatal explosion.

The explosion blew out the weakest structural element, in this case, the outside wall of the elevator and stair shaft, spewing forth bricks, which hit the adjoining buildings. An explosion typically involves a rapid air expansion followed by a suction as the air rushes back to fill the void. "After the blast, there was a tremendous suction that whipped open the doors of all the cabinets and closets," said Leonard Zuckerman, a jewelry manufacturer residing in an adjoining apartment building. The same suction force blew out every window of his building.

If any one of the other four tanks had been involved, if the additional pressure relief valve had been installed in Tank No. 2 on April 20, if the gas pipe had been located a few inches either way off its original position, if that side of that particular coupling in the gas pipe had been properly screwed in, if an employee arriving early had not tried to light a cigarette, or if an electric spark had not occurred in that particular switch . . .

Such a vaguely definable phenomenon as the Forty-fifth Street explosion in Manhattan is known in physics as a *Fermi problem*,

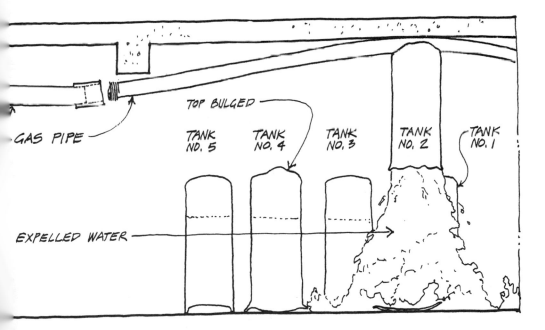

5.6   Ruptured Tank Striking the Gas Pipe

from the name of the Italian Nobel Prize physicist Enrico Fermi, the father of the nuclear energy era, who once stunned his advanced physics class by asking the question: How many piano tuners are there nowadays in Chicago? By intelligently guessing the values of the basic variables in the problem and by counting on some of guesses' being too low and others too high and hence compensating for the errors, he obtained an answer that closely matched the number of piano tuners in Chicago's telephone book. With a similar approach, it can be estimated that the chance of an explosion like that at Forth-fifth Street was at most one in thirty million, and probably much less. But this is why life is dangerous and always ends in death.

As was to be expected, without waiting for the verdict of the mayor's board of inquiry established immediately after the explosion, the owners and tenants of all the buildings damaged by the explosion initiated a class action in the New York State Supreme Court against the owners of 305 East Forty-fifth Street. In a class action the plaintiffs in a case act as a single "legal person," having agreed among themselves, or decided to agree at a later date, on how to share the recovered damages due them—in this particular case for physical and psychological damages, medical expenses to the wounded or shocked, and damage to the buildings' owners. About seventy people (the plaintiffs) sued the owners of the exploded building for a total of $680 million. The owners, of course, sued the photo lab, which countersued the owners.

Our firm, Weidlinger Associates, was approached by the attorney for the "plaintiff" in 1978 and agreed that besides basing our brief on the litany of code violations discovered by the mayor's inquiry board, his own (the attorney's) investigation, and the discovery of the investigations by the attorneys for the defendants (consented by law), we would rest our case on a mathematical deduction of the pressure in Tank No. 2 when it exploded. Having inspected the parts of that tank saved and stored by the fire department, we couldn't help noticing that the domed bottom head of the tank had been buckled by the pressure and had snapped through—that is, had been deformed from a dome shape to a soup dish shape (from a curvature down to a curvature up). Such snap-throughs occur at a value of the pressure determinable by a refined computer calculation that had become available only a few years before. It takes into account the change in the shape of the dome as the pressure increases gradually (in technical terms, it solves a nonlinear problem) and determines a lower limit of the pressure at which the dome curvature becomes inverted into a soup dish curvature.

Our calculation proved that the buckling pressure was substantially higher than the 70 psi (0.48 N/mm²) for which the tanks had been designed and even above the 110 psi (0.76 N/mm²) value at which the pressure relief devices had been illegally set by the installers, but less than the 130 psi (0.9 N/mm²) value that was the maximum discharge pressure of the pumps. With the usual steel coefficient of safety of 0.67, it was obvious that both the ultimate pressure of the tank (1.67 × 70 = 117 psi) and the 110 psi pressure set by the plumbers on the safety devices were not those allowed by the code. Moreover, since the bottom tank head *had* snapped through, we were confident that our calculation would prove why it did.

We had a tight case.

The reader anxious to find out how we fared and how the case was disposed of is referred to p. 251 for a blow-by-blow description of the court proceedings in "The Big Bang in Court."

6

The Day
the Earth Shook

> The frame and huge foundation of the earth
> Shak'd like a coward.
>
> William Shakespeare,
> *Henry IV*, Part 1

No natural event is more frightening than an earthquake. A hurricane announces its arrival with darkening skies, increasing wind velocities, and rain, all gradually growing more violent as the storm approaches. A plume of fiery gas and thickening clouds presage the eruption of a volcano. Responding to sight and sound, people often have time to prepare for the onslaught. But an earthquake strikes suddenly, without warning. Perhaps there is a rattle and a sharp crack as loose objects fall, but then buildings shake as the earth moves, unbalancing the firm foundation we have come to expect of terra firma. The destructive movements are all over in less than a minute, leaving behind fallen dreams and broken structures.

From ancient times earthquakes have taken on an aura of mystery. Strabo, living in Greece, where both earthquakes and volcanoes often brought destruction, recognized that earthquakes most frequently occur along a coast, but in speculating on their cause and leaving aside reason, he wrote of subterranean winds igniting combustible materials. More recently witnesses to the Charleston, South Carolina, earthquake of 1886 spoke of "vibrations of the mighty subterranean engine" and of "a subterranean roar that was heard." Voltaire in *Candide* attributed the cause of earthquakes to a subterranean fire. But although earthquakes obviously originate below the earth's surface, their cause is neither fire nor wind.

Plate Tectonics

The earth's crust is like a broken eggshell floating on the viscous inner magma of melted rock. Plate tectonics, the recently developed theory of movements of the earth's crust, offers the most plausible explanation for the existence of bands all over the globe along which most earthquakes occur. These bands contain *fault lines* or cracks that are, in fact, the edges of the tectonic plates and, as correctly observed by Strabo, occur primarily along continental coasts (Fig. 6.1). These giant plates move relative to one another

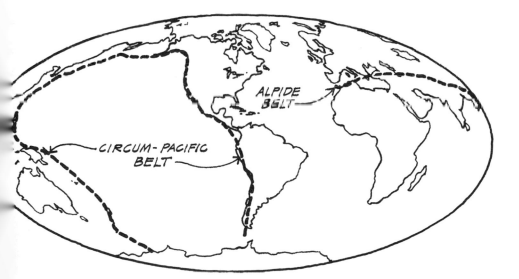

6.1 World Seismic Bands

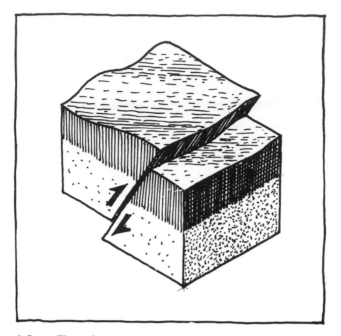

6.2a   Thrust

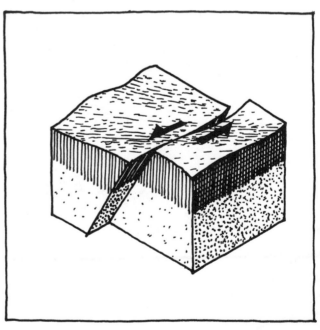

6.2b   Strike Slip

6.2   Tectonic Plate Movements

about as fast as one's fingernails grow, grind against each other both vertically (thrust) and horizontally (slip), and sometimes try to climb one above the other (subduction) (Fig. 6.2). Since the plate boundaries are not smooth, the movements are inhibited by friction, resulting in the storage of energy caused by the unreleased movement, somewhat like that in a stretched rubber band. Over time this energy accumulates until the frictional resistance generated by the roughness of the plate boundaries is overcome and the pent-up energy is suddenly released (the rubber band snaps), causing an earthquake. Predicting where, when, and how violently this event will take place is the major goal of geologists concerned with seismology (from *seismos*, Greek for "earthquake"). They are beginning to be quite successful in answering the questions of where and how violently, but not yet of when. They have correctly predicted the location and energy content of the last twelve major earthquakes in the world, but time uncertainty, despite rapid improvement, is still within thirty years.

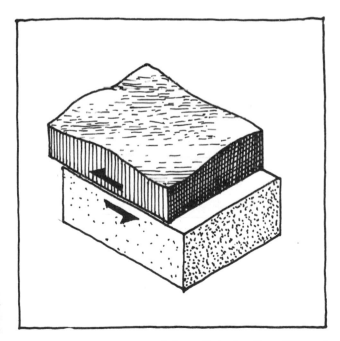

6.2c Subduction / Thrust

The Worst Earthquakes

Loma Prieta (a peak of the Santa Cruz Mountains) is on the 750 mi. (1200 km) long San Andreas Fault in California, which forms the boundary between the Pacific and North American plates and has been long identified as a region of seismic activity (Fig. 6.3). The best prediction for a major earthquake to occur in this fault was sometime between 1988 and 2018. The occurrence of moderate earthquakes in June and August 1988 led to greater watchful-

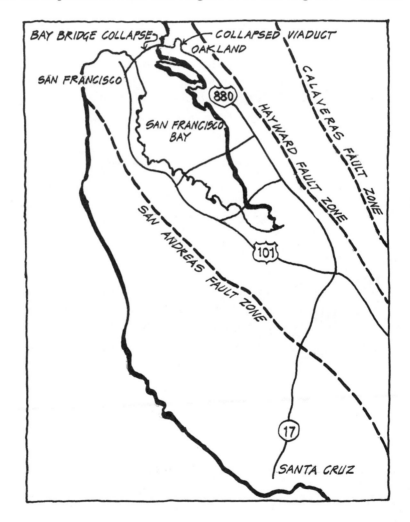

6.3   San Francisco Vicinity Map

ness by geologists, but these tremors were thought to be individual events, not foreshocks for *the* major quake. Then, on October 17, 1989, a strong shock of just five to seven seconds' duration toppled one section of a double-deck highway in Oakland, dropping the upper onto the lower deck and causing the deaths of forty-two people. There were twenty additional deaths and extensive destruction throughout the region, with more than six billion dollars in property damages and twelve thousand people displaced from their homes. With the two plates on either side of the San Andreas Fault moving against one another at the rate of 3 in. (76 mm) per year, the question remains whether the Loma Prieta earthquake was *the* big one or whether an even larger one is needed to release all the stored energy along the fault.

In the San Francisco earthquake of 1906, which resulted in a 275 mi. (440 km) long rupture along the San Andreas Fault, relative displacements of 9 to 15 ft. (3–5 m) were measured between the two sides of the rupture that caused major alterations in the landscape: Straight roads were displaced and interrupted, pipelines were severed, bridges were toppled, and communications were broken. But this was a quake with a forty-second duration and a Richter magnitude of 8.3* against Loma Prieta's 7.1. Measurements of earthquake *magnitude* on the Richter scale (developed in 1935) are based on energy release: Each higher whole number represents approximately a thirty-two times increase in energy. For instance, a Richter 6.3 is equivalent to about twenty thousand tons of TNT, the same order of magnitude but larger than the TNT equivalent of the atom bomb that destroyed Hiroshima.

In Japan, where the confluence of three faults occurs in Tokyo, earthquakes are a daily occurrence with an average of two measurable shocks per day. The western edges of the North and South American continents are also visited by numerous quakes through-

---

* Earthquakes are measured today by the logarithmic Richter scale, in which the *magnitudes* are exponents of powers of 10, as gauged by the amplitude of ground motion measured on the trace of a seismometer 100 km from the epicenter, the surface center of the earthquake. There are, in reality, several Richter scales, but the one most commonly used is that of the surface wave magnitude (M_s). An earthquake of magnitude 8 on this scale is a hundred times greater than one of magnitude 6, because 10^8 equals 100 million and 10^6, one million. A magnitude 8 earthquake is an annual occurrence in the world, while a magnitude 7 event is a weekly occurrence, but most of these high-magnitude earthquakes occur in sparsely populated areas, some even beneath the sea, causing little damage to man-made structures and few casualties.

out each year, but surprisingly the two strongest U.S. earthquakes
in recent history occurred not in California but in Missouri and
South Carolina. In December 1811, in the sparsely populated section west of the Mississippi that had been recently sold by France
to the United States for fifteen million dollars, a great earthquake
shook an area of at least two million square miles. Centered in
New Madrid, Missouri, the quake was followed by two others of
similar intensity in January and February 1812.

> The ground rose and fell as earth waves, like the long, low
> swell of the sea, passed across the surface, bending the trees
> until their branches interlocked and opening the soil in deep
> cracks. Landslides swept down the steeper bluffs and hill-
> sides; considerable areas were uplifted; and still larger areas
> sank and became covered with water emerging from below
> through fissures or craterlets, or accumulating from the
> obstruction of the surface drainage. On the Mississippi, great
> waves were created which overwhelmed many boats and
> washed others high upon the shore, the "returning current"
> (back traveling waves) breaking off thousands of trees and car-
> rying them into the river. High banks caved and were precip-
> itated into the river; sandbars and points of islands gave way;
> and whole islands disappeared.*

The most common buildings in the region were log cabins, which,
because of their flexible joints, were well suited to resist the shaking. A wooden house, properly braced and with all the parts carefully pinned together, will sway and stretch in response to an
earthquake, behaving essentially in an elastic manner. One family
living in a wooden house in Charleston claimed never to have been
aroused the evening of the earthquake and was not aware of any
unusual occurrence until stepping outdoors the next day. This does
not mean that all parts of a house will escape a permanent deformation—a door may not fit squarely in its frame or a window will
perhaps be stuck—but the structure will not break or fail in a catastrophic manner. This property of stretchability, technically called
ductility, is the most important measure of resistance to seismic
forces. Modern steel and reinforced concrete structures are carefully detailed to ensure the highest possible level of ductility.

Stone chimneys, being more rigid than the wood frames of the

---

* U.S. Department of Commerce, *Earthquake History of the United States* (Boul-
der, Colo.: NOAA, 1982).

houses, were generally knocked down. The shock was so strong that bricks were reported to have fallen from chimneys as far away as Georgia, a thousand miles to the east. In the town of New Madrid itself all the houses were demolished or so badly damaged that the town was totally abandoned.

It is estimated that the 1811 New Madrid quake would have registered 8.7 on the Richter scale, making it almost a thousand times more powerful than the Loma Prieta quake. The New Madrid Fault, evidence of which has only recently been found on Missouri farmland, is a six-hundred-million-year-old crack in the middle of the North American plate that never fully separated but that is now a weak spot and, like a partially cracked glass pane, can suddenly split in two. Predicting when or even if such a cataclysmic event could take place is not now scientifically possible. However, American Indians in the quarter century before the great quake predicted the event on the basis of the inherited tradition of a quake at an earlier time and the occurrence of a number of moderate shocks during the years before 1811, showing, once again, the importance of historical precedents.

The worst earthquake ever measured in number of casualties would be the quake of 1976 in Tangshan, China, in which about 350,000 people perished; the figure is approximate because the Chinese government refused to give official information to, and to accept help from, the outside world. It was acknowledged that in this tragic event, animals exhibited bizarre behavior before the quake, as had been rumored in many other cases.

The Charleston Earthquake and Base Isolation

In 1886 the population of the United States had swelled to an incredible fifty million people, many of whom participated in the ever-accelerating shift from a rural to an urban, industrialized society. Also, the country was shifting away from the divisiveness of the Civil War mentality, which had continued after the surrender at Appomattox twenty-one years earlier. South Carolina had been the first state to secede from the Union, and it was in Charleston Harbor that the first guns of the war were fired at Fort Sumter. Charleston, named after Charles II of England, contained many fine buildings in the eighteenth- and nineteenth-century styles,

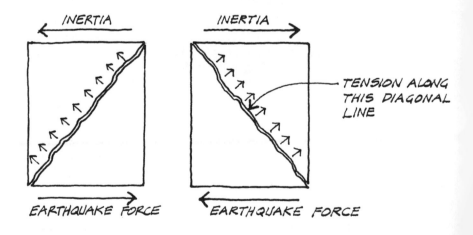

6.4 Diagonal Cracking of Masonry Wall

ranging from colonial to the various revival styles—Greek, Gothic, Romanesque, and Moorish—all part of an eclectic flowering. Laced with gardens interspersed in an eccentric seventeenth-century street pattern and bordering water on two sides, the city was a jewel of the Old South.

After supper on a sultry summer evening Carl McKinley was working on the second floor of the *News & Courier,* the Charleston newspaper, when he heard a sound he took to be of a heavy wagon rolling on the street below. The sound deepened, and he felt a tremor that grew in intensity, shaking him violently and causing furniture to be thrown about. McKinley and his co-workers rushed outdoors as the shaking subsided and were confronted by shrieks and wailing of survivors hidden from view by a dense whitish cloud of dust. He stumbled over piles of brick, trying to avoid the tangle of fallen telegraph cables. The greatest devastation was caused by falling masonry; it was estimated that as many as fourteen thousand chimneys fell that day. Although the main shock lasted not more than forty seconds, during that time few buildings escaped damage. Small wooden houses survived best, acting somewhat like a small boat riding out a storm. Masonry buildings performed poorly.

Bricks and concrete blocks joined with a cement mortar are very strong in compression but possess little tensile strength. An earthquake exerts a sudden push at the base of a masonry wall, which tries to stand firm by inertia and does not have time to flex. In the structural vernacular, a *shearing force* tries to slide an upper level of bricks over a lower one. The inertia of the structure, as if it were an invisible arm trying to hold back the movement of the upper level of bricks, causes the wall to crack along a diagonal line because there is tension between the upper and lower wedges of brick masonry (Fig. 6.4, see also p. 294). Since masonry is weak in tensile strength, the wall cracks, and since the alternating earthquake force acts to push the wall in a back-and-forth sway, the wall cracks in both diagonal directions, and thus totally disjointed, it eventually crumbles. It is characteristic of those masonry walls still standing after an earthquake to display X-shaped cracks between windows (Fig. 6.4).

Masonry walls supported on cast-iron columns and beams survived almost intact since the iron frame acted as a horizontal shock absorber, damping out the intensity of the seismic force before it reached the wall. This concept, known today as *base isolation*, represents an important approach in enhancing the earthquake resis-

6.5 Olive View Hospital: After the Earthquake

tance of buildings. Frank Lloyd Wright attributed the survival of his Imperial Hotel in the 1923 Tokyo earthquake to the flexibility of the pile-supported concrete mat foundation that absorbed most of the shock. In the San Fernando earthquake of 1971 the Olive View Hospital was seriously damaged (Fig. 6.5). The building, with four typical nursing floors, was supported by a colonnade of columns. Responding to the earthquake shock, the upper floors moved laterally as a rigid body, sustaining little or no damage but displacing the tops of the columns, which were too weak to absorb the resultant horizontal force. Consequently, the columns tilted sideways, carrying down the upper floors that partially crushed the first story; the upper floors were in effect isolated from the seismic shock by the flexible columns. In modern base isolation installations a building is supported on reinforced rubber pads that allow the earth to move under the building but that, unlike the Olive View Hospital columns, limit the possible lateral movement of the building. The piles in Frank Lloyd Wright's Imperial Hotel acted in this way since their movements were restrained by earth.

Liquefaction (Where Do We Stand?)

There are cases in which the earth totally fails in an earthquake because of *liquefaction*. This occurs in sandy soils completely saturated with water that suddenly become liquid when subjected to shaking from the quake. To demonstrate this action, place a weight on a pot full of sand to which water has been added almost to the top. Shaking the pot will cause the sand-water mixture to liquefy and the weight to sink and/or tilt. This is precisely what happened in Nigata, Japan, in 1964, when an apartment building tilted through an angle of 80° from the vertical without breaking up, so that after the movements stopped, the occupants were able to walk to safety down the face of the building (Fig. 6.6).

6.6   Nigata Apartment Buildings: After the Earthquake

Soil type under a structure greatly influences its behavior, a fact well illustrated in Loma Prieta in 1989, Mexico City in 1985, and Armenia in 1988. The greatest damage was suffered by structures on man-made fills (Loma Prieta), ancient lake bed sediments (Mexico City), or soft soils (Armenia). These conditions result in modifications of the incoming seismic wave, in particular, the amplification of certain frequencies of ground motion and the extension of the duration of the shaking. The sixty seconds of strong shaking in the Mexico City quake with a magnitude of 8.1 caused substantially greater damage than the five-second duration of Loma Prieta. In the San Francisco region, which was highly instrumented, differences in acceleration of up to 260 percent were measured between rock and soft soil sites during the Loma Prieta earthquake. Like a passenger in a car, a building responds to accelerations (changes in speed) rather than to velocity (speed). As the car accelerates, the body is pushed backward against the seat with a force proportional to the weight of the passenger. It is this force caused by inertia to which a building must respond in an earthquake, and the higher the acceleration, the larger the force that must be resisted.

The earthquake of December 7, 1988, near Spitak, Armenia, with a magnitude of 6.8, had a duration of strong motion of only ten seconds but was devastating, causing the deaths of more than twenty-five thousand people, most of them trapped in schools, apartment buildings, and public buildings. Of the three cities damaged by the shock, Leninakan, located farthest from the shock (20 miles [32 km]), was more severely damaged than Kirovakan, 16 miles (25 km) from the rupture zone. Leninakan lies in a broad alluvial plain and is underlain by deep sedimentary formations in what may have been an ancient lake. Kirovakan has a thin soil layer above a rocky base. The softer soils in Leninakan magnified the intensity of the shock and resulted in over 50 percent of the structures collapsing or having to be demolished. The most vulnerable structures turned out to be those consisting of precast concrete columns and beams joined to create frames nine to twelve stories high. Precast hollow-core concrete slabs spanned between these frames to create floors (Fig. 6.7). Almost all these housing blocks (there were 133 in Leninakan) collapsed or were so seriously damaged as to be unsafe and had to be demolished. An examination of the debris revealed that all the joints in the precast construction were weak; there was no connection between adjacent

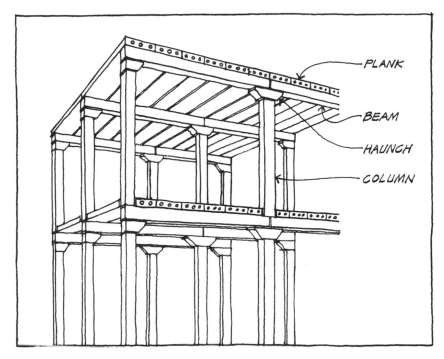

6.7 Precast Concrete Frame Construction

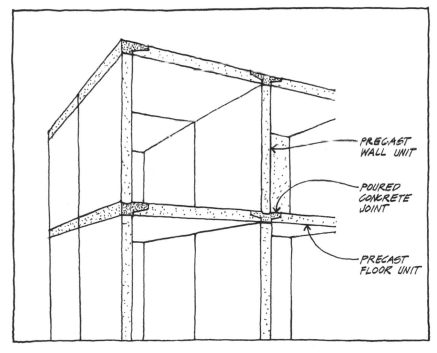

6.8 Precast Column Large-Panel Construction

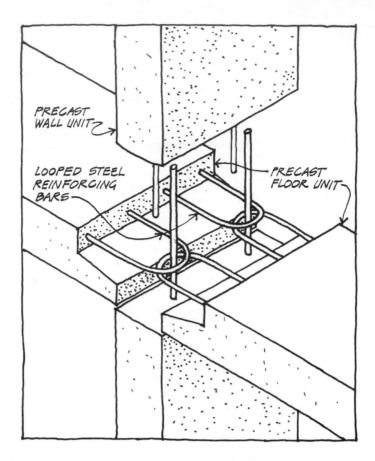

PRECAST
WALL UNIT

LOOPED STEEL
REINFORCING
BARS

PRECAST
FLOOR UNIT

6.9 Detail of Joint between Precast Concrete Wall and Floor Panels

hollow-core slab units and between the slabs and the beams. The structure was a loosely jointed assemblage with little or no resistance against lateral forces. In the case of a frame, the requirement of *ductility* mandated in modern seismic building regulations means that a joint must be able to undergo flexing without breaking. It was obviously lacking in the Armenian frame structures.

The precast large-panel system used for apartment buildings in Armenia performed well. These structures, nine stories high, were built of precast room-size floor and wall elements with poured concrete joints between them (Fig. 6.8). The lesson of Ronan Point (see p. 76) having been learned, the panels were interlocked by having looped reinforcing bars projecting from adjacent panels into the joint. These were locked together by a reinforcing bar threaded through all the loops. The quality of the concrete workmanship in filling the joint at the site was generally poor (Fig. 6.9), but in spite of this, there existed sufficient redundancy in the structure—i.e., different ways in which the forces could be resisted—and sufficient strength to result in a totally serviceable structure after the earthquake.

The major building damage resulting from Loma Prieta involved mostly masonry buildings founded on the *soft* soils in the Marina district of San Francisco. A number of four-story buildings with garages at the first floor behaved in the same way as the Olive View Hospital (Fig. 6.5). The large openings required for garage doors left only a slender frame to support the apartment structure above. Responding to the force of the earthquake, the frames were distorted laterally, with the garage doors acting as wedges to prevent the total collapse of the structure.

The Danger of Resonance

The most deadly collapse resulting from Loma Prieta occurred not in a building but in the double-decked section of the Nimitz Freeway in Oakland, known as the *Cypress Structure*. This structure consisted of 124 reinforced concrete frames spanning about 55 ft. (17 m) across the width of the highway. Between these two-level frames, cellular girders shaped like multiple horizontal tubes formed the roadway decks on both levels, spanning from 70 to 90 ft. (22–27 m) (Fig. 6.10). One of the sections of the Cypress Structure, 3,970

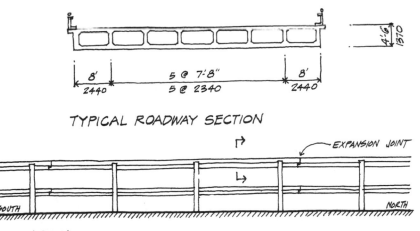

6.10 Cypress Structure Elevation and Cross Section

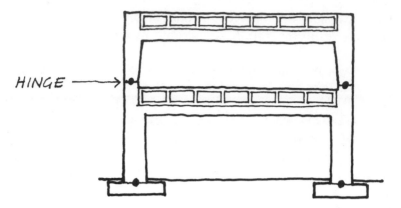

6.11 Cypress Structure: Typical Bent with Hinged Frames

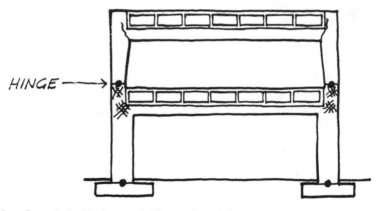

6.12 Crack Initiation at Hinge Location

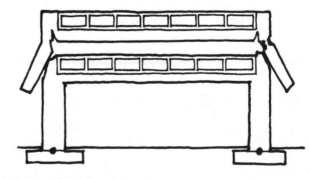

6.13 Typical Failure Mode of Bent

ft. (1210 m) long, was founded on *soft* soils about 550 ft. (167 m) above bedrock and was therefore subject to strong motions, actually four to six times the acceleration for which the structure had been designed in 1951. When the earthquake occurred, this particular section of the Cypress Structure collapsed as fifty of the frames broke (explained below), dropping the upper onto the lower deck of the causeway and crushing cars traveling northbound. All but two bays of the lower portion of this section remained standing and supported the weight of the debris of the upper roadway. "It was like a big, giant, long ocean wave," reported one witness, "and behind each wave a portion of the freeway collapsed." There was a delay between the first shock and the collapse, which allowed some motorists to stop their cars and, in some cases, get out. Those who did so generally stopped next to a column or under a beam, thinking those locations represented the strongest part of the structure. Unfortunately that was the worst choice they could have made since when the frames collapsed, no clearance was left under the beams.

The Cypress viaduct was not a structure with repetitive details throughout but had different frame configurations, with the predominant one having hinges at the base of the upper part of the frame as it rested on the lower part (Fig. 6.11).

How the failure took place is best explained through the sequence of events: With the passage of the first shock, the frame moved to the east, causing cracking to take place directly under the hinge points, which had little or no steel reinforcing to contain the concrete (Fig. 6.12). As the frame rocked back and forth, the upper columns slid off the crushed area at the hinge location and were pushed outward when the upper deck began to fall. The tops of the columns, directly under the uppermost beam, were bent out violently, causing an explosive failure of the concrete in that region (Fig. 6.13). The upper frame came to rest on top of the lower frame, with the upper columns splayed out like broken limbs of a tree after a storm.

This sequence assumes that the principal problem with the viaduct concerned its lateral rigidity. This, however, does not correlate well with the observation of "giant waves" rolling down the length of the structure and with the fact that the upper structure collapsed vertically. When one examines the vertical stiffness of the structure, specifically its principal mode of vibration in the vertical direction, a startling fact emerges. Consider, first of all, how a structure may vibrate differently in different directions.

Unlike the string of a violin, which is a linear element and vibrates primarily in one transverse direction to emit a specific tone with a particular frequency, a structure is a three-dimensional body. It has different stiffnesses in all three directions (up-down, front-back, and sideways) and will respond differently when "plucked" simultaneously in all three directions. These frequencies are the principal modes of vibration of the structure and are unique to each structure. In the case of the Cypress Structure, it turns out that the principal vertical frequency was almost identical to the frequency imposed by the earthquake at the site of the collapsed section. This coincidence led to a reinforcement, or amplification of the movements—i.e., *resonance* (see p. 272)—so that the structure and its supports moved with large amplitudes. This coincidence also explains the observed fact that the structure fell vertically with little lateral displacement, like the dog Pluto in a Disney cartoon, pushed down by inertia forces and with legs splaying outward.

Man and Earthquakes

There is little mystery in the response of structures to earthquakes. Masonry chimneys tend to break off above the roofs of houses; buildings with weak first stories tend to shear horizontally, as the Olive View Hospital did, distorting the first story and sometimes dropping the building above it to the ground; unreinforced masonry buildings tend to crack and sometimes collapse; masonry cladding tends to crack, peel off a building, and sometimes collapse to the ground. It is surprising that although each of these effects has been known to occur for centuries, each succeeding reconstruction often fails to account for them. Certainly modern seismic codes, in existence for less than a century, have evolved on the basis of earthquake knowledge. And certainly the survival rate of major structures in earthquakes has improved dramatically—evidenced by the many undamaged buildings in San Francisco, especially the tall towers waving harmlessly like trees in the wind in response to the ground shaking from Loma Prieta—yet brick chimneys are still built, as are unreinforced masonry structures. Like the farmer who returns to the base of the volcano after an eruption has destroyed his house, there remains in man a stubborn fatalism that negates experience.

7

Galloping Gertie

> The bridge seemed to be among the things
> that last forever; it was unthinkable that it
> should break.
>
> Thornton Wilder,
> *The Bridge of San Luis Rey*

From the day it was opened to traffic on July 1, 1940, the Tacoma Narrows Bridge had been nicknamed Galloping Gertie because of its undulating motions in the wind. Built at the beginning of the Second World War as a defense measure to connect Seattle and Tacoma with the Puget Sound Navy Yard at Bremerton, Washington (Fig. 7.1), the bridge spanned over a mile with a combination of a cable-supported suspension structure and steel plate girder approach spans.

Suspension bridges generally consist of main cables hung in a parabolic configuration from two towers and anchored at each end in heavy concrete blocks to resist the pull of the cables. The deck on which vehicles travel is connected to stiffening trusses or gir-

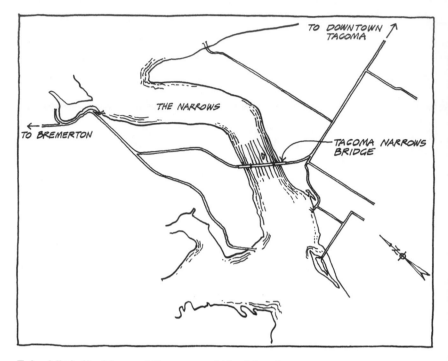

7.1   Vicinity Map of Tacoma, Washington

ders, which are, in turn, hung from the main cable with suspender
ropes (smaller steel cables) (Fig. 7.2).

The Tacoma Narrows Bridge consisted of two 420 ft. (126 m)
high towers, 2,800 ft. (840 m) apart (the main span), from which
were draped cables anchored 1,100 ft. (330 m) outboard of each
tower (the side spans). The design engineers anticipated a need for
some devices to control the oscillations of the bridge and, from the
time of its construction, repeatedly tried to take the up-and-down
sway out of the bridge. To this purpose, 1.5 in. (38 mm) *tie-down*
steel cables were attached to the bridge near each end and anchored
to fifty-ton concrete blocks, but when these cables were installed
on October 4, 1940, three months after the bridge had opened, they
snapped like cotton threads during the first windstorm. These tie-
down cables had neither significantly reduced the swaying and
bucking of the bridge nor, indeed, survived. And yet they were
reinstalled three days later with renewed optimism about their
effectiveness.

Other measures instituted to reduce the undulating motions included the installation of center stay, inclined cables connecting the main cables to the stiffening girders. Since the 8 ft. (2.4 m) deep stiffening girders were shallow in relation to the span, the Tacoma Bridge was three times more flexible than either the Golden Gate in San Francisco or the George Washington in New York, the only two bridges longer than the Tacoma Narrows at the time. But on the basis of the experience with the Bronx-Whitestone Bridge in New York, which also had a somewhat shallow stiffening girder, this flexibility was considered acceptable. An untuned *dynamic damper* (a piston in a cylinder) had proved successful in reducing torsional vibrations of the Bronx-Whitestone Bridge, but at Tacoma a similar damper failed immediately because the leather used in the pistons of the jack to provide a seal was destroyed by the sand blown into the cavity when the steel girders were sandblasted prior to painting. In any case, none of the remedial measures taken at Tacoma seemed to have an impact in reducing the bridge undulations.

Like a ship riding the waves, the bridge had pronounced vertical oscillations in even the lightest wind, causing passengers in cars to complain that they became seasick when crossing it. But it was not unusual for suspension bridges to exhibit some amount of movement; after all, the Golden Gate Bridge in San Francisco had

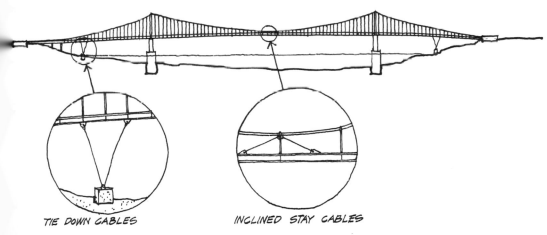

TIE DOWN CABLES   INCLINED STAY CABLES

7.2 Tacoma Narrows Suspension Bridge: Detail of Tie-Down Cables and Inclined Stay Cables

moved up and down up to 2 ft. (606 mm) in gale winds of 60 mph (96 km/h) two years earlier and up to 6 ft. (1.8 m) laterally in another windstorm. The main difference between the Tacoma oscillations and those of other suspension bridges was that these movements usually died out (were damped) rather quickly, whereas at Tacoma the movements seemed to last forever. This characteristic, which proved the Tacoma Bridge to have sixty times less damping than a typical suspension bridge, worried engineers so much that they decided to have a large-scale model of the bridge tested at the University of Washington, mainly to explore methods of improving its damping characteristics. Professor F. B. Farquharson, in charge of this study, decided also to monitor the bridge with instruments and movies while studying the problem on the model.

Observations continued throughout the summer and early fall of 1940 with records taken of wind velocities and the shape (mode) of the wavy motions of the bridge. They proved that the bridge vibrated, like a string, in a number of different modes, from a single undulation between the towers to a number of vertical undulations and one torsional, or twisting, oscillation. From the mounds of data collected, engineers were trying to understand why only certain winds would set the bridge deck into motions in no way proportional to the wind speed. Since the bridge had been designed by one of the outstanding world experts in suspension bridge design, Leon Moisseiff, there were few voices of alarm concerning its safety. Nevertheless, that fall, as the curious went to see and experience the galloping bridge, the engineers involved became increasingly uneasy because the stronger late-fall winds were beginning to blow north through the narrows.

On November 7, 1940, Franklin D. Roosevelt returned to Washington from Hyde Park, having just won an unprecedented third term as president of the United States. An estimated crowd of two hundred thousand cheered him on his victory over Wendell Willkie as he rode through the streets from Union Station to the White House.

That same morning Kenneth Arkin, the chairman of the Washington State Toll Bridge Authority, was awakened by the noise of the wind. He drove to the bridge after breakfast at 7:30 A.M. and read a 38 mph (58 km/h) wind velocity on an anemometer at the midspan of the bridge. He also observed that the bridge was bouncing noticeably, but not exceptionally, and that the tie-down stays on the west side of the span were loose and whipping in a circular arc. Shortly before 10:00 A.M. Arkin again checked the wind velocity and saw that it had increased to 42 mph (67 km/h) and that the movement of the bridge deck had heightened dramatically; by his count, the deck rose and fell at the center of the bridge 38 times per minute with a 3 ft. (0.9 m) amplitude. Greatly concerned, Arkin halted all traffic, and Professor Farquharson, who happened to be at the site that day, observed that the up-and-down motion of the center span consisted of at least nine vertical undulations while the bridge was also deflecting laterally by as much as 2 ft. (60 cm). Suddenly the bridge started twisting violently, and the nine-wave motion changed to a two-wave motion while the bridge deck near the Tacoma side appeared to twist to an almost 45° angle (Fig. 7.3).

7.3   Twisting Motion of Tacoma Narrows Bridge

Moments earlier a newspaperman, Leonard Coatsworth, trying to cross the bridge, had to stop his car near the quarter point of the span when the motions made it impossible to continue further. As the bridge pitched violently, the car careened across the pavement, and Coatsworth, jumping out of it, was thrown to the pavement. He tried to get up and run back off the bridge but was forced to crawl on all fours, while struggling not to fall over the edge because of the wild gyrations of the deck. Suddenly Coatsworth remembered leaving his daughter's cocker spaniel in the car and tried to go back, but by that time the motion was so violent that he couldn't. When he finally reached the shore, his hands and knees were bruised and bloody. Arthur Hagen and Rudy Jacox had also just driven onto the bridge when it began to sway. They jumped out of their truck and crawled to one of the towers, where they were helped to safety by workmen, as (in the words of Professor Farquharson) the bridge crumbled beneath them "with huge chunks of concrete flying into the air like popcorn."

During a momentary decrease in the violence of the motion Professor Farquharson attempted to drive Mr. Coatsworth's car to safety, but he abandoned this effort as the car "began to shift about in a most alarming manner." It was estimated that the amplitude of the twisting undulations from crest to valley was now 25 ft. (7.5 m). The bridge was tearing itself apart, suspenders flying high, ripping away a section of the deck near the quarter point and dropping Coatsworth's car and Hagen's truck into the waters of Puget Sound, 190 ft. (52 m) below. The only victim of the disaster was the helpless cocker spaniel, which went down with the car.

The crippled bridge, now severed, rested for a moment before resuming its dance of death. Then, with a deafening roar, a 600 ft. (180 m) stretch of the bridge tore away from the suspenders and fell into the water (Fig. 7.4). As each section fell, shock waves rippled along the remaining sections with a force sufficient to throw an observer violently to the deck. The side spans sagged, the tops of the towers tilted almost 12 ft. (3.6 m) toward each shore, and what was left of the once-graceful structure, at long last, came to rest.

When asked to comment, the designer, Leon Moisseiff, could only answer: "I'm completely at a loss to explain the collapse."

Moisseiff's credentials were impeccable. He had been consulting engineer for the Golden Gate Bridge, the Bronx-Whitestone Bridge, and the San Francisco-Oakland Bay Bridge. The methods of calculating forces in suspension bridges resulting from loads and winds that had been developed by Moisseiff and his associate Fred Lienhard were used by designers and engineers all over the world. Moisseiff had designed New York's Manhattan Bridge in 1909 and, in 1925, Philadelphia's Ben Franklin Bridge, the world's longest until construction of the George Washington Bridge twelve years later. After the collapse Clark Eldridge, the chief engineer of the Tacoma Narrows Bridge, bemoaned the fact that "eastern engineers" had been employed for the design but granted that they were "of national reputation." An editorial of the *New York Times* called Moisseiff an "outstanding engineer" and "not a reckless experimenter."

Yet the design of the bridge presented some unusual aspects that, had they been noticed, would have tied Tacoma Narrows to prior collapses.

7.4   Tacoma Narrows Bridge at the Moment of Collapse

A century before the Tacoma Narrows failure, a hurricane partially destroyed the 550 ft. (165 m) long Strait of Menai Bridge
joining the mainland to the island of Anglesey in eastern England,
along the post route from London to Holyhead. The bridge keeper
observed 16 ft. (4.8 m) high undulations in the deck before the
roadway broke up at a quarter point. The description of an eyewitness to the failure in 1854 of the 1,010 ft. (303 m) span bridge over
the Ohio River at Wheeling, West Virginia, could have been written about Tacoma: "For a few minutes, we watched it with breathless anxiety, lunging like a ship in a storm. At one time, it rose to
nearly the height of the towers, then fell, and twisted and writhed
and was dashed almost bottom upward. At last there seemed to be
a determined twist along the entire span, about one-half the floor-
ing being nearly reversed, and down went the immense structure
from its dizzy height to the stream below, with an appalling crash
and roar."

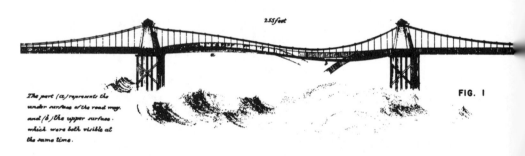

SKETCH Shewing the manner in which the 3rd Span of the CHAIN PIER at BRIGHTON undulated
just before it gave way in a storm on the 29th of November 1836.

255 feet

The part (a) represents the
under surface of the road way
and (b) the upper surface
which were both visible at
the same time.

FIG. I

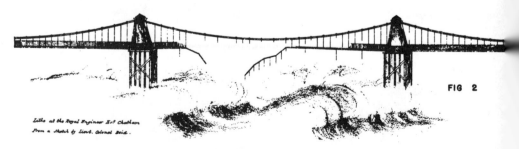

SKETCH Shewing the appearance of the 3rd Span after it gave way.

FIG 2

Litho at the Royal Engineer Est Chatham
from a Sketch by Lieut. Colonel Reid.

7.5 Brighton Chain Pier Collapse

Many suspension bridges failed in the eighteenth and nine-teenth centuries, capped by the fall of the 1,260 ft. (378 m) long Niagara-Clifton Bridge in 1889 in a windstorm with reported winds of 74 mph (118 km/h). Dr. J. M. Hodge, who had crossed the bridge a few hours before it failed, said it "rocked like a boat in a heavy sea and at times it seemed to tip up almost on its very edge."

The twisting motion before failure is a common characteristic of all suspension bridge collapses and was illustrated in a sketch of the failure of the Chain Pier at Brighton in 1836 by Lieutenant Colonel Reid (Fig. 7.5). Most of these spans were also very narrow in relation to their length, anywhere from 1 to 72 of the span for Tacoma and Niagara to 1 to 59 for Wheeling, ratios that may be compared with those of "fat" bridges, like the George Washington and Bronx-Whitestone, of 1 to 33, and of bridges considered "thin," such as the Golden Gate with a ratio of 1 to 47. Such slenderness makes the bridge very weak in torsion, like a long, narrow strip of steel, hence susceptible to torsional movements, particularly when combined with the absence of sufficient stiffening in the span direction that invites longitudinal "galloping." The shallow 8 ft. (2.4 m) girder of the Tacoma Narrows Bridge was less than half as stiff as the girder of the 500 ft. (150 m) *shorter* Bronx-Whitestone Bridge, with which it was often compared. It has been surmised that although it is the only modern bridge with plate girder stiffen-ers like the Tacoma, the Bronx-Whitestone Bridge was saved from the problems of the Tacoma because it is twice as heavy, twice as wide, and comparably stiffer.

The basic question remains: Even if so many other suspension bridges collapsed after undulating wildly, why did the Tacoma Narrows Bridge twist to its destruction under a relatively modest and steady wind?

The answer is fairly complex mathematically, although easy to understand physically. Because of its weakness in torsion, the Tacoma was destroyed by aerodynamic wind oscillations, of the same nature as those considered on p. 272. This weakness stemmed from two causes: the shallowness of its stiffening girders and the narrowness of its roadway, in relation to the span length.

The aerodynamic oscillations of the bridge can be easily dem-onstrated by a hair dryer blowing on a narrow strip of thin paper in a direction perpendicular to the strip. Depending on the incli-nation of the dryer to the plane of the strip, one can excite flutter in the strip of two kinds: a galloping (bending) mode or a torsional (twisting) mode, duplicating the motions of the Tacoma and of the earlier Wheeling and Niagara bridges.

It is not difficult to understand physically why spans weak in torsion are subjected to twisting motions. Since the wind is never perfectly horizontal, it may start hitting the span, say, from below, slightly lifting the windward edge and lowering the lee edge (Fig. 7.6a). The span reacts to this deformation and rotates back (like a twisted telephone cord when dangled), lowering the windward edge and lifting the lee edge. The wind now hits the span from above, pushing down the windward edge and raising the lee edge (Fig. 7.6b). The span reacts by twisting back, thus reinitiating the cycle, and the oscillations grow in amplitude progressively until the span breaks up. (These are *not* resonant oscillations, since a steady wind does not have a period [see p. 272] and, hence, *cannot* be in resonance with the twisting oscillations of the span, although these grow in amplitude with time exactly like resonant oscillations.*)

The reader might rightly ask us to answer a last question: Why did the Tacoma span choose to twist its two halves in *opposite* directions (Fig. 7.3)? The answer lies in one of the fundamental laws of nature, the law of minimum energy, or "the law of nature's laziness." Given the choice of two or more paths to reach a goal, nature *always* chooses the path of least resistance—i.e., the path requiring the minimum amount of energy to achieve the goal. In the case of the Tacoma span (and many other suspension bridges), the span may twist as a whole or split into two half spans that twist in opposite directions. Since it can be shown that the first option requires more energy than the second, nature prefers to spend

---

* Recent (1991) studies suggest that the cause may be attributable to vortex shedding, a phenomenon first described by Theodor von Karman. Spiraling vortices can be seen in the wake of a ship moving through water, and similar, though invisible, vortices trail an airplane wing in flight. Two kinds of vortices were shed by the twisting Tacoma Narrows deck. The first is called a Karman vortex street because the periodic shedding creates a continuous pattern of alternating vortices. However, these vortices were out of sync with the natural frequency of the bridge and therefore could not contribute to a buildup of motion. The second was a flutterlike complex pattern of vortices with a frequency coincident with the bridge's natural frequency that rapidly reinforced the destructive torsional oscillations. It is difficult to state whether the twisting oscillations of the deck caused these vortices or whether the vortices caused the deck oscillations, but at the present time this new assumption must be considered the best interpretation of the cause of the collapse.

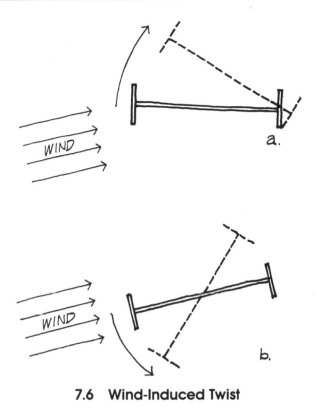

7.6 Wind-Induced Twist

less wind energy by twisting alternatively the two halves of the span, one clockwise and one counterclockwise.

Can one prevent the dangerous twisting and galloping suspension bridge motions that destroyed the Tacoma Narrows Bridge? Yes, and in many ways. To begin with, open stiffening trusses will allow the wind relatively freer passage through their openings not present in solid stiffening girders. Secondly, a larger ratio of roadway width to span will increase the twisting resistance of the span. Thirdly, one can increase the bending stiffness of the trusses or girders, thus also contributing to an increase in the twisting resistance of the span. Fourthly, if the bridge structure is damped, it will prevent the indefinite progressive increase in magnitude of the aerodynamic oscillations. And finally, the span oscillations can be counteracted by means of a dynamic damper (see p. 273), as was successfully done for the first time in 1990 in the Bronx-Whitestone

Bridge in New York by the American engineer Herbert Rothman. Unfortunately, in 1940, not even a great bridge engineer like Leon Moisseiff was aware of the danger of aerodynamic oscillations in suspension bridges, and none of these precautions was taken in the design of the Tacoma Narrows Bridge. Engineers would do well to look backward, sometimes, instead of only forward.

The $6.4 million Tacoma Narrows Bridge was finally scrapped two years after the disaster. Washington State received $500,000 for the salvage remnants.* The reconstructed bridge has stiffening trusses 25 ft. (7.5 m) deep and a box design for torsional stiffness; entirely aerodynamic, it has been free of any problems.

On September 3, 1943, three years after the failure of his bridge, Leon Moisseiff died of a broken heart.

---

* In one of those curious coincidences, the collapse of the Tacoma Narrows Bridge led to the discovery that an insurance agent named Hallett French, entrusted with forwarding the premium to the Merchants Fire Assurance Corporation, had diverted the money, using it temporarily for his own purposes, fully intending to forward the premium some weeks later. How could French have anticipated that such a large, seemingly strong, and well-constructed structure would ever fail?

8

When Metals Tire

> Like the tree that's in the backyard
> Blown and battered by the wind
> Our love will last forever
> If it's strong enough to bend.
>
> Beth Nielsen Chapman and Don Schlitz,
> "Strong Enough to Bend"

Let us consider two entirely disconnected events, the crash of an airliner and the collapse of a bridge, each a shocking failure and a puzzle to the experts charged with the investigation of their causes. We shall find they were due to a single, simple cause: metal fatigue or fracture.

The Exploding Comet

The Comet, designed by the famous British aeronautical engineer Captain Sir Geoffrey de Havilland, was one of the first commercial aircraft driven by jet propulsion developed during the Second World

War. Only twenty-one of the new amazing planes were built between 1952, the year of the Comet's introduction into commercial service, and 1954, when seven of them had crashed, it seemed inexplicably, killing a number of passengers. In May 1953 a Comet crashed under "mysterious circumstances" in a violent storm over Calcutta. Two more fell within months of each other in flights from Rome to London, the last, with thirty-five passengers and crew, thirty minutes after takeoff from Rome on a clear and sunny morning on January 11, 1954, falling into the sea between the islands of Elba and nearby Monte Cristo. The plane had reached an altitude of 29,000 ft. (8800 m) and was traveling at 490 mph (780 km/h) when, according to an eyewitness, a blast was heard, followed by a streak of smoke and the vertical plunge of the aircraft into the Tyrrhenian Sea.

By this time larger and more advanced models of the Comet were already in a development stage, to counter emerging competition from the United States against the British monopoly in long-distance jet flights. Thus the accidents were of most serious concern to the designer. To avoid suspicion that structural problems were the cause of the failures, the entire Comet fleet was grounded and examined. No evidence of structural weaknesses was found, and speculation of sabotage and hints of time bombs circulated.

The Tyrrhenian is relatively shallow near Elba, and the Royal Navy was charged with finding the wreckage, then discovering the cause of the disaster. On February 13 TV cameras scanning the seabed spotted the first pieces of the plane, and the navy started recovering the wreckage. Without waiting for the final results of the investigation, but after introducing fifty structural modifications, commercial flights of the Comets were resumed on March 23, 1954. Two weeks later another Comet crashed after takeoff from Rome, with a loss of twenty-one lives.

This tragic event energized the Royal Aircraft Establishment (RAE) into undertaking a historically intensive scientific investigation. Researchers first fitted together parts of the recovered plane onto a wooden framework, reassembling almost 70 percent of the plane at the Farnborough Research Station (Fig. 8.1a). More than sixty hypotheses about the cause of the disaster were examined, starting with sabotage, pilot error, and basic design, but most of them were discarded. The ghost of the reassembled plane was minutely examined, pressure tests on a section of the fuselage were conducted in a water tank, and additional experimental flights of the remaining Comets were undertaken by pilots defying the potential danger. At long last, after the researchers had discarded one theory after another, a cause was found to fit the facts: *metal fatigue,* the weakening of metals subjected to frequent reversal of stresses from tension to compression (from pulling to pushing) and vice versa. (You can demonstrate metal fatigue by bending a straightened paper clip in opposite directions; it usually breaks after ten to twenty alternating bends.)

Aircraft structures are particularly subject to fatigue, caused by the alternating pressurization and depressurization of the hull and the bending of the wings up and down as the plane flies through varying meteorological conditions. When failure resulting from fatigue occurs, its cause is often the age of the plane or questionable maintenance, and this is why planes are meticulously inspected at regular intervals. For example, the Aloha Flight 243 crash on

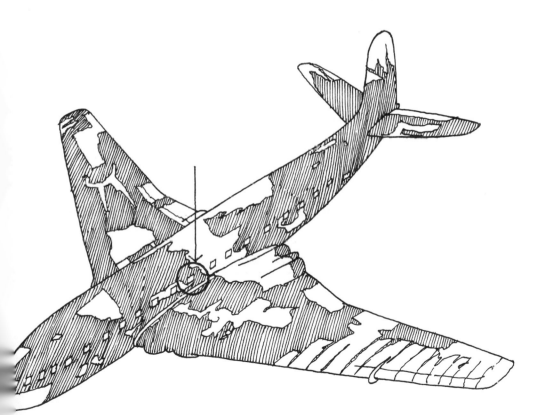

8.1a   Comet Airliner with Recovered Sections Shown Shaded

April 28, 1988, in Hawaii occurred to a plane that had completed ninety thousand flights in twenty years and, therefore, ninety thousand cycles of pressurization and depressurization. Suddenly a section of the fuselage was torn away as the plane was approaching its cruising altitude over the Hawaiian Islands, sucking out a flight attendant through the open ceiling of the first-class section. All passengers strapped in by their seat belts were saved by the extraordinary skill of the pilots, who safely landed the crippled craft.

Passengers on the Comet flight of April 6, 1954, were not so lucky. The fuselage of their plane suddenly ripped open, starting at the corner of a window (Fig. 8.1b). This area is particularly sensitive to fatigue since the weakening of the metal by fatigue occurs at a *smaller* number of stress alternations when the local stresses have *higher* values, and stresses *always* have higher values when their flow has to move around a corner or a hole, a phenomenon called *stress concentration* (Fig. 8.2). The analysis of the recovered Comet determined this stress to have reached a value equal to 70 percent of the metal's *ultimate stress*, the stress at which the metal fails. In the neighborhood of this value, metals do not behave *elastically*—that is, do not return to their original shape after removal of the load—but stretch *plastically*, remaining deformed after load removal (see p. 282). The Comet designers had not properly taken into account the possibility of stress concentration and the consequent danger of fatigue, and each time the plane was pressurized, the metal at the window corner stretched plastically, so that after one thousand flights it had no more give and it broke. The danger of fatigue is increased even by the unavoidable microscopic imperfections of the metal, such as minute pinholes or cracks, because stress concentration occurs at all these discontinuities.

De Havilland had tested samples of the corner panel and an entire fuselage section of each plane, concluding that in terms of fatigue the cabins were good for a service life of about ten thousand flights or ten years. After the accident a test performed by the RAE showed failure after only three thousand cyclic load applications. This result, although only one-third of de Havilland's estimate of the fuselage's fatigue life, was still three times larger than the thousand-load applications experienced by the last two crashed Comets. Why this incompatible difference? Because, first, the de Havilland test did not accurately represent the actual cabin since complete windows were not fitted into the test section. Then there

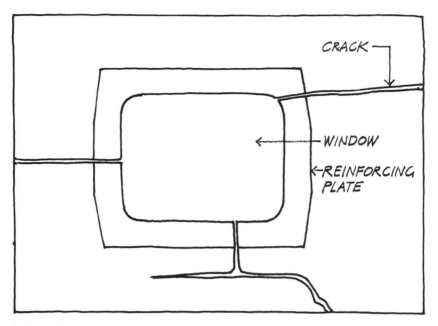

8.1b   Cracks around Window

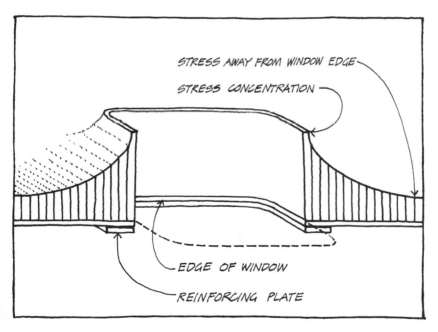

8.2   Stress Concentration at Window's Edge

were two more reasons: the additional stress concentration around a hole in the fuselage (needed for a rivet connecting a reinforcing plate to the window corner) and the difference between the smooth operation of a testing machine and the turbulent behavior of a plane in flight. In the machine test, through the ductility of the material, plastic behavior had time to redistribute the stresses concentrated at the window corner and thus to reduce their value, while sudden and violent stress reversals from a "bump" in flight could easily have triggered a sudden dynamic peak stress, initiating failure (see p. 272).

We mention all these subtleties only to show the reader that even though structural materials can only be pulled or pushed, they can do this in many different ways. A slight mistake on the part of a designer can cause a failure difficult to pinpoint. (A reader familiar with the Nevil Shute novel *No Highway* has already encountered the story, written *before* the Comet disasters, of a transatlantic flight that fell victim to metal fatigue. This is indeed an odd case of artistic insight into metallurgy!)

The Point Pleasant Bridge Failure

For forty years cars and trucks rolling westward on U.S. 35 from Point Pleasant, West Virginia, crossed the Ohio River over the Silver Bridge, so called because of the shiny aluminum paint used to prevent its steel members from rusting. At 5:00 P.M. on December 15, 1967, a cold day when the temperature dropped to 30°F (−1°C), several loud cracking sounds were heard by a witness on the western Ohio shore. The bridge was crowded with rush-hour traffic, normal for that time of day but swelled by Christmas shoppers returning home. Within a minute the three spans of the bridge, totaling 1,460 ft. (445 m) in length, began to fall, hesitating for a breathless moment before collapsing with a roar into the icy river and carrying with it thirty-seven vehicles of all types. The collapse started at the western span (Fig. 8.3), twisting it in the northerly direction (an indication that a member of the north-side trussed structure may have failed); the span crashed, folding over on top of the fallen cars and trucks. Loaded by the whole weight of the center span, which had become unsupported at its west end, the east tower fell westward into the center of the river, carrying with

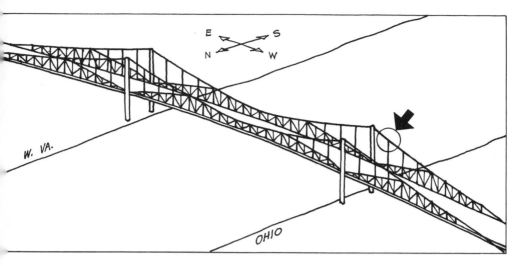

8.3 Point Pleasant Bridge

it the center span. The west tower then collapsed backward toward Point Pleasant, ending the destruction of the bridge. Forty-six lives were lost, the suddenness of the accident evidenced by the body of one victim, a taxicab passenger, who was found the next day clutching a dollar bill in his hand. While the replacement of the Silver Bridge was under construction half a mile from the site of the disaster, the bodies of an eight-year-old girl and of a forty-year-old man were still missing, apparently carried downriver by the swift current of the Ohio.

Modern suspension bridges use steel cables introduced by French engineers around 1830, but the Point Pleasant Bridge, like other U.S. suspension bridges of the time, was supported by two steel chains, each consisting of 50 ft. (15 m) long *links* with *two* parallel forged steel eyebars each. (A cable today generally consists of thousands of individual wires.) An *eyebar*, as the name implies, is an iron or steel bar with enlarged ends pierced by holes; a pin through the holes of adjoining links, 12 in. (300 mm) in diameter in the Silver Bridge, connects them to make a chain and is held in place with bolted cap plates (Fig. 8.4). The Silver Bridge had a central span of 700 ft. (213 m), with two 380 ft. (116 m) side spans, and approach spans supported by piers at either end of the bridge leading to the anchorages for the eyebar chains. As originally built in 1928, the two-lane bridge had a timber deck and two sidewalks. For added durability, the roadway was replaced in 1941 with a

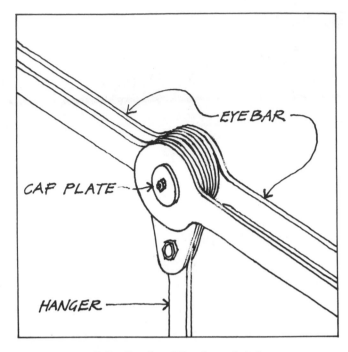

8.4   Typical Eyebar Joint

concrete-filled steel grid. The bridge was also unique in that the chains served both as suspension elements and as a portion of the top chord of the stiffening trusses (Fig. 8.5).

All suspension bridges have stiffening elements on the sides of the roadway, usually steel trusses or plate girders, to distribute the moving loads to the cables or chains and minimize their instability. Without such stiffening elements the cables or chains would

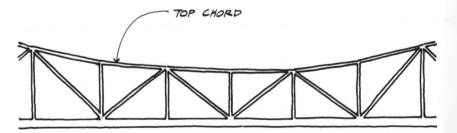

8.5   Stiffening Truss with Top Chord Eyebar Chain

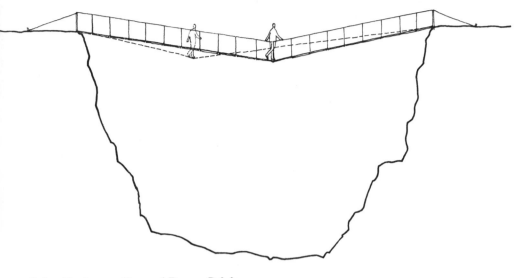

8.6   Deformation of Rope Bridge

deflect directly under the load and a car or truck would travel across
the bridge in a constant trough. The earliest suspension bridges in
the world, in China and South America, were "vine bridges" made
of vegetable fiber ropes that served as cables, hangers, and roadway. (At times the roadway was stabilized by tree trunks on which
to walk.) It is easy to visualize the changing shape of such light
bridges under the weight of a man walking across it, the bridge
dipping under his feet as the main cable tends to tighten into two
straight segments (Fig. 8.6). Even with stiffening elements there is
a certain give in any modern long suspension bridge span, and
Howard Boggs, one of the survivors of the Silver Bridge collapse,
stated: "The old bridge was bouncing up and down like it always
does. Then, all of a sudden, everything was falling down. My feet
touched the damned bottom of the river."

The failure of one or even several wires out of the thousands in
a cable is not in itself disastrous. During the wild wind oscillations
that led to the collapse of the Tacoma Narrows Bridge, more than
five hundred wires out of eighty-seven hundred were worn or broken in one of the main cables as the result of the scraping of the
steel band against the wires it held together, yet while the bridge
deck fell into the river, the cables survived. In the case of the Point

Pleasant Bridge, however, the failure of only *one* eyebar in a *single* link of the north chain caused the disaster, because the failure of any one eyebar resulted in a prying action on the joint of the parallel bars as well as the immediate doubling of force in the remaining eyebar of the link (Fig. 8.7).

The need to discover the cause of the Point Pleasant failure led to the decision to salvage and store as many elements of the fallen spans as possible. Fractured, bent, and rusting segments were reassembled into a giant jigsaw puzzle on a 27 acre (10.9 ha) field near the banks of the Ohio. The inquiry panel and its consultants, some of the best bridge engineers and scientists in the country, had the task of locating the bar that broke first. Laboratories were engaged in the conduct of microscopic examinations of the steel in

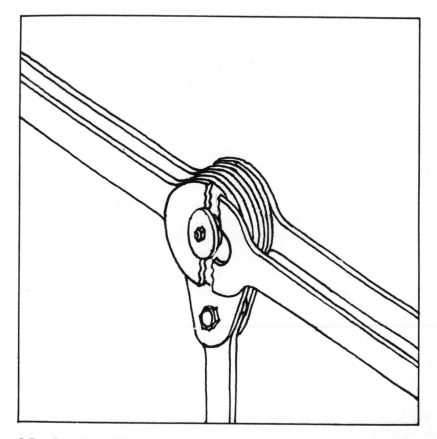

8.7 Cracked Eyebar

the neighborhood of fractures. As many as ten causes of the disaster were identified, and five were quickly eliminated—namely, overloading, sabotage, aerodynamic instability (see p. 117), displacement of a pier as the result of a barge impact, and underwater erosion of a pier support (see p. 146). Although the fracture of a specific eyebar was identified within the first year as the initiator of the collapse, the remaining causes were examined for three years before a final judgment was rendered.

At first it was suspected that the breakage of the "first" eyebar was due to metal fatigue caused by the cyclical application of the moving loads on the bridge. But it was further determined that the stress variations in the eyebars caused by the moving loads were small compared with the eight-time-greater stresses caused by the self-weight (the dead load) of the bridge. (The opposite was true in the case of the Comet.) Moreover, the total stresses in the eyebars were well within those allowed by the codes for the particular type of steel used in the forged eyebars, even when one took into consideration the stress concentration at the inside edge of the eyebar hole that raised the local stress by a factor of three. Extensive testing led to the tentative conclusion that only a brittle fracture, like that causing the breaking of glass (see p. 282), could have resulted in the kind of fracture appearing on the first broken eyebar. But the material of the eyebars was normally elastic and could stretch the expected amount—i.e., had the property called *ductility* in metallurgy. In fact, when a brittle fracture was induced experimentally, the sample showed a time delay between the instant appearance of the local crack and the complete separation of the metal on both sides of the joint. If this had been the case in the bridge collapse, a measurable length of time would have passed between the first indication of a crack and the total collapse of the structure. Why had there been no reports of any cracks following the last careful inspection of the bridge two years before the collapse?

The search was narrowing. The last unanswered question led to a microscopic investigation of the broken eyebar. It is well known that the main reason for an elastic material to fail in brittle fashion—i.e., suddenly—is stress concentration in the presence of initial tiny flaws or cracks in the material. The investigation revealed that such minor cracks as minuscule pinholes had existed in the eyebar ever since they had been forged and hammered into shape and then heat-treated to minimize the *hardness* or brittleness resulting from the forging and hammering process. The surface of the eyebar had indeed been *softened*, but a harder and hence more brittle layer still existed a fraction of an inch below the surface. This region, produced by too fast a cooling and shrinking of the material after heat treatment, allowed existing pinhole cracks to lengthen under the slightest application of a tensile stress. This particular phenomenon, called *stress corrosion*, was finally recognized as the *primary mechanism* of the Silver Bridge collapse.

In a standard test (called the Sharpy test) a pendulum hits a metal bar, notched to induce a stress concentration, from greater and greater heights until the bar breaks. The pendulum energy increases with height and measures the metal's resistance to stress corrosion, its *toughness*. The harder the material, the more brittle it is and the smaller is the amount of energy needed to break it by means of the pendulum impact. The Sharpy test measures, for example, the brittleness of cast iron and compares it with the softness of copper.

Toughness has the lamentable property of decreasing with temperature. Steel, for example, shatters like glass at −30°F (−34°C) but is already more sensitive to brittle fracture at 30°F (−1°C) than at room temperature, 70°F (21°C). During the Second World War a number of welded Liberty ships, conveying military supplies to the USSR, broke up in the Arctic Ocean, and old sailors preferred the uninterrupted creaky songs of riveted ships, telling them that the ships were still whole, to the crackling sounds of the Liberty ships, announcing the failure of a welded joint that often led to the breakup in mid-ocean of the entire ship.

The sequence of events leading to the collapse of the Silver Bridge can now be easily explained. The eyebars are forged, hammered, and heat-treated, but the process is not sufficiently controlled thermally; the core of the iron is still hard and therefore brittle; the eyebar presents initial flaws that appear insignificant under the assumption that the material is ductile; low winter temperatures cause the initial flaws to become larger under load alternations; the bridge goes through forty winter-summer cycles; the hidden cracks enlarge and merge, mimicking the process of *corrosion;* and as proved by tests, the steel becomes failure-sensitive at temperatures around 30°F (−1°C), which was the temperature on the fatal day. The bridge thus did not fail because of excessive loading; it succumbed to stress corrosion because of temperature cycling.

Even after the bridge collapse had been scientifically explained, diverging opinions were presented: "The failure was due to overload together with lack of lubrication between the eyebars and the connecting pins"; "no, it was essentially due to overload unless somebody up there was hacking away with a hacksaw!" Even in the field of modern technology, wherever more than one person express opinions, there is contention.

The Silver Bridge at Point Pleasant was one of two identical bridges. Its twin at St. Marys, also on the Ohio River, was dismantled in 1969 to preclude a future disaster. But costly blunders serve as useful learning experiences. President Lyndon Johnson, partly to counterbalance the tragic blunders of Vietnam, took time out from world affairs to order an inquiry into bridge safety throughout the nation. It was the beginning of the realization that our aging infrastructure needed urgent attention. More than seven hundred thousand bridges were inspected and classified by a president's panel on bridge safety. The process of bridge repairs is still under way and has become a continuous effort to rehabilitate our infrastructure.

9

Thruways to Eternity

They were thrown about like chaff before
  the wind;
When the fearful raging flood
Rushing where the city stood,
Leaving thousands dead and dying there
  behind.

"The Johnstown Flood,"
a ballad by an unknown author

The Mianus River Bridge Fall

On the fine morning of September 1982 Jerry White and his partner parked an orange Department of Transportation (DOT) truck near the twenty-five-year-old Mianus River Bridge on the Connecticut Turnpike. They were one of six two-man teams employed at the time by the DOT to inspect biennially over thirty-five hundred bridges in Connecticut. On average, each team was responsible for the inspection of almost three hundred bridges a year, more than one on some working days. To check the condition of the underside of a bridge deck when it was high above the water, 75 ft. (25 m) at the Mianus Bridge, White and his partner had a truck that normally carried a device on the end of an articulated boom. Called a *snooper*, the device hung under the bridge deck to allow them to view inaccessible spots. Unfortunately their snooper had been out of service for eleven months prior to this particular inspection, so White and his partner were compelled to check the bridge with binoculars from

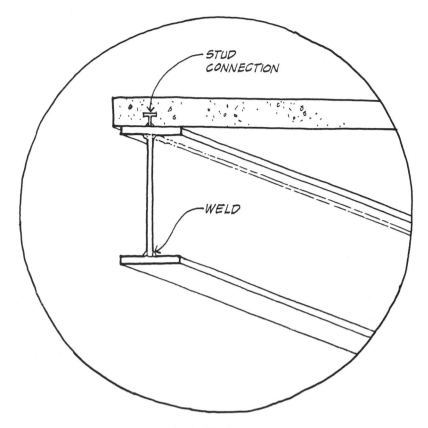

STUD
CONNECTION

WELD

9.1 Typical Welded Bridge Girder

the banks and to climb ladders up the piers for a better view of the steel structure.

They could also inspect the structure by walking along cat-walks hung from the bridge, one at the center of each of the two roadways and one between the roadways. To get closer to critical parts of the bridge structure, inspectors often walked on the bottom ledge formed by the inside flange of the I-shaped steel girders (Fig. 9.1), a precarious practice because of the pigeon excrement underfoot and the lack of safety hooks. That day White and his partner were looking as usual for signs of rusting of the steel girders and of disintegration of the concrete deck. Deterioration of bridges is a particularly severe problem in northern regions, where salts used to melt snow slowly destroy both steel and concrete. Chlorides in the salts attack steel, causing oxidation, rusting, through galvanic action of an electric current generated in the presence of water, as it is in a battery.

Where bridge piers stood in water, inspectors were also required, for bonus pay, of course, to make underwater dives to view the

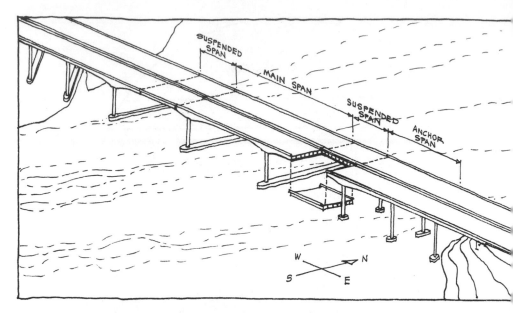

9.2 Mianus River Bridge, Showing Collapsed Section

condition of the foundations. Although not critical in the case of the Mianus River Bridge, such underwater inspections often detect possible foundation problems before they become critical (see p. 146).

Jerry White took penciled notes of his observations but did not forward them to the DOT office together with the standard completed inspection forms.

The Mianus River Bridge (Fig. 9.2) is a multiple-span structure carrying more than one hundred thousand cars daily over one of the most highly traveled routes in the world. It consists of two side-by-side three-lane bridges, one carrying westbound and the other eastbound traffic, of cantilevered construction, a type popular in the late 1950s. In cantilevered construction, steel plate girders (large I-shaped beams formed by welding plates together) run over two piers projecting beyond the face of the piers, like arms reaching out, to hold suspended spans. The Mianus bridges had two suspended spans, 100 ft. (30 m) long, on each side of a central span. The east end of the easterly suspended span was hung by means of a pin-and-hanger assembly from the ends of the east cantilever, and its west end sat in a cradle, called a *pillow block*, on a horizontal pin attached to the end of the cantilever from the central span (Fig. 9.3). Each hanger assembly consisted of two vertical steel plates pinned at the top to the cantilevered end of the anchor span and at the bottom to the end of the hung span (Fig. 9.4). Just

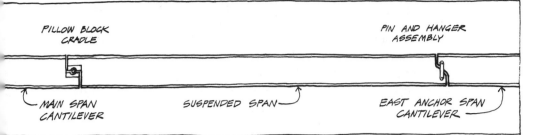

PILLOW BLOCK
CRADLE

PIN AND HANGER
ASSEMBLY

MAIN SPAN
CANTILEVER

SUSPENDED SPAN

EAST ANCHOR SPAN
CANTILEVER

9.3   Suspended Span Support Conditions

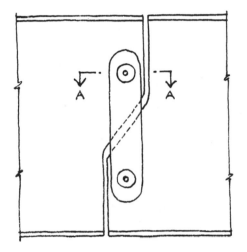

END DETAIL AT LINK

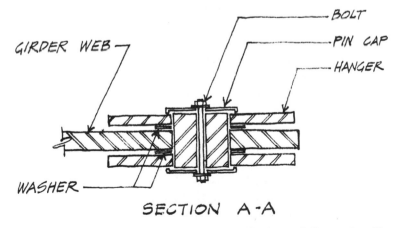

BOLT

PIN CAP

HANGER

GIRDER WEB

WASHER

SECTION A-A

9.4   Pin and Hanger Assembly: Elevation and Cross Section

like the ropes in a child's swing, the hanging plates tended to be in a vertical position but could swing from it, allowing the shortening of the hung girder in cold weather and its lengthening in the heat of summer. The failure of a single pin or bar in this assembly could cause the span to fall; it had *no redundancy* (see p. 55). The assembly had been recognized unsafe since 1968 and was not used in new construction. Many, but not all, new bridges built with pin-and-hanger assemblies were made safer by the addition of a steel yoke, or *sling*, which acted as a second hanger in case of failure of the first.

In the late spring of 1983 people who lived on the banks of the Mianus River, virtually in the shadow of the bridge, claimed to have heard shrill noises coming from it. For at least five or six years they had been finding on the riverbanks pieces of concrete and bits of steel from the bridge and had dutifully reported each of these findings to the Connecticut Department of Transportation. However, a new sound had been added recently to the rumble of the overhead traffic. "[A] high piercing [sound], like thousands of birds chirping," said a nearby resident. "It was very noticeable over the weekend [preceding the accident]."

Monday night, June 27, 1983, J. William Burns, the Connecticut commissioner of transportation, had been home packing for a trip to Scandinavia the next day. At 2:00 A.M. he was awakened by a telephone call. Within five minutes he was out of the house, shouting to his wife, "Honey, I don't think we're going to Sweden today." The call had come from a state trooper informing the commissioner that a bridge had collapsed thirty minutes earlier, taking several trucks and cars down into the Mianus River, killing three people and injuring three more.

Shortly before Commissioner Burns received the call, a resident in a nearby development had been rudely awakened by "a loud noise . . . like a clap of thunder." She added: "The house shook so much I knew something [terrible] had happened. I came out to [look at] the bridge and saw we had no bridge left." One of the two eastbound suspended sections of the bridge had fallen virtually intact into the river, and two cars and two tractor trailers lay crushed and twisted in the shallow water below. After surveying the wreckage and the bridge, Burns announced at the site that he saw a possible clue to the collapse: One of the pins connecting the fallen section to one of the cantilevered girders was missing. "If it had sheared off—he [Burns] said—it could have caused [the collapse]." A segment of the missing 7 in. (18 cm) pin was eventually recovered from the river, while the rest was found still connected to the cantilevered part of the bridge.

Was the pin the key to the failure, as Mr. Burns suspected, or were there additional causes? To help solve this riddle, Mr. Burns asked Dr. John Fisher, an engineer and a Lehigh University professor with a worldwide reputation in metallurgical research, to investigate the collapse. Three independent engineering firms and the National Transportation Safety Board were also brought in to ascertain the cause of the collapse; they were eventually joined by other engineers representing litigants in the court actions brought to recover damages. All the experts focused their attention on the hanger assemblies, although, as is not unusual, each came to emphasize different causes and reach different conclusions.

The bridge's assembly consisted of steel bar hangers, shaped like a doctor's tongue depressor, with a hole at each end to accept pins; washers to separate the hangers from the face of the steel girders; and a locking device to hold this sandwich together (Fig. 9.4). The locking device consisted of a cap on each end of the pin, secured by means of a threaded rod passing through the length of the pin's axis and tightened with nuts at each end. These caps, supposedly restraining the hanger from slipping off the pin, appeared to be "rather flimsy" to all the experts: Several caps were *dished out*, changed from original flat disks to saucer-shaped configurations, as if bent out by a powerful force pushing them out. They were only 0.3 in. (8 mm) thick, totally out of proportion to the substantial dimensions of the pin. Calculations proved the caps' thickness was less than one-half that required by the design regulations in force at the time of construction (1957).

The heavy concentration of rust found throughout the various parts of the hanger assembly appeared to be another probable cause of trouble. When Mr. White, the inspector, had walked along the catwalk, looking toward the outside hanger assembly, he could have seen the dishing of the pin cap from 20 ft. (7 m) away by using binoculars, but he could not have observed the extensive rusting *behind* the cap plate. (Removal of the cap plate was not part of the inspection procedure then, nor is it required at the time of this writing.) Examination of the recovered portions of the hanger assembly revealed that the surface between the hanger plate and the pin was severely corroded, as were the surfaces between the spacer washer and the girder (Fig. 9.4). This implied a reduction in thickness of the hanger plate in contact with the pin and hence that the *stress* in the essential parts of the assembly had substantially increased. This high stress could well be one of the collapse causes. Moreover, when rust builds up in a confined space, it increases in volume and exerts a tremendous pressure. Rust could easily have caused the observed dishing of the pin cap plate. (This action is similar to what happens when water freezes, increasing in volume as it turns into ice. Taking advantage of this force, stonemasons used to drill holes in blocks of stone to be split, filled them with water, and let winter's cold exert the splitting force.)

The unusual amount of rust found in the Mianus Bridge hanger assembly led the investigators to look for the source of the water responsible for it. It was discovered that ten years before the accident the drains on the roadway had been paved over, allowing water, salt, and dirt to flow through the joint between the cantilevered and suspended spans, dropping directly onto the hanger assembly and causing accelerated rusting of its steel.

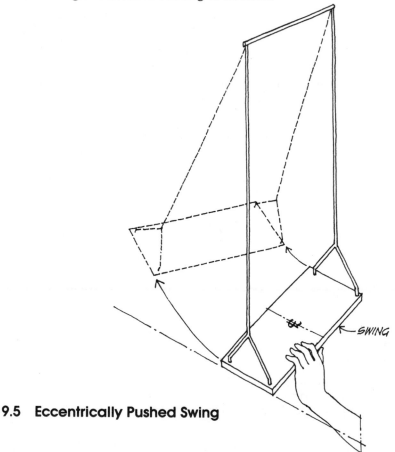

9.5 Eccentrically Pushed Swing

The suspended span, even if it had been rectangular in plan, would have imposed sideways forces on the four corner supports because the accelerations or braking forces of vehicles on the bridge are never perfectly centered on the roadway. As anyone who has ever pushed a child on a swing with hands placed even slightly off center will recognize, the swing *twists*, and if that twist is restrained, sideways forces occur (Fig. 9.5). In the Mianus Bridge, these lateral forces were almost six times larger than the reactions on a rectangular bridge because the bridge was skewed at an angle of almost 54° with respect to the direction of the river.

We can now reconstruct the events leading to the collapse of the Mianus Bridge. Over the bridge's twenty-five years, corrosion builds up between the hanger plates and the pins because of the constant wetting action of rain, brought on by the paving over of the floor drains. Each time a car or truck passes over the bridge, the skew effect imposes a lateral force on the hanger plates, contributing to the tendency of the hanger plates to be pushed off the pin. At the southeast corner of the suspended span, the force of corrosion, aggravated by the skew effect, is so large that it causes the restraining pin cap to dish out and possibly pop off. Sometime before the collapse, hours or days earlier, the bottom of the inside hanger plate slips off the pin (Fig. 9.6), causing a transfer of the

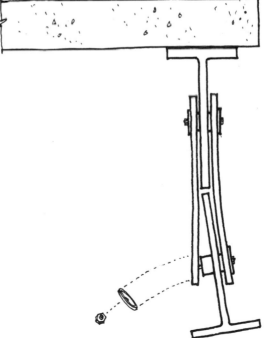

9.6 Failure of Hanger

load to the outside hanger plate, which must now carry twice the load for which it was designed. It also causes the southeast corner of the span to drop slightly, creating a step to the cantilevered span. (A truck going east and passing that point not more than thirty minutes before the accident reported striking a bump about 4 in. [10 cm] high.) The outside hanger plate also bends out because of the prying action of the now-eccentric load replacing the load equally balanced between the two hangers. Repeated pounding of traffic causes a fatigue crack (see p. 123) to develop at the top of the upper pin, which eventually breaks off, initiating the collapse. The end comes quickly after this condition develops. A trailer truck in the curb lane, a car in the median lane behind it, and another truck in the center lane start to move across the span. Their weight bends the cracked pin, which tears apart, causing the outside hanger to fall. There is a sudden flash of light as the streetlamps go out, their wires severed by the scissorlike action of the suspended span moving down against the cantilevered girder. The east end of the span is now supported by the remaining hanger assembly at the northeast corner, which cannot carry the added load and breaks, causing the span to rotate downward, carrying the three vehicles with it. As the span rotates, it lifts off the pillow blocks on the west end and slips eastward, continuing its downward plunge. The leading truck, unable to halt its forward motion, is impaled on the "expansion fingers" of the cantilevered span (a serrated steel plate covering the joint in the roadway), causing the top of the cab to be ripped off. The car and second truck fly off the falling span into the river, striking the pier of the standing structure.

In the aftermath of the disaster the inspector, Jerry White, "panicked" and altered the notes he had made during his last inspection, lest his inspection be deemed insufficiently thorough. He made about twenty additions to the notes ("needs snooper," "laminated rust," "vertical cracks," etc.), made copies of the falsified notes, turned them in to his superiors, and burned the originals. Because he used a finer pencil to make the corrections, he was found out, but in recognition of his long record of good service, he was only reprimanded and given a one-year probation.

The Schoharie Bridge Catastrophe

The Erie Canal was first proposed in 1724 to join the Hudson River to the Great Lakes, but its construction did not start for almost a century. A technical marvel of nineteenth-century technology, the Erie Canal cuts a 363 mi. (581 km) path through wilderness and forests, dug by hand labor and horse or ox-drawn plows and scrapers. Although the vertical difference along its route does not exceed 675 ft. (206 m), a total of eighty-three locks were required to accommodate it to the rolling terrain. Rising westward from Albany to Utica demanded fifty-three locks; after the canal ran the length of the Mohawk Valley and crossed the Genesee River on an aqueduct, another twenty-five locks permitted it to reach the level of the great Genesee. Finally, a flight of five locks brought the canal into Lake Erie. When completed in 1825, it was the longest canal in the Western world, and proud New Yorkers proclaimed:

> 'Tis done! 'Tis done! The mighty chain
> Which joins bright Erie to the Main,
> For ages, shall perpetuate
> The glory of our native State.

The first canalboat to arrive in New York on November 4, 1825, carried a keg of water from Lake Erie, which Governor De Witt Clinton poured into the Atlantic to celebrate the "marriage of the waters." The last boat traveled the canal's length in 1918.

A stone aqueduct built in 1841 to carry the Erie Canal over the Schoharie Creek (near its confluence with the Mohawk River) stood for a century, 4,000 ft. (1200 m) downstream of a bridge that today carries the New York State Thruway over the creek. Founded on a base of limestone blocks supported by heavy timbers driven into the ground, called *spiles*, the aqueduct survived numerous floods until in 1940, after two decades of disuse and neglect, the first of its fourteen arches collapsed as the result of the undermining of its foundation by the creek's current (Fig. 9.7).

In the vicinity of the Erie Canal aqueduct, a number of other bridges were built over the Schoharie Creek between 1880 and 1930, and many also collapsed partially or completely because of floods, including a state bridge that fell in 1987 six days after one of the most tragic bridge failures in New York State, that of the Thruway bridge over the Schoharie Creek.

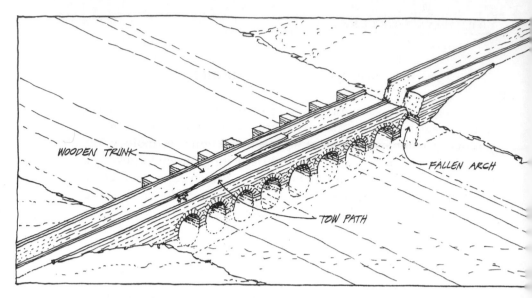

9.7a Schoharie Creek Aqueduct

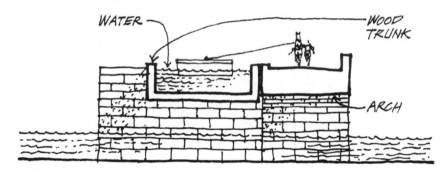

9.7b Section through Aqueduct

The New York Thruway between New York City and Buffalo, built in the 1950s as part of a nationwide network of limited-access highways linking every state from the Atlantic to the Pacific Coast, is the twentieth-century transportation answer to the nineteenth-century Erie Canal. The 540 ft. (164 m) long Thruway bridge at Schoharie Creek consists of five spans of steel girders supporting a concrete deck and carries both east- and westbound lanes (Fig. 9.8).

On the morning of April 5, 1987, thirty-five years after the bridge was constructed, the third from the west of its four concrete piers collapsed into the fast-moving waters of Schoharie, as reported by two witnesses, with the sound of "an explosion or thunder." Two spans of the bridge were carried down 80 ft. (25 m), ending at the

9.8 Thruway Bridge at Schoharie Creek

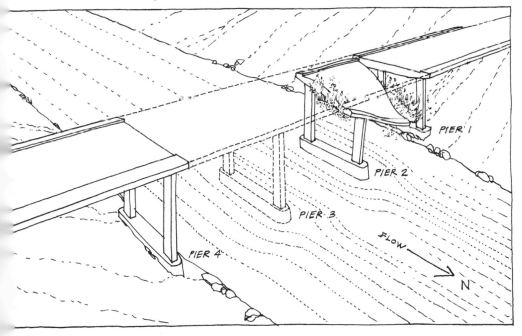

9.9 Collapsed Schoharie Bridge

bottom of the creek, together with a car and a truck. Within a minute three more cars had dived into the murky waters, and within ninety minutes the second pier from the west (Fig. 9.9) and another span of the bridge had also collapsed. The power of the rushing waters was so great that one vehicle was swept downstream 4,700 ft. (1500 m) before coming to rest, and the body of one of its passengers was never found. Altogether, ten people were killed in the accident, which occurred on a stretch of road carrying an average of sixteen thousand vehicles a day.

As a result of the Silver Bridge collapse in 1967, national bridge inspection standards requiring the biennial inspection of all bridges in the nation had been established. New York State requirements, more stringent than the national standard, mandated annual inspections of Thruway bridges and diver inspections of underwater elements at five-year intervals, none of which had yet been carried out at Schoharie, although one was scheduled for 1987, the very year of the collapse. The yearly inspections never aroused suspicion of an existing problem at the bridge, although *riprap* (broken stones thrown together irregularly around the base of the piers to protect them) had remained visible only on the downstream side of the piers as early as 1977. A report prepared in that year had recommended the replacement of the missing riprap, but in the contract issued in 1980 for maintenance work, all reference to new stone riprap had been deleted by a nonengineer state employee who decided, after viewing the site from shore, that it was unnecessary. Further evidence of the force of the rushing water was shown by the fact that the rocks used for the riprap, weighing about 1,100 lb. (500 kg) each, had over time been carried well downstream. Was this force considered in the design?

When the bridge was built, cofferdams (boxes of interlocking steel plates) had been placed around the areas at the base of the piers to keep out the water during construction and allowed space for riprap stones. According to the original design, and as stated during the postcollapse investigation, the cofferdams were intended to remain in place, containing the stones and protecting the piers against erosion. (However, the design documents did not clearly state this requirement.)

Scour is experienced by anyone who stands on the beach in a fast-flowing undertow from a receding wave. The sand on the up-beach side of the feet is washed out by "scouring," and the parts of the feet thus unsupported sink into the sand (Fig. 9.10). Under Pier

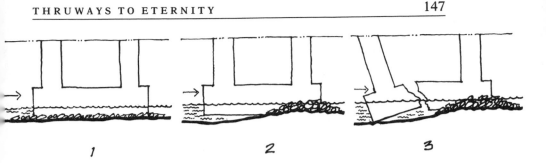

9.10 Effect of Scour on Bridge Piers

3 of the Schoharie Creek Bridge the depth of scour on the upstream side, measured after the collapse, was as much as 9 ft. (3 m), causing the pier to tip upstream into the scoured hole and the bridge girders to slip off their supports, falling to the river. If the girders had been *continuous*—that is, in one piece for the full length of the bridge—the failure of one pier would have resulted in the sagging of the girders, a clear warning of impending failure.

A bridge over the Inn River at Kufstein, Austria, suffered the loss of a pier under circumstances almost identical to those at Schoharie, with one crucial difference: The bridge was a continuous concrete box with five spans from one abutment to the other. On July 11, 1990, a motorist noticed a sag in the bridge and notified the authorities, who closed the span without any accidents or loss of life. A pier had failed, sinking into the river, but redundancy had provided the warning signs. This *redundancy* might have been just enough to save the lives of the ten victims of the Schoharie Creek collapse.

The Hatchie Bridge Tragedy

Two years after the Schoharie Creek disaster a furniture van and several cars were driving north on U.S. 51 near Covington, Tennessee, and rolling over a 28 ft. (9 m) section of a bridge over the Hatchie River when suddenly the span dropped into the water 25 ft. (8 m) below the roadway. One car hurled through the gap and came to rest 80 ft. (24 m) farther north under the bridge. The furniture van followed the car, hitting the next two bridge supports as it flew through the air, causing additional spans to fall and burying the van and a total of three cars under a hundred tons of debris. On that fateful evening of April 1, 1989, the bridge was fifty-five years old, certainly within the expected useful life of such a structure.

Unlike the Schoharie Bridge, the Hatchie River span had a foundation of timber piles, a modern version of the spiles used under the old Erie aqueduct. Although both bridges failed as a result of scouring and undermining of the foundations, the Hatchie also suffered from long-term *meandering* of the river channel, which had migrated 83 ft. (25 m) northward since the bridge was built. On the day of the failure the Hatchie River was 3 ft. (1 m) above flood stage and had spread across the flat plain to almost three times its normal width. It appeared to the investigators of the collapse that one or more bridge piers had been undermined by the scouring action of the water. The pier that failed was unprotected from scour, since it was originally not in the main channel, although two prior field inspections noting the migrating channel had recommended that such protection be added.

In the final analysis, a *technical* fault, *lack of redundancy*, and a measure of *human* failing share the blame for the collapses of the Mianus, the Schoharie, and the Hatchie river bridges. Can these tragic failures be avoided in the future? The ever-deepening research into material properties and natural phenomena will certainly contribute to minimize damage caused by incomplete knowledge, but human nature and economic difficulties must be considered as unavoidable obstacles to perfect construction.

10

The Weaknesses of Mother Earth

[A] foolish man ... built his house upon
the sand: And the rain descended, and the
floods came, and the winds blew, and beat
upon that house; and it fell. . . .

Matthew 7:26–27

S oils often act as the very worst structural materials, yet we
must entrust the support of all our buildings to their strength
(at least until we decide to levitate them in electromagnetic fields). Some soils are weak, as is loose sand permeated by water, which exhibits *liquefaction* under load when water
is squeezed out of it by superimposed weights; others are hard as
rock and can support over 40 tons per square foot (3,800 kN / m²);
others are tricky, like clay that is hard when dry and slippery when
wet; and most of them have properties that vary from spot to spot.
Luckily, in the last fifty years the relatively young science of soil
mechanics, originated in Austria and Germany in the early 1800s,
has made rapid progress in determining soil properties vital to the
construction and the structural design of buildings.

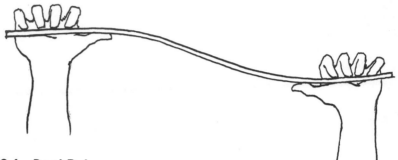

10.1   Bent Ruler

Why should we all be interested in soils? Because soil instability can endanger skyscrapers as well as one-family houses and bridges as well as harbors and can be responsible for minor as well as disastrous structural failures. No contemporary structural engineer would dare design a building, any building, without first obtaining from a soil engineering report detailed information, including the difference in settlements to be expected at points on a site. Large *differential settlements* may damage any structure, as you may prove to yourself by grabbing at both ends a thin ruler (to represent a beam) and lowering one hand with respect to the other until it breaks (Fig. 10.1). Or by putting a cereal box (to represent a building) on a piece of cardboard (to represent the soil surface) and tilting the cardboard (simulating the settlement of the soil) until the "building" topples. Or by placing on the cardboard two cereal boxes next to each other and bending the cardboard to simulate the splitting apart of a wide building when it stands on soil that is weaker on one end than on the other.

The following cases of soil problems will show you what may or even may not happen to buildings because of unexpected soil properties. From now on we hope you will not be surprised by earth movements that atavistically we are inclined to deny because if *even* the earth moves, what can we rely on to stay put?

A Strange Case
of Gentle Settlement

When walking into the main square El Zócalo, a first-time visitor to Mexico City in 1940 would probably have been attracted by the crowds milling around day and night, by the sight of the ancient cathedral—begun in 1573—and by the National Palace with murals by Diego Rivera, José Orozco, and David Siqueiros. Eventually the visitor would have wandered to the Alameda and noticed the Palace of Fine Arts, a majestic building with a massive concrete structure clad in heavy Italian travertine, built between 1900 and 1934 and containing the magnificent thirty-five-hundred-seat Opera, the National Theater, and the Art Museum. The visitor would have been surprised to notice that while all the other buildings on the square were built at the square's level, the theater stood at that time 6 ft. (1.8 m) *below* it so that one had to go *down* a staircase to enter. But upon inquiring of a Mexican friend about this unusual feature, the visitor would have learned that like the other Alameda buildings, the theater had been built on grade, on the loose sand permeated with the water of ancient Lake Texcoco, but that the enormous weight of the palace had slowly squeezed the water out from under it, compressing the soil and lowering the theater in due time by 6 ft. (1.8 m). Surprisingly the building was not damaged, because the sandy homogeneous soil was squeezed down *equally* under the weight of the building, uniformly distributed over its plan area, and its stiff structure allowed the theater to move *rigidly*—that is, without dangerous distortions.

But if our visitor had returned to the Alameda in the 1960s, he would have noticed, to his greater surprise, that the National Theater had moved again. One still entered it by way of a staircase, but now one went *up*, because the theater was 6 ft. (1.8 m) *above* the level of the square, having risen, undamaged, 12 ft. (3.6 m). His Mexican friend, noticing the surprised expression on the face of the visitor, would probably have asked him to look around the square. Did he notice any changes in the landscape? Yes, a number of tall buildings had been erected around the square since he had been there twenty years earlier. This time the weight of the skyscrapers had squeezed the water out from under their foundations and pushed it back under the theater. This enormous but simple hydraulic system was responsible for the theater's rising above the level of the square. It is one of the rare occasions when soil motions of this magnitude have done *no* damage to a building. But not all soils are this considerate, and not all buildings are that stiff, and as the reader will learn, much smaller motions can cause real catastrophes.

The Florida Pancake

The superficial layers of soil along the east coast of southern Florida consist of a conglomeration of solidified dirt and sea vegetation of varying thickness, on which light buildings have been safely founded. In the 1950s a large condominium and hotel complex was designed for a site on this coast, and the soil engineers consulted by the engineering designer advised that the building should be supported on piles. Piles of wood, reinforced concrete, or steel are used to reach a compact or hard (rocky) soil strong enough to sup-

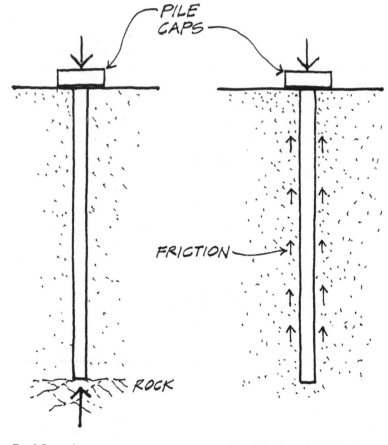

a   **End-Bearing**   b   **Friction-Supported**

10.2   Piles

port a building's weight as transmitted through its columns. These piles may act in two different ways. In *thin* layers of weak soil above layers of strong soil, the piles are designed long enough to transmit directly in compression the loads from the *pile caps* to the strong layers. In *deep*, stiffer soils the piles are supported by the friction developed between their outer surface and the soil (Fig. 10.2).

Before the Florida complex was designed, a square grid, 50 ft. (15 m) on a side, was laid out on the site by the soil consultants (geotechnical engineers), and samples of the soil were drilled out at each corner of the grid. The geotechnical engineers examined the soil samples and determined that 30 ft. (9 m) long friction piles would safely support the heaviest building on the site, a twenty-five-story hotel. The ordered piles were being driven in at column locations when suddenly the operation had to be stopped . . . because a pile had disappeared into the soil after the last drop of the pile driver's weight! An inspection of the hole at that particular spot showed that the soil was Florida pancake, weakly supported by loose sand saturated with water. Additional exploration showed that to reach a solid layer, the piles had to be up to 140 ft. (42 m) long! It goes without saying that in this case the variation of soil properties was so great from point to point that sampling from a 50 ft. (15 m) square grid, usually considered conservative, had been too scattered to detect the variable soil characteristics. Had it not been for the disappearing pile (and one might not have disappeared only a few feet away), a catastrophe might have ensued.

The delay in construction caused by this incident was responsible for contractors' compensation from the owners of hundreds of thousands of dollars. A few additional samples and longer piles would have been less costly.

Did the Tower Stop Leaning?

The lovely Tuscan town of Pisa was originally a Greek colony on the banks of the Arno River where it flows into the Tyrrhenian Sea and later an Etruscan city and a part of the Roman Empire. It became a powerful maritime republic in the eleventh century, dominating the Mediterranean against its rival republics, Genoa and Venice, and the Arabs until it was defeated by Florence at the naval Battle of Meloria in 1284. It fell to Florence in 1406.

10.3 The Leaning Tower of Pisa, Italy

Now six miles from the coast, Pisa boasts such an incredibly beautiful square that the Pisans refer to it as the Field of Miracles. It is surrounded by the superb cathedral, the baptistery, and the famous Leaning Tower, all clad in white marble in the Pisan Romanesque style popular between the twelfth and the fourteenth centuries (Fig. 10.3).

Amateur scientists visiting these monuments cannot forget that Galileo Galilei, first a student and then a professor at the local university, discovered the *isocronicity* (equal time) of pendulum oscillations—i.e., that their duration or period is independent of the size of their swings—by measuring against his pulse the period of the hanging chandelier of the baptistery. They also remember that the velocity of bodies falling under the action of gravity is independent of their weight. Galileo proved this by dropping wood and iron balls from the top of the Leaning Tower of Pisa, which, most obligingly, already leaned toward the south with its top displaced by about 15 ft. (4.5 m) from its base.

The tower had never been straight. Started in 1174 by Bonanno Pisano (a Pisan Goodyear), it began leaning slightly to the north from the start of construction because of unstable soil conditions, as shown by the slanted cut of the stone blocks of its inner structure and the wedge-shaped layers of mortar used in trying to straighten out its upper part. It soon shifted, leaning to the south, and continues to do so to this day. The tower's inner structure consists of an outer cylinder of heavy stone blocks, an inner cylinder of porous, weaker stone blocks, and a fill of stone chips and lye mortar. A clockwise staircase runs to the top of the tower inside the interior structure, with opening onto the balconies. The exterior of the tower is subdivided into eight segments: a solid basement, six balconies ornamented with arch openings, and a bell tower that also served as lookout against enemies. The tower is 200 ft. (60 m) high and stands 193 ft. (58 m) above ground (Fig. 10.4).

In view of the tower's inclination, it is of interest to learn a few details about the three layers of soil under it. The first, about 33 ft. (10 m) thick, is composed of variable thickness, mixed layers of mud, compressible clay, and sand; the second, 33 to 70 ft. (10–21 m) thick, is composed of four layers of compressible clay, hard clay, sand, and, again, clay; the third, of a layer of sand, 67 ft. (20 m) thick, saturated with water (Fig. 10.5).

In 1174, when construction had almost reached the level of the ceiling of the third terrace, it was stopped, most probably owing

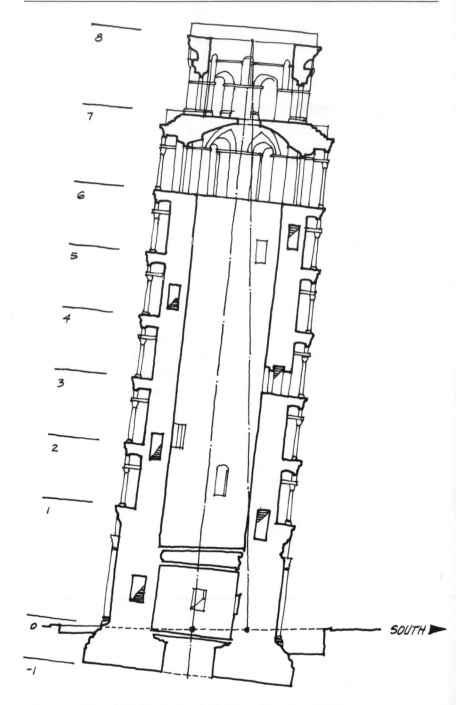

10.4   Section through the Leaning Tower of Pisa

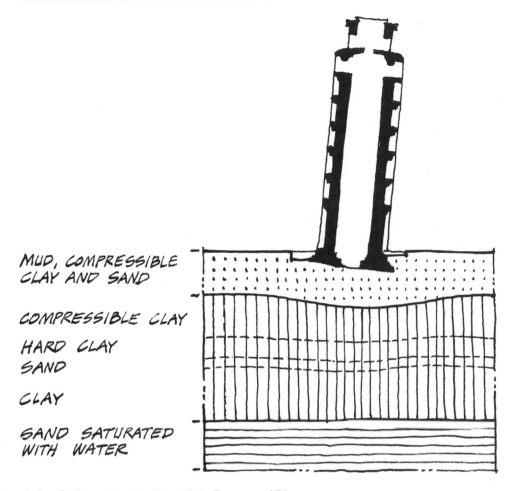

MUD, COMPRESSIBLE
CLAY AND SAND

COMPRESSIBLE CLAY

HARD CLAY

SAND

CLAY

SAND SATURATED
WITH WATER

10.5 Soil under the Leaning Tower of Pisa

to Pisa's perpetual state of warfar'e. It was not continued until ninety-four years later, in 1272, when it reached the level of the sixth-balcony ceiling. In an attempt to counteract the leaning (by now pronouncedly southward) of the first construction, 1 ft. (0.35 m) at its top, the rest of the tower was built at a slight angle to the north with respect to the lower part, a difference distinguishable to the naked eye. But the tower kept leaning more and more to the south, and the bell tower was added, at the same inclination, between 1360 and 1370.

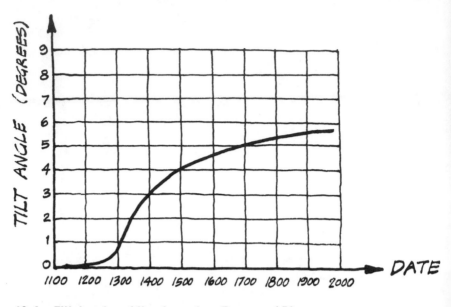

10.6   Tilt Angle of the Leaning Tower of Pisa

The graph of Fig. 10.6 shows the increase in the inclination angle of the tower between 1174 and 1980: The tower leaned slowly at first, had the most pronounced rate of inclination around the beginning of the thirteenth century (1300), and has continuously reduced its leaning rate up to the present time.

The Pisans have always loved and cared for their tower, but until recent times they did not know what radical measures were needed to stop it from tilting. Had it not been for the long initial interruption of construction, which allowed the slow consolidation of the clay layers by the weight of the lower part (6,730 short British tons, or 5,780 metric tons), the tower would probably have been finished in less than fourteen years . . . and then collapsed. Luckily the Pisans could only fix the marble exterior, changing four balcony columns in 1394, restoring the balconies extensively between 1797 and 1808, and building a raised masonry platform around the base in 1838 to facilitate entrance into the tower and stop the surface water from percolating into the soil. To their dismay, this work, instead of improving the situation, accelerated the leaning. In 1935 the Corps of Civil Engineers (a civilian agency of the Italian government) injected with mortar the original foundations of *dry masonry* (built without mortar), with the shocking result of suddenly *increasing* the tower inclination by 33 seconds of a degree (less than one-hundredth of a degree) at a time when the yearly leaning rate averaged only 5 seconds of a degree (less than 1.5 thousandths of a degree). In 1990 the displacement at the top of the tower was 10 ft. (2.97 m), the inclination 5 degrees 21 minutes, and the settlement of the foundations 8.33 ft. (2.5 m).

In 1965 a thorough investigation of the tower's condition was finally performed by a ministerial committee, which published its results in three volumes. The main conclusion of this exhaustive report indicated that the water level under the tower was *below* sea level and could be explained only by the large amount of water pumped daily from deep wells in the area. The report's recommendation, to limit the amount of water to be pumped in the future, was accepted, with minuscule positive results.

At long last in 1990 Dr. Carlo Cestelli-Guidi, a professor of soil mechanics at the University of Rome and the first scientist to establish a soil mechanics laboratory in Italy (in 1928), reviewed with Dr. Giovanni Calabresi all the available evidence on the basis of today's knowledge and came to the surprising but welcome conclusion that the tower was in *stable* condition and that none of the suggestions (proposed by the sixteen participants to a 1972 international competition called to study how to stop the leaning) was warranted and most of them would, almost certainly, be risky. But . . .

The Italian experts have informed the world that during the first three months of 1991 the tower leaned by 4 / 100 in. (1 mm), more than it did in the preceding twelve months. While a permanent solution to the continuing lean is still being sought, temporary strengthening of the base of the tower has been implemented. This consists of the installation of a girdle of posttensioning wires to prevent local buckling of the highly stressed lower part of the tower. When dealing with soils and old buildings, one never knows what to expect.

Recent rumors about disagreements between the Pisan administration and the Italian Ministry of Public Works may have suggested that the tower was in danger of collapse. Nothing is farther from the truth. The tower was temporarily closed to the public in 1989 to allow restoration of its marble exterior, badly damaged by industrial pollution, a needed action that was resented by a city administration eager not to lose, even in part, the two million dollars a year it raises from crowds converging from all parts of the world to visit the Leaning Tower.

On the other hand, it has been reported at the time of this writing (1991) that the tower has been righting itself possibly because of recent heavy rains that have saturated the earth and that the tower has been temporarily stabilized by means of inclined steel cables connected to concrete blocks in the ground.

Of course, the Pisans never wanted the tower to be straightened out. Who would travel halfway around the world to see the Straight Tower of Pisa?

11

Valley of Tears

See yonder vale, as morn breaks o'er the
scene,
Bedeck'd with fragrant flow'rs and nature's
sombre green,
Tho' now the sun shines o'er the scene, and
after many years
We'll ne'er forget that awful day, within
that vale of tears.

William Thomas

The storage of water in reservoirs to ensure continuous supplies for domestic use or crop irrigation has been used since earliest times. *Earth embankments*, artificial hills consisting of rocks and soil built across river valleys, were used in Ceylon (now Sri Lanka) as early as 504 B.C. to store water from rains falling in monsoon periods and to release it during periods of drought; one such dam at Padavil-Colan, Ceylon was an incredible 11 mi. (18 km) long and 70 ft. (21 m) high.

Huge earthen dams on the Tigris, the more eastern of the two great rivers in Mesopotamia, and a large masonry dam on the river Nile survived hundreds of years after their construction in prehistoric times. In the valley of the Orontes, near Homs in Syria, an earthen dam was already old when visited by Strabo, the Greek geographer, two thousand years ago and was finally reconditioned in 1934, having suffered from *piping* (the development of tubular leak-causing cavities) beneath its foundation. The rehabilitated dam narrowly survived a close brush with disaster when a windstorm, following record rainfalls that caused the water level in the reservoir to rise above the crest of the dam, resulted in *overtopping* of its embankments.

The Romans built numerous masonry dams throughout Italy and North Africa, generally characterized by a width at the base of three to four times their height. But only in the nineteenth century did the Scottish engineer William Rankine develop the scientific basis for the design of modern masonry dams, showing that their base width need be no more than their height.

In the recent war with Iraq the allied military command considered destroying the 429 ft. (130 m) high Mosul Dam on the Tigris River. The resulting massive flood would have engulfed Baghdad and much of southern Iraq. Only the potential of countless civilian casualties prevented this monstrous act from being implemented.

The earliest record of a dam failure is that of an earth embankment near Grenoble, France, which failed in 1219 after twenty-eight years of service. Of a total of 1,764 dams built in the United States before 1959, an incredibly high 1 in 50 failed for a variety of causes, ranging from defects in construction to poor maintenance and, most often, to the inadequacy of technical knowledge at the time. On the other hand, the strength of certain types of dams was demonstrated during the Second World War, when in March 1943 the Royal Air Force bombed dams in the Ruhr Valley of Germany. A masonry gravity structure and an earth embankment, both with a width at the crest of more than 50 ft. (15 m), were barely damaged by the bombs, while the Möhne Dam, a thinner concrete structure, was breached, devastating towns down the valley when the great volume of stored water was suddenly released.

Yet the worst dam disaster in the United States occurred as late as 1889.

The Destruction of Johnstown

Nestled in the Allegheny Mountains of central Pennsylvania lies the picturesque city of Johnstown. It is not surprising that the first settler, Joseph Jahns, a Swiss pioneer after whom the city was named, was attracted to the charming site on the banks of the Conemaugh River, surrounded by high hills reminiscent of his homeland. The city thrived in the nineteenth century with the exploitation of coal mining and the development of a steel industry, but its bucolic calm was rudely shattered on May 31, 1889, when the South Fork Dam, built 14 mi. (22 km) upstream of the city, suddenly burst following a period of unprecedented rain. A roaring 40 ft. (12 m) "ball" of water smashed into the city with incredible fury at a speed of 20 mph (32 km/h), completely destroying Johnstown and seven other towns in the valley. Buildings, bridges, trees, animals, and human beings were swept up in the path of the rushing waters. Locomotives were tossed about like cockleshells, and a mountain of debris, piled against a railroad bridge below the town, caught fire, becoming a funeral pyre for the living and dead trapped within it. Almost three thousand lives were lost in the flood and the fire, and thirty-five thousand people were left homeless. As the worst peacetime disaster in the nation's history the Johnstown flood soon became legend, inspiring poems and ballads, many of which survived through the generations thanks to an oral tradition.

Construction of the South Fork Dam was started in 1839 and, after a ten-year interruption (from 1841 to 1851) for lack of money, was completed in 1853. It was originally built to provide a reliable source of water for the Pennsylvania Canal, which ran from Philadelphia to Pittsburgh and included lengths of canal and one portage railroad. The dam, almost 900 ft. (270 m) long and 72 ft. (22 m) high, created a reservoir that could supply enough water to pass "two hundred boats per day for one hundred and thirty days without any augmentation from rain," according to an article by Alfred Pagan. In the original design, a spillway 150 ft. (45 m) wide allowed water up to a depth of 10 ft. (3 m) to pass over the dam, but the built spillway averaged only 110 ft. (33 m) in width (Fig. 11.1). Water could also be fed into the canal through five 2 ft. (600 mm) diameter outlet pipes. Four years after completion of the dam, railroads began to take over as the primary means of transportation in the area, and the canal and dam, no longer needed, were sold to the Pennsylvania Railroad. The dam was seldom used and in a sad state of disrepair by the time it was sold again (in 1880) to the South Fork Hunting and Fishing Club of Pittsburgh, which counted among its members such illustrious figures in industry and philanthropy as Andrew Carnegie and Henry Clay Frick. The dam repairs requested by the new owners modified it dangerously: The outlet pipes, no longer needed to feed the canal, were removed, the dam was lowered by 2 ft. (0.6 m) in order to accommodate a wider roadway on its top, a trestle bridge was constructed across the spillway to allow the road to go from one end of the dam to the other, and a screen was placed in front of the trestle to prevent the loss of fish when water overtopped the spillway (Fig. 11.2). The reduced width of the as-built spillway, together with all these modifications, reduced the capacity of the spillway to almost one-third of that intended in the original design. The scene was set for a disaster.

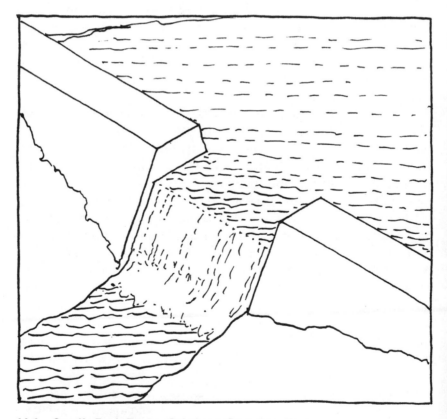

11.1 South Fork Dam: Original Construction

On May 30, 1889, it started to rain at 9:00 P.M. When the resident engineer engaged by the South Fork Club, John G. Parke, Jr., awoke the next morning, he noted that the water in the lake behind the dam had risen about 2 ft. (0.6 m). Concerned by the continually rising water level, he kept observing it while eating breakfast, then rode by horse to the South Fork village and sent a telegram to warn officials in Johnstown of the dangerous situation. By noon, when he returned to the dam, water was already flowing over it, and "as I crossed the breast (the roadway along the crest of the dam) at this time [I] found the water was cutting the outer face of the dam." The water was already 7.5 ft. (2.25 m) above the normal lake level, almost at the top of the cut-down dam.

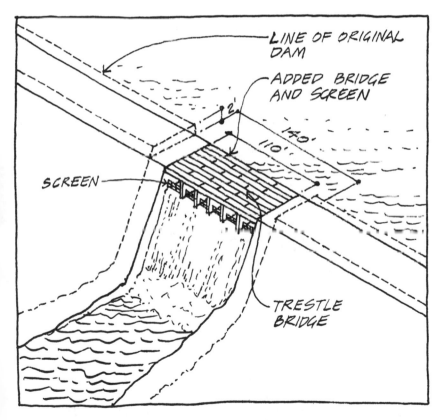

11.2   South Fork: Modified Dam and Spillway

After eating lunch, Parke returned to the dam to find that:

> the water on the breast had washed away several large stones on the outer face and had cut a hole about 10 ft (3 m) wide and 4 ft (1.2 m) deep on the outer face. The water running into this hole cut away the breast both horizontally and vertically, and this action kept widening the hole until it was worn so near to the water in the lake (thinning the dam) that the pressure of the water broke through. The water then rushed through this trough and cut its way rapidly into the dam on each side and at the bottom. Before long, there was a torrent of water rushing through the breast, carrying everything before it: trees growing on the outer face of the dam were carried away like straws.

This continued, and in forty-five minutes the lake was fully drained. The pressure of water behind the dam could not be resisted by the damaged structure, and the flood of water, after collapsing the dam, demolished Johnstown and six other villages in the valley.

The dam as originally designed, and even as built, would have safely handled the flow into the reservoir from so heavy a rainfall (about 5 in. [130 mm] fell in a thirty-hour period). The modifications required to satisfy the comfort of a select few was the only cause of the disaster. In court actions undertaken after the catastrophe, the event was deemed to be a "providential visitation," and it is ironic that the only plaintiff against the Pennsylvania Railroad requested compensation for the loss of ten barrels of whiskey.

The Malpasset Tragedy: The First Collapse of an Arch Dam

The Johnstown disaster was one of the most tragic in terms of lives lost in the United States, but one of the most dramatic dam failures in recent history occurred above a town on the French Riviera. The Malpasset Dam was designed in 1951 by the firm of Coyne & Bellier, led by the most innovative dam designer of the time, André Coyne. When the Temple of Ramses II at Abu Simbel in Egypt was threatened with submersion in the new Aswan High Dam reservoir, Coyne proposed building an earth and rock-fill dam 230 ft. (69 m) high and elliptical in plan to isolate the temple, but this daring proposal was eventually rejected in favor of an Italian scheme

11.3 Malpasset Dam

that involved cutting the temple loose from the rock and raising it to a new platform above the reservoir level. (It was approved and paid for by the Italian government.)

The Malpasset Dam across the canyon of the Reyran Valley was built in the shape of a thin concrete arch curved both in plan and in vertical section, like a shallow dome turned on its side (Fig. 11.3). It was 200 ft. (60 m) high at its crest and spanned almost 635 ft. (190 m) between *abutments*, the parts of the dam immediately adjacent to the canyon walls. The dam abutted a rock face on the right bank and terminated in a concrete wing wall on the left bank, closing a gap between the dam and the canyon wall (Fig. 11.4). In order to save concrete, the dam, besides being curved vertically, was differently curved on the upstream and downstream faces, resulting in its thickness's increasing from top to bottom and

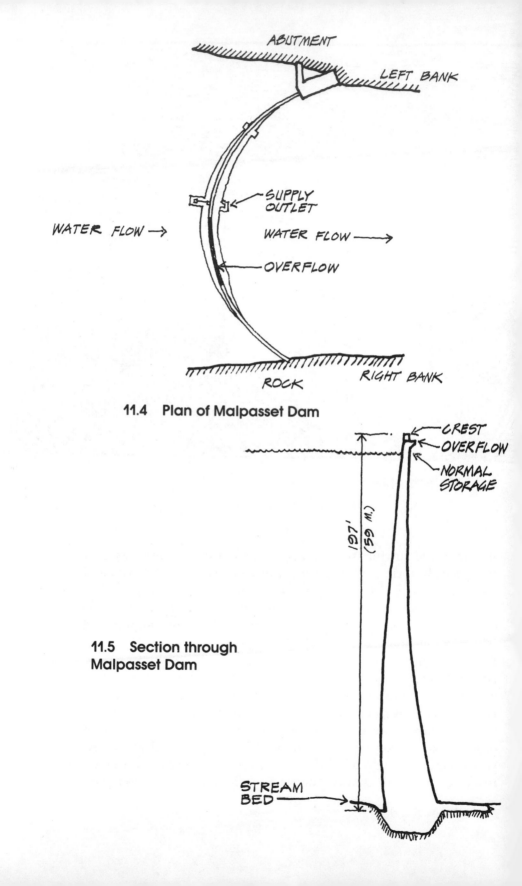

ABUTMENT

LEFT BANK

WATER FLOW →

SUPPLY OUTLET

WATER FLOW →

OVERFLOW

ROCK

RIGHT BANK

11.4   Plan of Malpasset Dam

CREST

OVERFLOW

NORMAL STORAGE

197' (59 M.)

11.5   Section through Malpasset Dam

STREAM BED

somewhat complicating its construction (Fig. 11.5). It was the thinnest arch dam ever built: 22.6 ft. (7 m) thick at the base and 5 ft. (1.5 m) at the crest, a direct descendant of a dam built in 1926 at Stevenson Creek in California to test the arch dam theory. While Malpasset was still under construction, Coyne designed Le Gage Dam, a double-scale reproduction of the one at Stevenson Creek and a dam with calculated stresses more than twice those predicted for Malpasset, showing that Malpasset was safely within the limits of technological feasibility.

Concrete dams are generally built by pouring the concrete in huge blocks—in this dam, 44 ft. (13 m) long and, on average, 5 ft. (1.5 m) high—abutting one another. To ensure water tightness of the joints between the blocks, as well as between the blocks and the rock foundation, copper or steel barriers were placed across the joints, which were filled with a dense mortar. Because a dam, particularly an arch dam, radically alters the preexisting stresses in the rock around the foundations, a thorough understanding of the geology of the dam site is vital to its safety. This study is usually entrusted to a geotechnical engineer, a specialist who examines rock samples obtained from *borings* retrieved by drilling into the rock and relates the samples to the overall geology of the region to reach realistic conclusions about the capacity of the rock to sustain the added load of the dam.

The Malpasset Dam was completed in 1954, bottling up the steeply banked valley of the Reyran River and retaining thirteen billion gallons (fifty-five billion liters) of water behind its thin concrete shield.

During the night of December 2, 1959, following five days of heavy rainfall, the five-year-old dam suddenly cracked like an eggshell and burst, releasing the impounded water, which rushed down the valley and demolished everything in its path, including roads, rail bridges, and a new four-lane highway. On their way to the Mediterranean, the waters smashed into the town of Fréjus, which was founded by Julius Caesar in 49 B.C. (and was where Octavian built the ships that defeated Antony and Cleopatra at the Battle of Actium). Nearly four hundred sleeping villagers, almost 5 percent of the town's population, drowned or otherwise died in the flood, and the town, with its priceless ancient monuments, was heavily damaged. The incredible force of the rushing water can be appreciated by the fact that blocks of concrete from the dam, weighing as much as three hundred tons, were scattered almost 1 mi. (1.6

km) downstream. The site of the dam was deeply scarred. The left bank was totally destroyed, its wing wall swept away. A stepped outline on the right bank followed the joints between the original concrete blocks, and a pitiful low-level barrier survived at the bottom of the valley from which the elegant dam had risen.

To quell the hysteria of the surviving population, investigators charged by the minister of agriculture quickly eliminated as causes of the disaster sabotage, earthquake, meteorites, or an explosion of munitions on the lake bed behind the dam. The first reports from the site—that the dam had started breaking near the center of the arch—led investigators to suspect that an abutment may have shifted. (An arch is especially sensitive to shifting of its lateral supports that causes tension to develop and hence cracks to appear on its face because concrete is weak in tension [Fig. 11.6].) The original design of the dam was thoroughly reviewed and found to be entirely satisfactory. Records of the construction were checked, and the physical evidence was examined to determine whether the dam

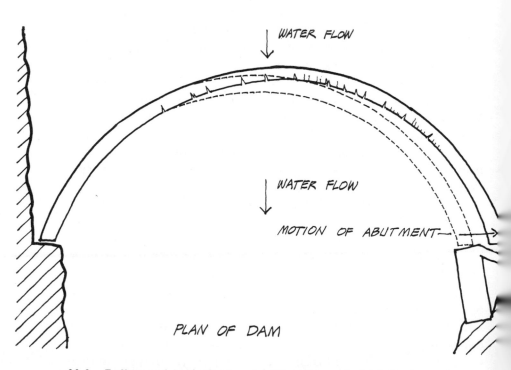

WATER FLOW

WATER FLOW

MOTION OF ABUTMENT

PLAN OF DAM

11.6   Failure of Arch Owing to Displacement of Abutment

was correctly built. Blocks of concrete were found still attached to pieces of bedrock, indicating that the concrete-to-bedrock joint had not failed. When joints between concrete blocks were tested and found to be as strong as the blocks themselves, joint failure was excluded as a possible cause of the disaster. Thus a fault or weakness in the rock under the left embankment was left as the most likely cause of the collapse. While further tests were undertaken to locate the specific fault, a legal investigating panel was appointed by the examining magistrate to determine the responsibility for the collapse.

While these investigations were proceeding, the Kariba Gorge arch dam in Rhodesia (now Zimbabwe) was dedicated and the highly acclaimed Roseland Dam in the French Alps was nearing completion, both successfully designed by the Coyne & Bellier firm. However, their construction brought no satisfaction to André Coyne. Dejected by the shattering failure at Malpasset, the sixty-nine-year-old engineer died six months after the disaster.

A final report issued the following year by the magistrate's panel led to the surprising indictment of Jacques Dargeou, the engineer charged with accepting the dam on behalf of the Agriculture Department; he was charged with involuntary homicide by negligence. Questioning the technical validity of the panel's conclusions, Dargeou demanded a new investigation by a different group of experts. After much legal wrangling, the second panel started its investigation and issued its report in 1963. It found Dargeou negligent in not having adequately explored the dam's foundation before construction but suggested for the first time that the designer himself, André Coyne, should have been more thorough in gathering foundation information. To complicate matters, the previous autumn the first panel had quietly issued an administrative report attributing the failure to an *unpredictable* shift of the rock under the left embankment.

A long trial ensued with a judgment issued in late 1964 that led to the acquittal of Jacques Dargeou. But this was not the end of the story. Under French law, crime victims (or their relatives) can sue a responsible party directly on criminal charges, bypassing the public prosecutor. The Fréjus Victims Association, a group of 240 relatives of the victims, brought suit against four engineers, including Jean Bellier, a partner and son-in-law of the late André Coyne, and two new facts surfaced in the new trial. A month before the collapse a photo survey of the dam had revealed changes at twenty-eight separate locations in the shape of the dam and in its foundation from its originally built dimensions. The engineer who succeeded Dargeou had received this information, did not consider it significant, but nevertheless had written Coyne suggesting an inspection of the dam. (Unfortunately this letter was in the mail when the dam broke.) A second revelation came from a watchman who suggested that blasting for a highway as close as 260 ft. (78 m) from the dam may have weakened its foundation. He claimed having felt strong shock waves from the blasts, which involved as much as two and one-half tons of dynamite each and were judged by experts to be *eight times* above a safe limit.

This last brief trial resulted in the acquittal of the four indicted engineers: Bellier was considered a "cog in the machine" of the Coyne firm, and the other three defendants only minor players in the constructions process. Legal battles for damages in *civil proceedings* continued for another two years, but the conclusion of the criminal proceedings still left open the question of responsibility. What became perfectly clear, after so many court fights, was the cause of the dam failure. A thin, clay-filled seam in the rock adjacent to the left bank of the dam had acted as a lubricant and caused the foundation to shift slightly; *this* displacement had cracked the dam. Perhaps Max Jacobson, the head of the first investigating panel, put his finger on the real cause of the disaster when he said, "M. Coyne had been misled by his own genius"; he had trusted his intuition rather than guarantee the solidity of the dam through geologic tests.

12

The House of Cards

Things fall apart; the centre cannot hold.

William Butler Yeats

E very year thirty-nine out of one hundred thousand American construction workers die in work-related accidents, a higher rate than in many other Western countries: fifteen in the United Kingdom, sixteen in Greece, eighteen in Finland, eighteen in New Zealand, twenty-five in Spain, thirty in France. Construction is, in fact, one of the most hazardous industries in the world, and although not all construction accidents are related to structure, many are.*

Therefore, when in 1987 the first reports appeared of a construction accident in Bridgeport, Connecticut, it was not considered an unusual event but rather like a daily report of crime in the tabloids. But this was no ordinary event: Twenty-eight construction workers had been killed in Bridgeport, the second-worst construction accident in American history, after the collapse of a reinforced concrete cooling tower in 1978 at Willow Island, West Virginia, in which fifty-one workers had died.

---

* Exceptions being always newsworthy, in 1933 newspaper readers were informed not only of the spectacular speed of construction of the world's tallest building, the Empire State Building, but also of the fact that not a single worker had died in its construction.

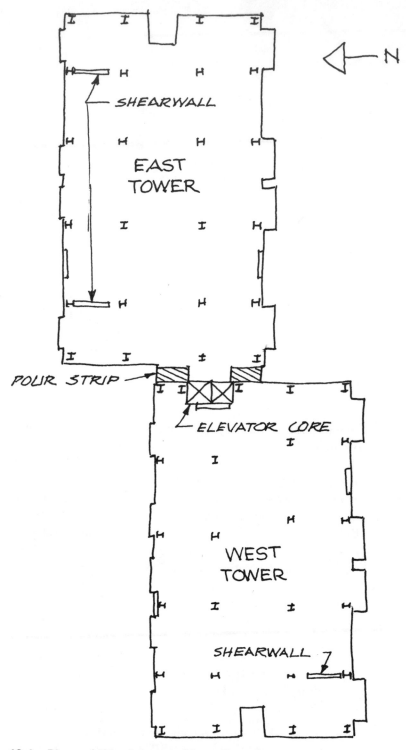

12.1 Plan of L'Ambiance Plaza Towers

L'Ambiance Plaza in Bridgeport was to be a sixteen-story apartment building with two offset rectangular towers linked by an elevator core (Fig. 12.1). The building, with steel columns and flat *posttensioned* concrete slabs, was being constructed using the lift-slab technique.

The lift-slab technique, invented in 1948 by Youtz and Slick in the United States and used since the early 1950s, consists in first casting all of a building's posttensioned slabs on the ground, one on top of the other like a stack of pancakes, then lifting them, one or more slabs at a time, up the columns with hydraulic jacks at a rate of 5 ft./hr. (1.5 m/h) until each slab reaches its final position, is locked in place, and permanently attached to the columns. Posttensioning involves placing greased high-strength steel wires wrapped in plastic along the length or width of a slab, pouring the concrete, and, when it is sufficiently hard, pulling the wires with hydraulic jacks against the edges of the slab and finally anchoring the wires. The process imposes on the concrete a compression that balances out the tension resulting from the loads acting on the slab; it thus eliminates the tensile weakness of the concrete (Fig. 12.2).

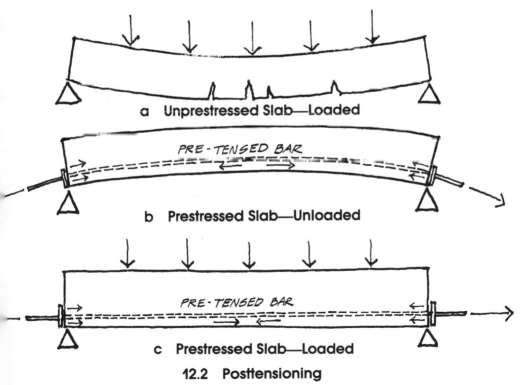

a **Unprestressed Slab—Loaded**

b **Prestressed Slab—Unloaded**

c **Prestressed Slab—Loaded**

12.2 Posttensioning

Although the joint between the slab and the columns provides a
degree of rigidity, the connection is not "perfectly" rigid, and a lift-
slab building must rely on concrete walls, known as *shear walls*
(see p. 302), to provide lateral stability and resistance to wind and
seismic forces.

On April 23, 1987, the L'Ambiance tower structure was more
than half completed. All the slabs had been poured, and a number
of upper-floor slabs, lifted to the top of the columns, had been
"parked" at the ninth level above the basement slab (Fig. 12.3). On
that day workmen were pouring concrete for shear walls, and at
approximately 11:30 A.M. three slabs had been lifted to the top of
the columns of the west tower at the ninth-floor level. Workmen
were installing wedges between the columns and the slabs, to hold
the slabs in position temporarily, when suddenly a loud metallic
noise and a snap or crack were heard, followed by a rumbling noise,
like that of rolling thunder or the passing of an overhead jet aircraft.

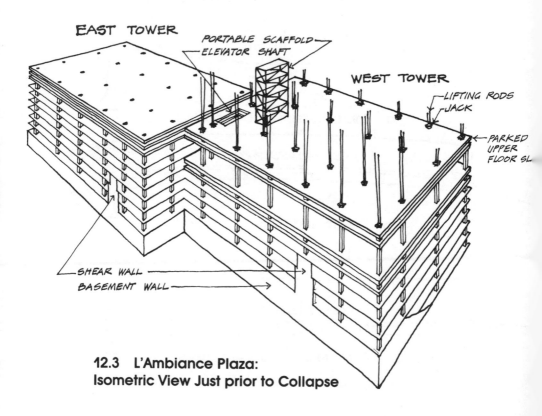

**12.3 L'Ambiance Plaza:
Isometric View Just prior to Collapse**

Kenneth Shepard, an ironworker standing near the center of the west tower on the sixth floor to install wedges locking in place one of the recently parked stack of slabs, looked up and saw the slab overhead "cracking just like ice breaking." Miraculously protected by the scaffolding around him, he survived the harrowing ride as he was carried down to the ground with the collapsing structure. The west tower fell first. Each top slab fell on the one immediately below and momentarily stopped the progress of the collapse. But unable to carry the added load, lower slabs in turn failed, and all the slabs fell one after another in an unstoppable chain reaction. The east tower, whether struck by falling debris or destabilized by the lateral pull of the completed links connecting it to the falling west tower, also collapsed. Shepard's partner, who was welding previously placed temporary wedges at the time of the collapse, did not survive. According to eyewitnesses, the total collapse took place in about 5 seconds, only about twice the 2.25 seconds it would have taken an object to fall freely from the ninth floor to the ground, thus proving that the structure offered almost no resistance to the fifteen hundred tons of falling slabs raining down as concrete rubble on the twenty-eight unsuspecting workers scattered throughout the building.

The day after the collapse, as rescue workers still searched for survivors, investigators from the National Bureau of Standards and representatives of the professionals involved in the design and construction of the building arrived on the scene of devastation, seeking clues to the failure. By a strange coincidence many stayed at the local Hilton Hotel, a building constructed by the same lift-slab method that had caused the disaster they came to investigate.

Considered first was the possibility that a differential settlement of the footings under two of the columns might have caused the collapse. This theory was rejected for lack of physical evidence. The lateral stability of the structure was then investigated as the main cause of the failure because until shear walls are locked in place, the structure of a lift-slab building is like a house of cards supported by toothpicks, a system with little, if any, lateral resistance and therefore unstable. (Because of this temporary condition, a lift-slab building under construction in Canada had collapsed twenty years earlier in a sudden windstorm.) The contractor had the responsibility of stabilizing the building, by stretching temporary diagonal steel cables between the columns, but apparently had not done so.

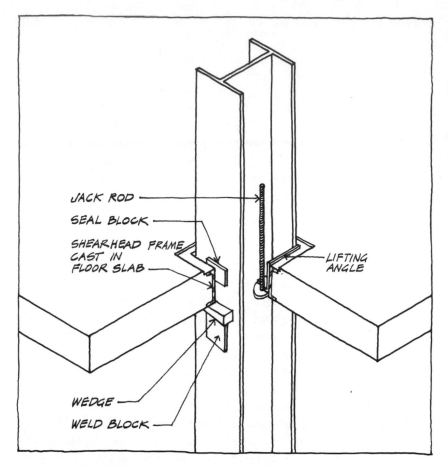

12.4 Typical Shearhead Arrangement

The slabs' lifting assembly was another suspect element. Slabs are reinforced at each column by a steel assembly called a *shearhead* that provides both an attachment point for the lifting mechanism and a means of transferring the vertical loads from the slabs to the columns. A typical shearhead (Fig. 12.4) incorporates a frame of channel-shaped (]-shaped) steel members cast into the concrete slab, leaving a hole inside which is a steel lifting angle with slots in the horizontal leg to allow the lifting rods to pass through. Jacks attached at the top of the columns pull on lifting rods, which in turn push up on the horizontal leg of the steel lifting angle by means of a lifting nut screwed tightly against it (Fig. 12.5). The whole mechanism works very much like a car jack, with the ground replaced by the top of the column and the car replaced by the concrete slab.

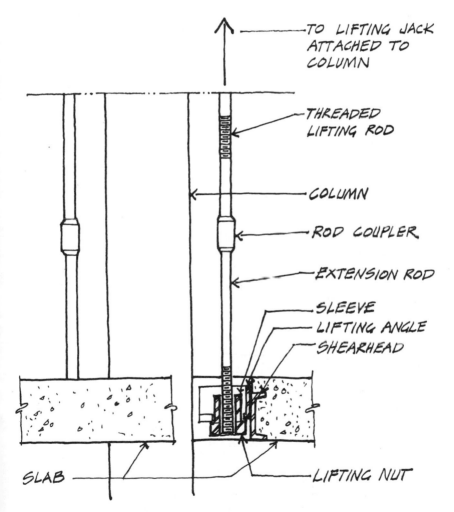

TO LIFTING JACK
ATTACHED TO
COLUMN

THREADED
LIFTING ROD

COLUMN

ROD COUPLER

EXTENSION ROD

SLEEVE
LIFTING ANGLE
SHEARHEAD

SLAB

LIFTING NUT

12.5 Lifting Rod Attached to Jack

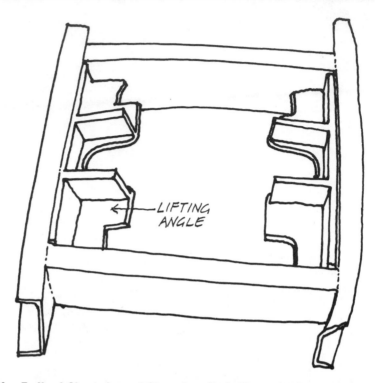

LIFTING ANGLE

12.6   Failed Shearhead Showing Rotation of Lifting Angles

Investigators examining the wreckage found a shearhead that had a bent lifting angle with scraping markings, suggesting that the lifting nut had slipped out of the slot provided for it (Fig. 12.6). This particular shearhead had fallen from a column of the west tower, exactly where Mr. Shepard and his partner were installing wedges at the time of the disaster.* What Mr. Shepard apparently heard was the lifting rod slipping out of the lifting angle and hitting the column (Fig. 12.7). Once this support failed, the slab transferred the load from the lost support to other columns, which were unable to carry the additional load and failed in turn. Since all the slabs caved in toward the center of the building, physical evidence suggested that the collapse was due to failure of a lifting assembly that caused progressive failure of adjacent interior assemblies.

---

* Thornton-Tomasetti, the consultants originally retained by the city to investigate the collapse, suggested recently (1991) that the initiating factor was the loss of a wedge needed to support the slab temporarily until it was welded to the column. The wedge may have fallen out and caused the slab to sag suddenly, initiating the catastrophic series of events.

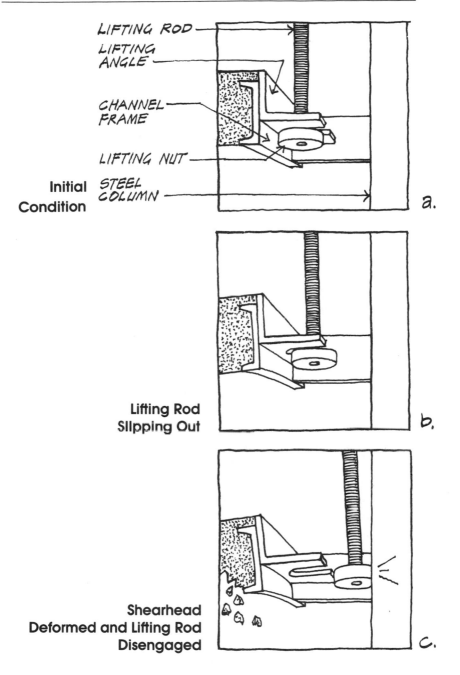

LIFTING ROD

LIFTING
ANGLE

CHANNEL
FRAME

LIFTING NUT

Initial STEEL
Condition COLUMN

a.

**Lifting Rod
Slipping Out**

b.

**Shearhead
Deformed and Lifting Rod
Disengaged**

c.

12.7   Failure Sequence

Some construction accidents are predictable, and unfortunately warning signs of lift-slab failures at other construction sites had been ignored. In 1954 a 250-ton roof slab had fallen 16 ft. (4.8 m) while being lifted at Sierra High School in San Mateo, California. Safety measures were thereafter mandated in California. These included placing *cribbing*, temporary posts to support the slab before the attachment to the column is completed, and *sway bracing*, cables to keep the stack of floors from shifting sideways. The bracing, as noted above, was required but not used in the L'Ambiance Plaza construction. In 1956 an eight-story lift-slab garage under construction in Cleveland tilted 8 ft. (2.4 m) out of vertical in a brisk wind, setting off a scramble to keep it from toppling. News accounts related that "as darkness fell, engineers had apparently won their frantic struggle to prevent their structure from crushing the two-story building next door. Cables attached to four winch trucks, telephone poles, and other objects had stopped the building from listing farther." Within the year prior to the L'Ambiance collapse, two incidents at other lift-slab projects had taken place. One in Stamford, Connecticut, involved a lifting rod that slipped out of the lifting angle at a shearhead, causing a sudden transfer of load to an adjacent lifting rod and snapping it. Luckily the failure did not progress further, and the building did not collapse. Also during the prior year the "lift-slab" company had issued a directive advising its personnel that slabs *must* be lifted evenly because recent projects had shown that uneven lifting could cause serious accidents, especially with posttensioned slabs that are particularly sensitive to uneven lifting.

The small town of Pontelandolfo, Italy, had sent its sons and daughters to Waterbury, Connecticut, for one hundred years and now mourned ten of its own who died in the collapse. All twenty-eight men who died in this tragedy had spent a lifetime working on construction sites. "They pounded nails, they poured concrete, and they found joy in the effort. They had a nearly primal urge to be outdoors," said the *Hartford Courant*. Perhaps this is why sons follow fathers in the dangerous construction trades and new workers keep filling the ranks of their fallen comrades.

13

Structural Dermatology

The flesh, alas, is wearied.

Stéphane Mallarmé

Skin Problems

New Yorkers have recently become used to seeing the ground floors of many of their buildings (mostly those with brick facades) covered by scaffolds that obscure the entrance and support masons and materials going up and down. Often, to their unpleasant surprise, the smiling faces of the workers appear at the windows, peering in at tenants still in bed after 8:00 A.M. or just getting dressed. The cause of all this inconvenience, at least in New York City, is Local Law 10, which requires, since 1980, that facades of all buildings over six stories high be inspected every five years to ensure that their components would not fall on passersby or on cars parked at the curb.

Shortly before Local Law 10 was passed, a number of bricks, stones, and heavy ornaments had fallen with increasing frequency on the streets of New York from the facades of old buildings. Luckily most of these falling objects did not injure people or damage property, but when a stone window decoration dropped on a Columbia University student from a building belonging to the university and killed her, an uproar started on the campus, eventually leading to the passage of the law.

Prior to that time brick facades had been inspected at infrequent intervals, mostly for the purpose of locating the origin of water leaks. Over time, rain, snow, ice, and industrial pollution disintegrate the mortar in the joints binding the bricks together. To retard this process, a variety of chemical sealants is sprayed on such walls, but unfortunately these are washed away after a year or more by the polluted rains of the city and do not eliminate the danger of loose elements dropping off. Moreover, such sealants seldom stop disintegration of the mortar, and eventually the crumbling mortar must be removed and the joints "pointed" with fresh mortar.

Water infiltration from cracks in facades, terraces, and roofs is sometimes the cause of serious structural damage, particularly in buildings framed with columns and beams of steel. The water penetrating through the narrowest cracks reaches these structural elements by *capillarity* (the property of water to flow, even upward, through capillary cracks as thin as hair), and unless beams and columns were carefully protected by painting at construction time, they may rust over the years until most, if not all, of their strength is lost. The same phenomenon occurs in reinforced concrete buildings, in which capillary cracks are expected to occur and water can reach the steel reinforcing bars if the concrete is too porous. One such occurrence took place in France in the 1930s, when the sudden collapse of a reinforced concrete water tank showed that most of the reinforcing bars had rusted into a fine powder of iron oxide.

The use of additives, capable of improving the strength and compactness of concrete, has been the cause of many brick facade failures because the chemical components of some of them facilitate the oxidization of steel in the presence of minimal amounts of water in the form of humidity. Such additives are not damaging when the recommendations of the manufacturer *and* the requirements of good engineering practice are followed in construction, but when these are ignored and construction becomes "sloppy" (under the pressure of time and money demands), extensive damage may occur within a few months or years. Recently this kind of damage, involving a single type of additive, has been responsible for numerous court cases with demands of hundreds of millions in damages against the additive manufacturer, even though no failures could be proved to be due to its use when correct construction procedures had been strictly followed.

The cost of facade damage is dramatically emphasized by the millions of dollars and the years of remedial work required to fix the brick and terra-cotta tile skin of the historic high-rise building built for General Electric in Manhattan.

In the recent past brick skin deficiencies could also be attributed to the decreasing skill of the limited number of masons entrusted with enclosing, brick by brick, the thousands of square feet of modern buildings. But today many brick facades consist of prefabricated panels that are manufactured in specialized factories and are supposed to satisfy all the requirements of the governing codes *and* of good practice. The finished panels, which often incorporate layers of insulation, are hung from the steel or concrete structure, and here lies a source of problems in "structural dermatology." In the United States the design of a building's skin is the responsibility not of the structural engineer but of the architect. The architect may (or may not) consult with his or her structural engineer on the complex details of panel connections but more often trusts the suggestions of the panel manufacturer, who in turn may (or may not) have consulted a technical adviser on this or prior occasions. This practice is just one frequent cause of panel failure.

Panels are hung from the structure of a building by means of bolts and nuts that are often fully tightened to guarantee their stability, and here lies another cause of failure. Panels exposed to temperature variations that, even in a mild climate, may range from $-10°F$ ($-23°C$) in winter to $+100°F$ ($+38°C$) in summer tend to expand and contract in daily and yearly cycles. Under these conditions an unrestrained panel 10 ft. (3 m) high and 20 ft. (6 m) wide expands and contracts 0.06 in. (1.5 mm) vertically and 0.12 in. (3 mm) horizontally. A panel cannot "breathe" when it is tightly connected to the structure of an air-conditioned building that to all practical purposes remains at a constant temperature. It tends to crack in tension, when prevented from shrinking in winter, and to crush the mortar, when prevented from expanding in summer.

Thus an incorrectly hung panel fails for social, economic, and physical causes. Thermally caused cracks in incorrectly hung panels can be avoided only if one allows all the bolts to be "hand-tightened" so as to slide vertically *and* horizontally into vertically and horizontally elongated (slotted) holes, except for "wrench-tightened" bolts at one location needed to guarantee the stability of the panel (Fig. 13.1).

Roman wisdom humorously states that of course, a fire may be stopped with water but asks: "What can you stop water with?" The solution of leak problems in roofs and facades requires such specific technical knowledge that it has given rise to a new architectural and engineering specialty, that of *waterproofing consultant*. Some readers, because of sad personal experiences, may understand why the new consultants are in such high demand.

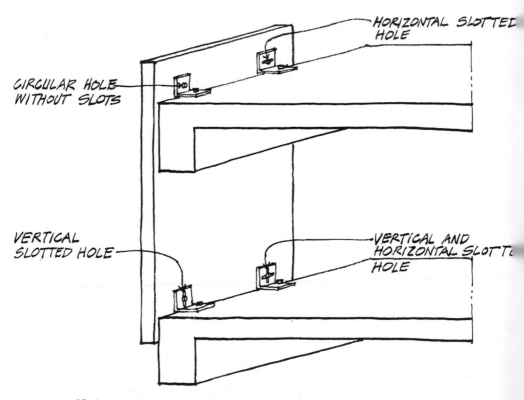

13.1 Attachment of Precast Panel

A brick facade is not the only problematical type of skin. While light *curtain wall* panels of steel or aluminum and glass are less likely to loosen from the structure, they may still cause water leaks and break or buckle if not carefully designed and correctly hung. This is true as well for elegant marble, travertine, or granite facades. One of the most glamorous high-rise buildings in New York's luxury midtown area, with a vertically curved curtain wall facade of tinted glass, has part of the stiffening trusses (resisting the wind forces) at the corners of the steel frame covered by large panels of travertine. Shortly after the end of construction a few of these heavy panels fell to the street in the early-morning hours, luckily without causing damage or injuring people. An inspection of the building revealed that the design of the panels' connection to the frame was correct but that a number of bolts had not been installed, a fact unnoticed by inspectors on the site. After the panels were replaced, passersby noticed some people who, upon reaching the west corner of this building, crossed the street from the north to the south sidewalk, only to cross back to the north sidewalk after reaching the building's east corner (or vice versa), thus avoiding a walk under the south facade of the building. These pedestrians could not know that the avoiders were members of the consulting engineering firm responsible for the design of the building structure, some of the very few people in the city aware of this unpublicized temporary failure that fortunately caused no harm or damage.

This is all to caution the reader that even if our skin troubles may not always be worth worrying about, those on the outside of our buildings deserve the best care from knowledgeable consultants and experienced construction workers, as illustrated by the following stories.

An Expensive Skin Graft

The Standard Oil of Indiana office building in Chicago, started in 1971 and inaugurated in 1974, was designed to be a high tech model among the world's skyscrapers. With eighty-two stories aboveground on one-quarter of the site, the building, now renamed the Amoco Tower, reached 1,123 ft. (342 m) into the sky from a square base 186 ft. (57 m) on a side. Its shaft, with a ratio of height to width of 6.2, was entirely clad in white Carrara marble. The recently developed technology for cutting thin marble panels had allowed

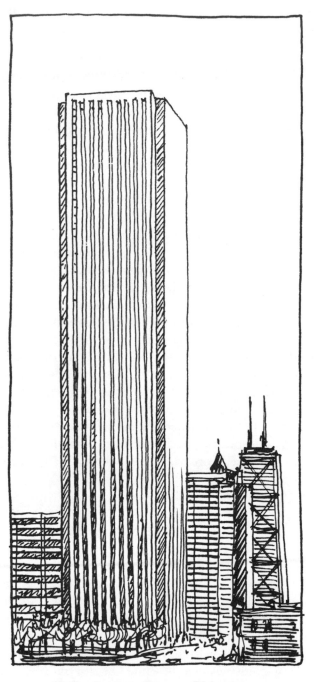

13.2   Amoco Tower, Chicago

the delivery from Italy of forty-three thousand panels, 50 by 45 in. (1.27 × 1.14 m), 1¼ to 1½ in. (32–38 mm) thick, to be connected to the steel structure by through bolts. The shiny appearance of the tower was enhanced by four cutout corners, 14 ft. (4.4 m) on a side, that made it look like an even more slender tower with a height to width ratio of 7.1 (Fig. 13.2).

The design engineers minimized the cost of the steel structure needed to resist gravity, wind, and earthquake loads by means of an ingenious structural design never used before. As we show in Appendix D, the horizontal displacements or *sway* of a high-rise building must be limited in order to avoid the embarrassing effects of airsickness to tenants of high floors. This is usually done by increasing the stiffness of the steel-framed structure—that is, by using heavy steel columns and rigid connections between columns and beams. In forty- to fifty-story frames, this increased stiffness requires the use of approximately 30 to 40 pounds of steel per square foot (1.5–2 kN/m²) of floor area and is entrusted to the bending resistance of the frame (when not helped by that of concrete shear walls). But if the resistance to the horizontal forces is instead entrusted to *vertical* steel trusses, as in the John Hancock Building in Chicago, buildings twice as high, of up to one hundred stories,

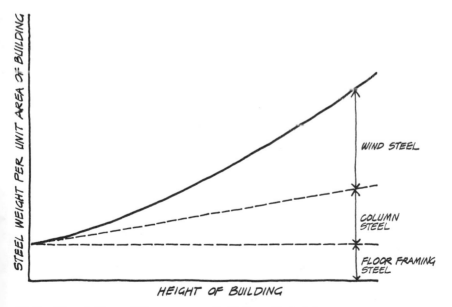

13.3 Steel Quantities versus Building Height

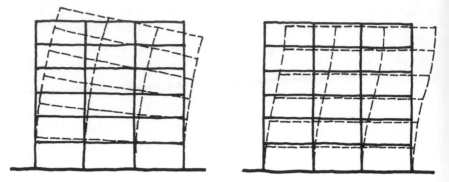

a   Caused by Bending   b   Caused by Shear

13.4   Building Drift

can be stiffened by the same amount of wind steel per unit area
(Fig. 13.3). It must be added that the wind or earthquake deflections of a framed building consists of two components: the bending
deflections of the frame's columns and the *drift* or shearing deflection of each floor relative to the floor below it (Fig. 13.4). The engineers of the Amoco Tower minimized both components of the
horizontal deflection by building the four walls of the tower out of
thin steel plates, thus creating a tube. (Buildings with stiffened
external walls are now called *tube buildings*.) Slit windows make
up less than 50 percent of the facade without unduly decreasing its
stiffness. The tower oscillates horizontally with a period of 8.3 seconds, slow enough to prevent drift problems to the tenants.

The steel plate of the tube tower was too thin to carry to the
ground, without buckling, the loads usually supported by the outside columns of a frame. In the Amoco Tower thin-plate "chevrons"
of steel (Fig. 13.5), connected to the tube in the spaces between the
windows, constitute hollow triangular columns capable of carrying vertical loads to the ground, besides incorporating the vertical
water pipes and the ducts of the mechanical systems. Fireproofing
and thermal insulation were also attached to the chevrons, and a
marble veneer was bolted over this structural sandwich. With one
more refined thought, the entire steel structure was bolted by means
of only two types of bolts, thus avoiding the not unusual occurrence of misplacing a bolt chosen for a specific location among a
large variety of bolts.

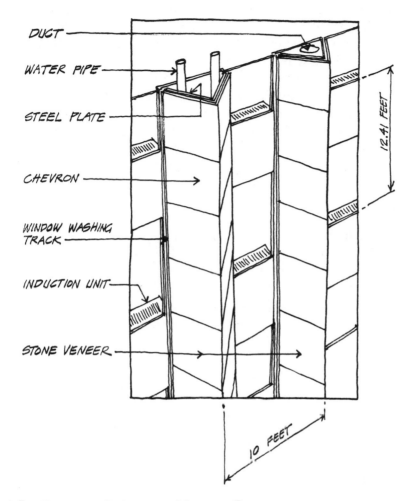

DUCT

WATER PIPE

STEEL PLATE

CHEVRON

WINDOW WASHING
TRACK

INDUCTION UNIT

STONE VENEER

12.41 FEET

10 FEET

13.5 Chevron Columns of Amoco Tower

The technical press gave deserved recognition to this interest-ing, innovative design. The $120 million Amoco Tower was con-sidered a success. But . . .

Shortly after the building was completed, Amoco Corporation engineers noticed that the marble panels were beginning to buckle outward. By 1988, 30 percent of the panels had bowed out more than ½ in. (13 mm) and some as much as 1½ in. (38 mm). For safety reasons, all were immediately bolted through to a steel clip attached to the structural frame. Tests then proved that many panels had lost a large part of their strength. Marble is a limestone, a sedimentary rock wholly or in large part composed of calcium carbonate and mostly formed by the deposition and consolidation of the skeleton of marine invertebrates, successively metamorphosed into solid rock by heat and pressure. Like all limestones, marble is corroded by the humidity and the acid fumes of a polluted atmosphere and loses strength, buckling out even under its own weight, as shown by some old marble tombstones set up vertically.

In addition to the chemical action of corrosion, the panels of the Amoco Tower were subjected to the compressive stress resulting from the partial prevention of free thermal expansion by the semirigid bolt connections. These stresses were particularly high in the Windy City, where temperatures extremes go from $-27°F$ ($-35°C$) in winter to $+102°F$ ($+39°C$) in summer. The horizontal displacements of the tower under the high winds of Chicago (up to 69 mph or 111 km / h) may also have contributed in a minor way to the panels' failure.

On the other hand, there is no question about the reduced thickness of the panels' being a major contributory cause of their failure. The buckling strength of a compressed, thin structural member is measured by a dimensionless geometrical parameter L/r, *called the slenderness ratio*, where L is the length of the member and r, the so-called *radius of gyration*, measures the stiffness of the member cross section. In the Amoco Tower the L/r of the panels varied between 104 and 138, while most building codes, in order to guarantee against buckling failures, require values of L/r not greater, and often smaller, than 120. Physical proof of the influence of the panels' thickness on their longtime behavior is given by the marble panels of the General Motors Building in New York, which are 1¼ to 1½ in. (32–38 mm) thick but bonded to thick concrete panels, so as to have an L/r lower than that required by building codes.

In 1989 the Amoco Corporation decided to substitute *all* the marble panels with 2 in. (50 mm) thick granite panels from Mount Airy in North Carolina. Besides being much stiffer, these panels are less subject to chemical corrosion by polluted air because granite is a granular rock composed chiefly of hard crystals of quartz, solidified from molten rock or *magma*, from the hot core of the earth. The sound performance since 1963 of similar 2 in. (50 mm) thick panels from Vermont quarries, used to clad the building of the Columbia Broadcasting System in New York, gives assurance that the skin graft to be performed on the Amoco Tower will give satisfactory results.

There is a sad moral to this story. The unusual care of the architectural and engineering designers of the Amoco Tower, addressed to both the safety and the economy of construction of their splendid building, could be said to have been diminished by a minor saving in the choice of the cladding (less than 1 percent of the original cost). If one ignores inflation, the cost of the granite skin graft is estimated at more than half the original cost of the entire building. Although the case between the owner and the designers has been settled out of court, the cases between the owner, the general contractor, and the various subcontractors were still pending in 1990. Even before the final verdict is in, it is obvious that the recladding of the Amoco Tower in Chicago will be one of the most expensive among high-rise buildings in the United States.

The newly developed science of *chaos theory* shows how a minor change in the initial conditions of a smooth process (physical, chemical, biological, or economic) may change it into a suddenly chaotic catastrophe. Chaos scientists say, tongue in cheek, that the unexpected beating of a butterfly wing in Oslo today may be the cause of a hurricane in South America tomorrow. Perhaps architects and engineers should apply chaos theory to their design and construction practices inasmuch as a ½ in. (13 mm) difference in the thickness of a cladding panel may avoid an unforeseen future expense and eliminate the chaos of protracted litigation.

Skin Shedding

The city of Rochester, New York, could boast, until recently, of two magnificent high-rise buildings. One, the Xerox Tower, forty-two stories high, had improved upon the innovative design of Eero Saarinen's Columbia Broadcasting System Building in New York, by utilizing a naked concrete structure supported on four enormous corner pylons. The dark color and its visible structure give the Xerox Tower an imposing architectural presence.

The other high rise, Rochester's Lincoln First Bank, also forty-two stories high, had a steel frame entirely covered by large slabs of white Italian marble, quarried from the same Apennine Mountains above Carrara that supplied Michelangelo 450 years ago with the marble for the *Pietà* in St. Peter's and his other sculptural masterpieces. For a few years the glittering appearance of the Lincoln First Bank Tower dominated the cityscape of Rochester and vied with that of the majestically dark Xerox Tower. But what glitters is not necessarily sound and stable. Slowly, one by one, the marble panels of the Lincoln First Bank Tower began to buckle outward, opening vertical cracks and causing water leaks first at a few floors and, progressively, over almost the entire building (Fig. 13.6). The bank, concerned about the stability of the panels, erected heavy scaffolds all around the tower to protect passersby and requested Weidlinger Associates to investigate the cause of this dangerous failure.

We inspected the facades of the bank building, moving up and down on a scaffold hanging from the roof, and noticed that the panels had been connected to the steel frame by bolts. We were surprised to notice that the 39 to 75 in. (1–1.9 m) wide by 50 in. (1.27 m) high panels were only 1 in. (25 mm) thick. It was our belief, even so, that the facade was not in immediate danger of shedding its panels, and advising the bank not to yield to the clamoring of the local press by making hurried repairs, we requested that all the design documents be forwarded immediately to our office.

A careful perusal of the architectural, structural, and shop drawings revealed a number of interesting features concerning the

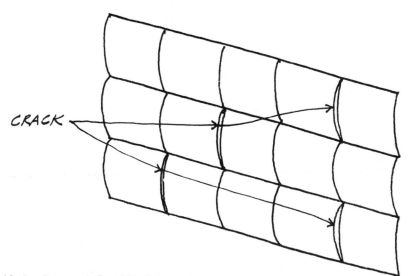

13.6 Bowed-Out Wall Panels

evolution of this curtain wall design. It was found that the marble panels first considered were *2 in. (50 mm) thick* and connected to two-story-high steel "cages," which were to hang alternately from the external columns of the structural frame and the *spandrel beams* (the beams connecting to each other the external columns at the floors). The final drawings showed instead *1 in. (25 mm)* panels hung from one-story-high cages, much lighter than the original ones. Both the original and the final cage designs called for connections of the panels to the cages by means of bolts fully tightened in circular holes (of the same diameter as the bolts) at the top and with hand-tightened bolts in vertically elongated (slotted) holes at the bottom. Such connections allowed the "breathing" of the panels under code-dictated temperature variations from 20°F (−7°C) to 120°F (49°C). Hence an initial suspicion that the panels had buckled under compression, caused by the fixity of the supports' preventing their expansion and contraction, had to be discarded. On the other hand, there was little doubt that the panels *had* buckled and that the unacceptably high value of their slenderness ratio (173) was an obvious indication of why they all had bowed out up to ½ in. (13 mm) vertically but only slightly horizontally, causing water penetration at all floors. This observation suggested the need to examine the comprehensive manual issued by the Italian Marble Exporters Association (*Marmi Italiani*, 1982 English-language edition), which lists all the physical characteristics of each Italian marble. It was discovered, most unexpectedly, that the *water absorption* coefficient of the marble used at the Lincoln First Bank Tower, an Acquabianca marble from the Lucca (Tuscany) quarries, was *three times* as large as that of other Italian marbles of the same type. Since absorption of humidity from a polluted atmosphere lowers the strength of marble, it was easy to conclude that the Acquabianca compression strength had been lowered to such an extent by the industrially polluted air of Rochester that the thin panels of the tower had buckled *under their own weight*. Such slow bowing out, called *creep*, was accelerated by the method of panel support at the bottom on *shelf angles* (Fig. 13.7), as well as by their large slenderness ratio. To eliminate the danger of this type of failure, the Italian marble manual suggests that panels be anchored at half height on their vertical boundaries, thus cutting in half the slenderness ratio. This precaution had been apparently ignored by designers of the bank tower.

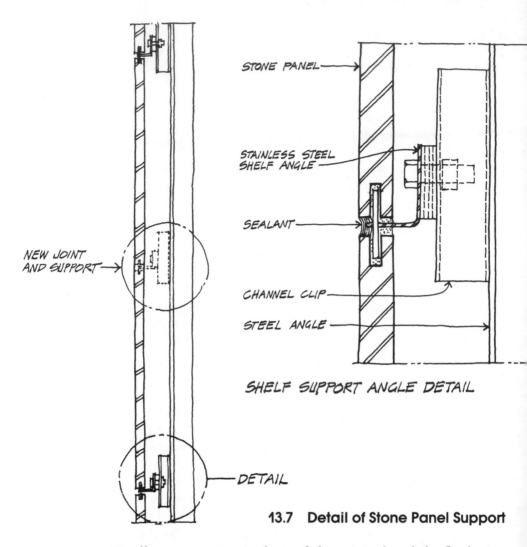

STONE PANEL

STAINLESS STEEL
SHELF ANGLE

SEALANT

CHANNEL CLIP

STEEL ANGLE

NEW JOINT
AND SUPPORT

SHELF SUPPORT ANGLE DETAIL

DETAIL

13.7 Detail of Stone Panel Support

Finally, a computer analysis of the original and the final cage designs proved that under their own weight, the weight of the panels, the wind loads, and the thermal gradients of the Rochester building code, no bars in the cages would have failed in the original design, but many bars would in the final thin-panel design. The cages as actually built had large deflections under load, larger than those accepted by good engineering practice, and added one more cause to the failure.

Sometime after receiving this kind of technical information, the tower owners decided to change the panel system, and we submitted a study showing that the Acquabianca panels could be reused by being tied to the cages at top and bottom, after they were cut in half vertically, thus reducing their slenderness ratio to an acceptable value of 86. The owners, unable to postpone the fixing of the pervading water leaks and to wait out the outcome of court cases that could last for months or even years, decided instead to substitute aluminum panels for the marble panels, at a higher cost but with a greater guarantee of quick and safe results.

When the cases between the owners on one side and the architects, the general contractor, and the many subcontractors on the other reached court, attorneys were quick to point out that the panel thickness was not only a structural deficiency but also a violation of the Rochester building code, which required a minimum thickness of 1¼ in. (32 mm) in marble panels and, moreover, did not permit their use above a height of 40 ft. (12 m). The attorneys also reminded the defendants that the code demanded written approval of the curtain wall design by the Rochester director of buildings, a document that seemed to have disappeared if it ever existed. As a result of these technical and legal problems, all cases were settled out of court without assigning blame. Damages were assessed at about half the cost of the Amoco Tower damages, a verdict that seems to be more or less fair since the Lincoln First Bank Tower has an external surface approximately one-half that of the Amoco Tower, but the owners were left holding the bag for most of the repairs' cost.

Structural dermatology remedies are certainly more expensive than human dermatology treatments.

When Everything Happens

The Hancock Tower, headquarters of the John Hancock Mutual Life Insurance Company in Boston, designed by Henry N. ("Harry") Cobb of the renowned architectural office of I. M. Pei & Partners in New York, received a high honor in 1974 from the American Institute of Architects and in the same year was awarded the Harleston Parker Medal from the Boston Society of Architects as "the most beautiful piece of architecture in Boston in the year 1974." The building well deserved these recognitions. A sixty-story structure, framed in steel and totally clad with floor-to-ceiling panels of reflective glass, it became, on a clear winter day, a gigantic screen reflecting the majestic stone facade of Trinity Church under an ever-changing flow of white clouds, which made it part of both the permanent fabric of the city and the transient life of the sky.

13.8   John Hancock Tower, Boston, Massachusetts

But despite its elegant appearance and the dominant role it played in the Boston skyline, the Hancock Tower had been plagued by serious problems that started the day construction began and lasted over two years. The ensuing litigation between all parties involved in its construction was settled with a legal agreement of "nondisclosure in perpetuity" that started an unending set of unconfirmed rumors. Eventually the construction fraternity, a closed corporation to outsiders but a first-rate grapevine to its members, was able to put together a reliable story of the events and explain why the dean of Boston structuralists William LeMessurier could assert that the Hancock Tower was "one of the safest buildings in the world" (Fig. 13.8).

The Hancock Tower is a 790 ft. (234 m) tall building with a conventional steel frame clad with 4½ by 11½ ft. (1.35 × 3.45 m) double-glazed glass panels. The panels, available since the 1960s but never used on such a tall building before, had the inside face of the outer glass sheet (or *light*) coated with a thin layer of reflective material and a lead spacer around the edges to separate the inner from the outer glass lights (Fig. 13.9). The panels' exceptional vertical dimension allowed for the first time continuous glass

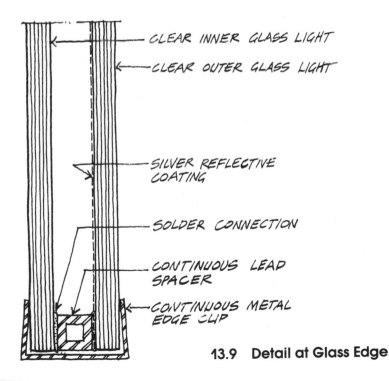

CLEAR INNER GLASS LIGHT

CLEAR OUTER GLASS LIGHT

SILVER REFLECTIVE COATING

SOLDER CONNECTION

CONTINUOUS LEAD SPACER

CONTINUOUS METAL EDGE CLIP

13.9   Detail at Glass Edge

surfaces over the entire facades of the tower. (Recent fire codes, following the development of sprinkler and other fire prevention systems, had made possible these beautiful facades by not requiring spandrel beams to prevent flames developing on one floor from reaching the floor above.) The tower satisfied *all* the requirements of the governing codes, but it must be noticed that one of the most essential requirements of high-rise construction—the limitation of wind sway at the top of the building—was not then, nor is it now, regulated by the code; it is left, instead, to the judgment of the structural designer. In the Hancock Tower, a building with an asymmetrical plan 300 ft. (92.4 m) by 104 ft. (30 m) in the shape of a thin rhomboid (Fig. 13.10), the wind sway in the short direction was within the dictates of good engineering practice but larger than that usually chosen by conservative structuralists.

The first of what were to be called four difficulties in the construction of the tower became apparent during the excavation of the site. It produced serious settlements in the adjacent streets and structural damage to Trinity Church, built from 1872 to 1877 across the street from the tower. The sheet piling and the lateral braces of the excavation, designed to prevent the collapse of its vertical cuts, moved laterally as much as 3 ft. (0.9 m), and careful monitoring of Trinity Church's movements showed them to be perfectly correlated with the progress of the excavation. The Hancock company accepted full responsibility for this damage.

Then, on the night of January 20, 1973, a windstorm of unusual severity hit Boston, and a number of the glass panels being erected on the tower were blown out. The falling panels, caught in the air

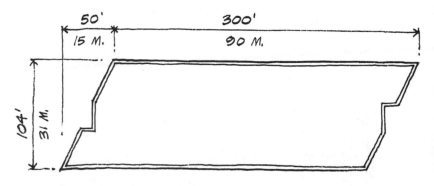

13.10 Plan of John Hancock Tower

turbulence around the building, hit and cracked numerous other panels, which were dismantled to avoid further breakage. Eventually about one-third of the erected panels were replaced with temporary plywood panels, ugly advertisements of the facade failure that looked like patches over blind eyes and inspired jokes about the "world's tallest wooden building." If the excavation problems had not unduly worried the construction team and were quickly remedied, the facade failure started a series of investigations that eventually required radical changes in both the structure and the curtain wall of the tower.

When glass panel damage occurs in a high-rise building, structuralists assume that it is due to the lateral deflection of the steel frame under the action of the wind, unless it is caused by unusual settlements of the soil. Experts from the faculty of the civil engineering department at the Massachusetts Institute of Technology (MIT) were called to give their opinion on the tower's facade failure, but their measurements of the wind displacements of the frame, coordinated with measurements of wind speeds at the top of the tower, did not explain the damage to the panels. Instead, they raised doubts about the magnitude of the displacements and the safety of the tower itself during a windstorm. As we point out in Appendix D, the acceleration of the wind oscillations has an influence on the physiological reactions of the occupants: Resonant accelerations make people airsick, and from this point of view, the accelerations measured on the Hancock Tower seemed to have unacceptable values. Since wind effects on buildings depend not only on their structure but on their shape, the shape of the surrounding buildings, and the lay of the land, wind tunnel tests were requested of Professor Alan Davenport of the University of Western Ontario, Canada, a world authority on structural wind problems. The tests confirmed that the wind sway was not responsible for the panel failures but rather was the cause of motions unacceptable for the comfort of the occupants. As expected, these motions were characterized not only by large displacements in the short direction of the tower but also, and most unexpectedly, by *twisting motions* caused by the narrow dimension of the building in the short direction and partially by the rhomboidal shape of its plan. The tower oscillations *had* to be damped.

William LeMessurier, following tunnel tests on the design of the slender Federal Reserve Building in New York City (which was never built), had been advised by Davenport: "Bill, you've got to attack damping directly; there is no way you can do it simply by putting on more steel." LeMessurier, following Davenport's advice, had designed a *tuned dynamic damper* (see p. 000) for the Federal Reserve Building and had also been successful with a similar damper for the Citicorp Building in New York City (Fig. A1). For the Hancock Tower he designed two tuned dynamic dampers consisting of two masses of lead, each weighing three hundred tons, to be set on a thin layer of oil near the opposite ends of the fifty-eighth floor of the tower. The dampers were connected to the structure by springs and shock absorbers, which allowed oscillations of their masses in the short direction of the building. When the tower oscillated mainly in the short direction, both dampers oscillated together also in the short direction, but in opposition to the building, thus damping the bending motions of the tower (Figs. 13.11a and b); when the tower developed essentially twisting oscillations, the dampers moved in opposite directions to each other and counteracted the opposite oscillations of the two ends of the tower (Figs. 13.11c and d).

Yet, according to LeMessurier, Professor Robert J. Hanson of the civil engineering department of MIT at the time still "was carping away at the ultimate safety of the building," and Harry Cobb decided to ask the advice of a world authority on the dynamics of structures, Professor Bruno Thurlimann of the Eidgenössiche Technische Hochschule of Zurich, Switzerland, who as a student had attended the outstanding research center on steel structures at Lehigh University. Thurlimann made a surprising discovery: The tower was not only very flexible in the short direction but also too flexible *in the long direction*. This unusual characteristic had not been noticed by the structural designers because they had neglected (most competent engineers would probably have done the same thing) the so-called *P-Delta effect* caused by the action of the building's weight during the wind oscillations. As the wind bends the building in a given direction, the weight moves in the same direction and adds its bending action to that of the wind (Fig. 13.12). The resulting oscillations are equivalent to those of a building with a *longer* period—that is, with a *weaker* structure. To remedy this new problem, the steel frame stiffness in the long direction was *doubled* by means of 1,650 tons of added diagonal steel bracing. This was a difficult decision for all the structuralists to take because the *measured* deflections indicated a stiffness in the long direction *triple* that *computed* mathematically by Thurlimann. In computing

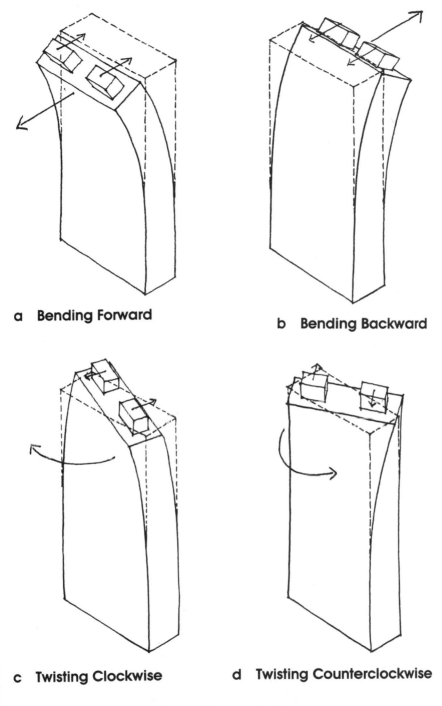

a **Bending Forward**

b **Bending Backward**

c **Twisting Clockwise**

d **Twisting Counterclockwise**

13.11 Tuned Dynamic Dampers

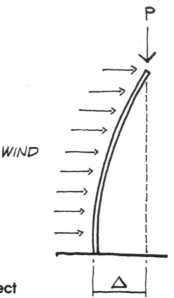

13.12   P-Delta Effect

it, Thurlimann had taken into account only the contribution to the building stiffness provided by the frame and neglected any contribution from the curtain wall and the concrete block walls of the core. Ignoring the P-Delta effect, he had found a period of fourteen seconds for the longitudinal motions of the tower, while the *measured* period of these oscillations was eight seconds. But the crisis of public confidence created by the glass problem made it imperative to take drastic precautions, while it was inconceivable to all concerned structuralists to rely on a glass curtain wall or on a cement block wall, *unconnected* to the frame, for the safety of the tower. The remedial action, despite its cost, was approved by all the designers, but Michael Flynn, I. M. Pei's technical expert, said: "It was like putting your socks on after your shoes."

Through all this, the glass panel failure remained unexplained. It was understood only thanks to the persistence of the I. M. Pei office who continued to study the problem. Research proved that the panels had been correctly installed, while the Davenport tests had shown that the cracks in the glass were not due to the wind motions, and the panels had *not* cracked at the "hot spots" located on the facades by the wind tests. The true cause of the panels failure was revealed from test results obtained during this time by an independent laboratory that simulated the thousands of wind oscillations and thermal stress cycles caused by the expansion and contraction of the air between the two glass lights of the panels. It was noticed that while the two lights were identically supported and designed to share equally the wind pressures and suctions, the wind loads in most cases first cracked the *outer* light both in the lab tests and on the tower facades. The lab researchers, looking at the edge of the lead solder binding the reflective material sheet to the spacer (Fig. 13.9), found that it had chips of glass in it. The researchers were finally able to prove that the lead connection around the panel's edge had developed fatigue because the bond obtained by the melted lead solder between the *reflective coating* and the *outside* light, as well as that between the reflective coating and the lead sealer, was so strong that it did not yield and transmitted the motions to the *outer* light, cracking it first. It was the strength of these bonds that had done them in. Had they been weaker, less well researched, the panels would have been safe!

Unfortunately too late, a last investigation showed that the material of the reflective panels had given the same kind of trouble in previous installations on smaller buildings. *All* the 10,344 identical panels of the Hancock Tower were replaced with single-thickness tempered glass.

Is there a moral to this story? There is indeed. It is well known to all creative designers and was clearly articulated by LeMessurier: "Any time you depart from established practice, make ten times the effort, ten times the investigations. Especially on a very large-scale project."

14.1 Campanile of San Marco, Venice, Italy

14

Old-Age Death

Deep-hearted man, express
Grief for thy dead in silence like to death;
Most like a monumental statue set
In everlasting watch and moveless woe,
Till itself crumble to the dust beneath.

Elizabeth Barrett Browning

Towers

Pavia is one of the jewel towns of northern Italy. Fifty miles south of Milan, at the confluence of the turbulent waters of the Ticino River and the placid waters of the Po, it was known as Ticinum during the Roman Empire. After vying with Milan as capital of the Lombard kingdom, Ticinum became a free commune in the twelfth century. Its law school, started in the ninth century, developed into a widely known center of culture, and by 1361 Pavia had established the university that later honored Petrarch and Columbus. Rival noble families of the papal Guelph and the imperial Ghibelline factions asserted their dominance over the town by erecting so many towers that Ticinum was called *Pappia, civitas centum turrium* (Pappia, the town of one hundred towers). The duomo, or cathedral, started in 1488, was meant to rival St. Peter's in Rome and, although unfinished, has the third-largest church dome in Italy.

Pavia was not the only Italian town to sprout high towers in the Middle Ages. San Gimignano had seventy-two of them and was known as San Gimignano dalle Belle Torri (San Gimignano of the beautiful towers) until more recently it acquired the nickname of the New York of Tuscany, although only thirteen of them survive to this day. Siena could alert its citizens of the danger of a Florentine attack by ringing the bells of the Torre de Mangia (the eater's tower), so called from the nickname of one of its bell ringers famous for his appetite. Crowned in white marble, it stands 286.5 ft. (87.33 m) above the brick town hall. Venice looked on the doges in the *Bucentaur*, the gilded state galley, marrying by papal license the "Most Serene Republic" to the sea, from the lagoon and from the top of the Campanile di San Marco, St. Mark's bell tower, 324 ft. (99 m) above it (Fig. 14.1). Pisa gloried in its tower, which leaned dramatically without falling. Bologna, the first university town in Europe, attended by ten thousand students by 1088, could be proud of the Torre degli Asinelli (tower of the Asinelli [little donkeys] Family), which tried unsuccessfully to emulate the tower of Pisa by leaning slightly and reached 321 ft. (98 m) toward the sky. And Cremona erected the highest of them all, Il Torrazzo (the big tower), 364 ft. (111 m) tall.

All of them pure status symbols and all but one of them (in Pisa) square in plan, the medieval towers of Italy varied in height roughly between 131 ft. (40 m) and 360 ft. (110 m), in width between 15 ft. (4.5 m) and 29 ft. (8.5 m) and in height-to-width ratio between 9 and 13, slenderer than most modern skyscrapers, which seldom dare ratios of more than 7 or 8. They were identically structured with a skin one or two bricks thick, hiding thick walls of rubble-and-mortar concrete, which varied in thickness along the height. The height of the towers was the status symbol of their owners, but no private tower was allowed to be taller than the communal tower. The proudest towers were either cut down by an edict of the commune or decapitated by a rival family jealous of any tower taller than theirs.

In Bologna the punishment of "tower decapitation" (head cutting), mostly politically motivated, as in all other medieval towns, was inflicted by a simple procedure guaranteed not to damage the surrounding neighborhood. The tower to be demolished was propped up on two or three sides by means of inclined wooden poles and then weakened on the same sides by large openings. When the kindling set on top of platforms right under the propping poles was set on fire and burned the poles, the tower collapsed in the desired direction and "justice" was done. So infallible was the procedure that it was used in 1272 to demolish half a tower belonging to the heirs of Guidotto Prendiparte (the Fat Guy of the Partisans Family), guilty of having helped their father in the homicide of Ugolino Bonacosa Asinelli (Little Hugh of the Goodthing Smalldonkeys Family), while leaving undamaged the other half of the tower belonging to the innocent half of Guidotto Prendiparte's family.

Most, but not all, of the communal towers stood proudly, some for almost one thousand years, but when one came down, it collapsed in a most dramatic manner. The Campanile di San Marco (Fig. 14.1), started in 888 and finished between 1156 and 1173, crumbled suddenly and most unexpectedly in 1902 after being repeatedly hit by lightning. Luckily it fell without killing or even hurting anybody, but it damaged the lovely *loggetta* (small covered balcony) at its base designed by Sansovino. Too famous the world over to disappear forever from the *piazzetta* (the small piazza, as against the large Piazza of San Marco), where it had been admired and loved for so long, the campanile was rebuilt exactly as it had looked, after a five-year fierce debate between the modernist and the classicist factions, but with a modern structure (Fig. 14.2).

One of the oldest towers, built in 1060 in "the town of the one hundred towers," collapsed at 8:55 A.M. on March 17, 1989. The Civic Tower of Pavia (Fig. 14.3), the only tower ever erected to serve the needs of both the commune and the church, to alert the Pavesi of the approaching Milanese enemy and to ring the bells of the duomo, the love and pride of all the Pavesi, failed in a matter of minutes. It *disappeared* in a cloud of red dust under the eyes of the terrified citizens crossing the cathedral square or walking along the narrow streets of the historic center. The roar of the collapse and the shaking of the ground were so horrific that the rumor spread instantly: "An earthquake has destroyed our cathedral."

On that March 17 the pigeons resting in the belfry of the tower suddenly abandoned it at 8:45 A.M. and began fluttering above it in a mad carousel. Giuseppina Comaschi, the newspaper vendor who had been looking at the tower from her stand the best part of her life, was the first to hear the crackling and to notice the bulging of its walls. She grabbed the phone to give the alarm, but before

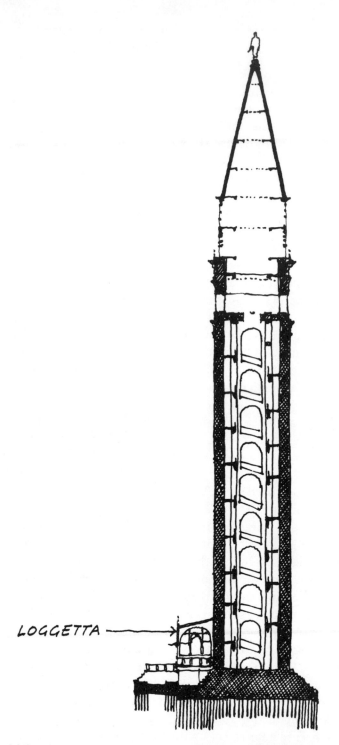

LOGGETTA ———→

14.2   Section through Campanile of San Marco

14.3   Civic Tower of Pavia, Italy

she could finish dialing, she was buried under the flow of debris invading the square and died. Mercifully Giulio Fontana died of a heart attack in a barber's chair while waiting to be shaved by Salvatore La Spada, the shop owner, as the avalanche of bricks and concrete invaded the shop. Signor La Spada himself could not avoid getting his legs trapped in the debris; five hours later the men of the fire brigade freed him, but not before seriously considering whether to amputate his legs. The dogs of the canine police squad from the neighboring town of Bergamo were unable to sniff the bodies of Barbara Cassani, seventeen, and Adriana Uggetti, eighteen, until four days later, when, on the afternoon of March 21, they were extricated from the rubble of a store cellar, tragically ending the agony of their families' vigil in the bishop's residence. His Excellency, upon hearing the roar of the collapse, had rushed into the square just in time to save Letizia Calvi, who had been hit in one leg by a flying brick and could not move. Almost miraculously only four people died and fifteen people were hurt by the collapse. The fire commissioner stated that a difference of five minutes either way would have killed tens of people.

As usual in such circumstances, each eyewitness description of the failure differed from any other. To Signor Stefano Gerard the tower seemed "to swell and the columns of the belfry to vibrate" before the fall. Signora Venera Silvestri Di Martino noticed "two bricks spit by the tower" and saw "the tower open up as if hit by a tremendous whiplash"; to one witness the tower seemed "to fall down straight"; to another "to curl up on itself." All agreed that bricks and chunks of concrete had been falling from the tower, but some said for days, others for years.

Professor Giorgio Macchi of the civil engineering department of Pavia's university, now in charge of one inquiry on the causes of the collapse, declared more than a year later he is unable to state why the tower failed. On the other hand, the members of the structural engineering department of the Polytechnic of Milan have already given the supervising magistrate their three-volume report on the failure. All evidence and reports have been sealed by the court magistrate to protect the rights of the claimants against the town, and eighteen months after the tragedy, nobody knows officially why the tower came down. The state has appropriated money for preliminary studies, but only the newly established (and so far penniless) Association for the Monuments of Pavia has declared that the tower *must* be rebuilt. Meanwhile, Pavia's Fraccaro Tower, found to be in serious danger, has been equipped with the latest electronic gadgets to transmit every four hours to Professor Macchi's lab information about the "breathing" of cracks, the leaning angle of the tower, and the settlements of the soil under it (none so far). Everybody in Pavia worries about at least one more tower, the Tower of St. Dalmatian, and the damaged cathedral waits to be fixed while, in 1990, the cathedral square was still encumbered by debris that the court did not allow to be removed. The question heard everywhere is simply: Why did the tower fall?

A convergence of causes is obviously responsible for the collapse, some of long standing, other relatively recent, some of chemical and others of structural origin. We can only list them here in decreasing order of importance and in the simplest possible terms.

1. As slow chemical reactions between the old and the more recent mortars used in the tower lowered the compressive strength of the concrete walls, these began to crumble and increased in volume to such an extent as to burst the brick skin that had contained them and hidden the growing damage. (For the exclusive information of the few readers familiar with the chemistry of concrete, we may add that the calcium sulfate in the gypsum of the brick walls interacted chemically, at an extremely low rate, with the more recent hydraulic lime or cement mortars used in successive repairs, giving rise to two compounds, called *ettringite* and *thaumasite*. The first causes such an increase in the volume of the lime mortars that they slowly crumble, while the second is the cause of their dramatic decrease of compressive strength. Such chemical changes are known to accelerate with humidity.) The experts consider these chemical interactions to be the main cause of the collapse.

2. The air pollution resulting from the numerous industrial establishments in Pavia have also accelerated the weakening of the compressive resistance of the lime concrete in the tower, contributing to the bursting of the better-built brick skin.

3. The construction of the sixteenth-century belfry (Fig. 14.4), very much debated at the time, increased the tower height and consequently the wind forces on it. It also added a dead load to the tower masonry, dangerously increasing the compressive stresses in the weakened concrete. Moreover, the bell vibrations generated stress waves in the concrete, disintegrating it mechanically over a period of three hundred years.

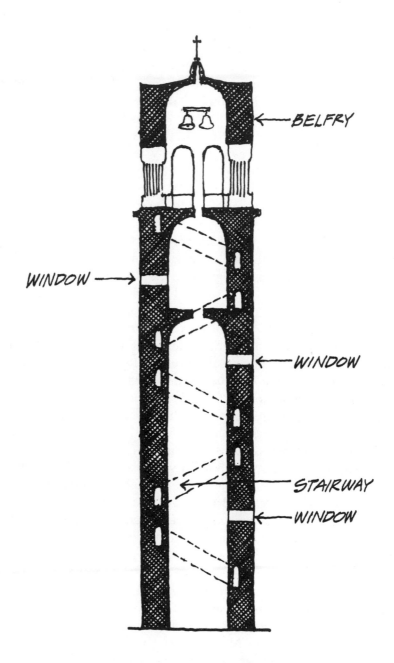

14.4   Section through Civic Tower of Pavia

4. The stairway leading to the belfry (Fig. 14.4) was dug out of the tower walls, substantially weakening their compressive strength.

5. The windows and other openings in the concrete walls (Fig. 14.4) and the brick skin of the tower generated a flow of *stress concentrations* in the structure, analogous to the faster flow of water around the piers of a bridge (Fig. 14.5), which facilitated the opening of cracks, particularly in the brick skin.

6. Recent car and truck traffic generated vibrations in the soil below the tower, which contributed to the loosening up of the skin bricks.

7. Although soil settlements have not been discovered recently in the area of the tower, it is most probable that the lowering of the *water table* (the water level) in the past may have disturbed the tower foundations.

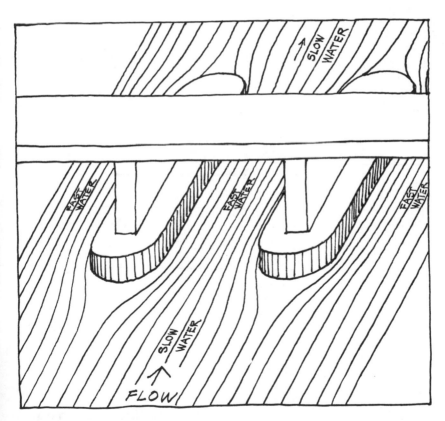

14.5   Flow of Water around Bridge Piers

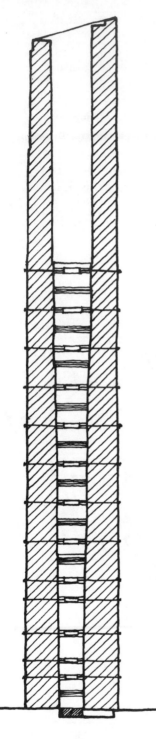

SECTION

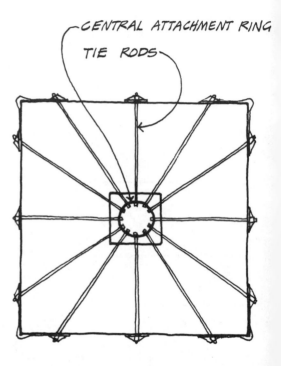

CENTRAL ATTACHMENT RING

TIE RODS

PLAN

14.6 Proposed Strengthening of Fraccaro Tower in Pavia, Italy

All these causes, taken together, explain how the venerable tower lived so long and died so suddenly.

The Civic Tower cannot be repaired, but a brilliant solution to a similar problem has been proposed by Professor Engineer Giulio Ballio of the BVC structural office in Milan to strengthen the endangered Fraccaro Tower in Pavia (Fig. 14.6). It consists in restraining the walls of the tower from bulging and bursting out by means of prestressed radial stainless steel bars pulling the walls together from inside the tower. The bar pulls would generate a state of compression in the four walls, just as the tensed spokes of a bicycle wheel generate a state of compression stiffening the rim.

Once all the highly technical causes of the collapse and the proposed remedies have been studied by experts and (vaguely) understood by laypersons, people in the street might be satisfied with the simple explanation, and the feeling of resignation, offered by a citizen of the Most Serene Republic of Venice on the occasion of the collapse of the campanile: "It died of old age." Even the experts agree that after standing for one thousand years, a medieval tower is old.

The Ages of Buildings

Human beings are said to have three ages: a chronological age, measured from the day of birth in the West and from the day of conception in the East; a physiological age, established by medical investigations; and a psychological age, defined by the way each of us feels. Buildings also have three ages: a chronological age, measured from the day construction ends; a structural age, established by engineering investigations; and an economic age, determined by the building's capacity to be profitably used. The table at the end of this section (p. 219) gives the chronological age of a number of buildings, some of which, although old, are structurally young, some of which are in ruins, and others of which have disappeared altogether.

The life-span of a building depends very much on the culture that built it. For example, the Japanese temples, like those of the Nara Monastery and others, although built of a most perishable material like wood, are kept eternally young by a continuous process of rejuvenation. The fifth-century Shinto shrine in Ise has been rebuilt every twenty years without alteration (Fig. 14.7). On the other hand, some New York City brownstones, built between the end of the nineteenth and the beginning of the twentieth century, have crumbled before age one hundred. In the 1960s the facade of one of them on East Eighteenth Street fell unexpectedly in the early hours of a cold winter morning, leaving the building intact and the tenants, still in bed, exposed to passersby. An investigation of the collapse tentatively suggested that the brick facade had been shaken and weakened by vibrations emanating from pile drivers used to build the foundations of an adjoining building. The Deauville Hotel in Atlantic City, New Jersey, a building in the Art Nouveau style of the 1920s, still in perfect structural shape but by then unprofitable,

14.7   Shrine of the Sun Goddess at Ise, Japan

AGES OF MONUMENTS

Name	Site	Age (in Years)	Comments
Pyramids	Gizeh, Egypt	4,670	Almost intact
Temple of Amon	Luxor, Egypt	3,540	Restored ruins
Stonehenge	Salisbury Plain, England	3,500	Megalithic monument
Knossos	Crete, Greece	3,500	Restored Minoan monument
Nuraghe	Sardinia, Italy	3,250	Prehistoric monument
Lighthouse	Pharos, Greece	2,700	Destroyed by earthquake in fourteenth century
Ephesus	Celçuk, Turkey	2,540	Restored ruins
Parthenon	Athens, Greece	2,420	Damaged by gun shells
Pantheon	Rome, Italy	2,140	Temple used today as church
Colosseum	Rome, Italy	1,910	Arena damaged by man
Hagia Sophia	Istanbul, Turkey	1,453	Museum, former church, and mosque
Horiyuji	Nara, Japan	1,390	Temple
Chichén Itzá	Yucatán, Mexico	1,000	Restored site
Civic Tower	Pavia, Italy	890	Crumbled 1989
St. Mark's Tower	Venice, Italy	842	Crumbled 1902, rebuilt 1912
Santa Maria del Fiore	Florence, Italy	556	Church in use
St. Peter's	Rome, Italy	364	Church in use
Taj Mahal	Agra, India	342	Intact tomb
Brownstones	New York, New York	100	Some in use
Housing	New York, New York	70	Dynamited for profit
Hotel Deauville	Atlantic City, New Jersey	40	Dynamited for profit

was dynamited by demolition specialists in the 1960s in such a spectacular show that to this day it is frequently shown on national television. The Bridge of Santa Trínita over the Arno River in Florence, the sixteenth-century masterpiece of Bartolomeo Ammannati, was ruthlessly dynamited during the Second World War by the retreating Nazis, despite heroic efforts to save it by the Italian partisans. Its reconstruction after the end of the war as an exact replica of the original was paid for by an international subscription.

We mention on p. 239 the destruction of the Cathedral of Coventry in England during World War II, but it would take a separate volume to list all the historical or otherwise significant structures destroyed by the wars men have fought. Hence we shall end our description of willful demolition by mentioning the recent case of four houses in the Times Square area of New York City that is particularly significant both because one of these structures had housed the temporarily homeless and because the demolition was sneakily executed at night just a few hours before a freeze prohibiting all demolition was due to be imposed by the city. Although the developer responsible for this action was fined two million dollars by the city's building authorities, he was allowed to build on the site so cleverly "cleared" a high-rise hotel worth hundreds of millions of dollars.

Thus do nature, time, incompetence, human folly, and greed conspire to tear down structures man has spent so much love, time, thought and energy to put up.

15

The Worst Structural Disaster in the United States

> The bad end unhappily,
> the good unluckily.
>
> Tom Stoppard,
> *Rosenkranz and Guildenstern Are Dead*

I n July 1980 the plushiest and most modern hotel in Kansas City, Missouri, the Hyatt Regency, was ready for occupancy after two years of design and two more years of construction. Kansas City's "first citizen," Donald Hall, of Hallmark greeting cards fame, bought it from the developers, and his management company started one of the most ambitious and popular programs to be found in an American deluxe hotel. Service in the 750 rooms and suites was refined and fast, food in the many restaurants exquisite, and the tea and dinner dances in its grandiose atrium were soon attended by elegant crowds.

The Hyatt Regency complex consists of three connected buildings: a slim reinforced concrete tower on the north end, housing the guests' bedrooms and suites; a 117 by 145 ft. (34 × 44 m) atrium with a steel and glass roof 50 ft. (15 m) above the floor; and at the south end a four-story reinforced concrete "function block," containing all the service areas—meeting rooms, dining rooms, kitchens, etc. (Fig. 15.1). The tower was connected to the function block by three pedestrian bridges, or *walkways*, hung from the steel trusses of the atrium roof: two, one above the other, at the second- and fourth-floor levels near the west side of the atrium and one at the

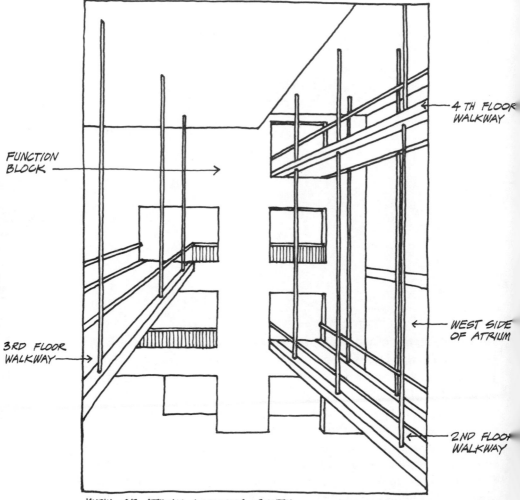

FUNCTION
BLOCK

4 TH FLOOR
WALKWAY

WEST SIDE
OF ATRIUM

3RD FLOOR
WALKWAY

2ND FLOOR
WALKWAY

VIEW OF ATRIUM LOOKING SOUTH

15.1 Atrium of Hyatt Regency Hotel, Kansas City, Missouri

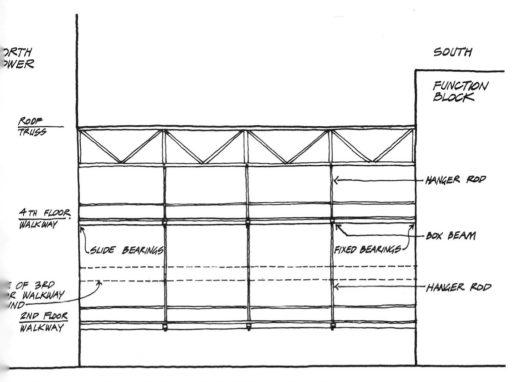

15.2   Elevation of West Side Atrium Showing Second- and Fourth-Floor Walkways

third-floor level near the east side of the atrium (Fig. 15.2). Restaurant service was available at a bar set *under* the two stacked walkways on the west side of the atrium. The main purpose of the walkways was to permit people to pass between the tower and the function block without crossing the often crowded atrium.

At 7:05 P.M. on Friday, July 17, 1981, the atrium was filled with more than sixteen hundred people, most of them dancing to the music of a well-known band for a tea dance competition, when suddenly a frightening, sharp sound like a thunderbolt was heard, stopping the dancers in mid-step. Looking up toward the source of the sound, they saw two groups of people on the second- and fourth-floor walkways, observing the festivities and stomping in rhythm with the music. As the two walkways began to fall, the observers were seen holding on to the railings with terrified expressions on their faces. The fourth-floor walkway dropped from the hangers holding it to the roof structure, leaving the hangers dangling like impotent stalactites. Since the second-floor walkway hung from the fourth-floor walkway, the two began to fall together. There was a large roar as the concrete decks of the steel-framed walkways cracked and crashed down, in a billowing cloud of dust, on the crowd gathered around the bar below the second-floor walkway. People were screaming; the west glass wall adjacent to the walkways shattered, sending shards flying over 100 ft. (30 m); pipes broken by the falling walkways sent jets of water spraying the atrium floor. It was a nightmare the survivors would never forget.

The following day the press mentioned 44 dead and 82 injured, but the last victim to be reached alive, a World War II navy pilot who was in a wheelchair on the second-floor walkway, succumbed from chest injuries five months later. The final count reported 114 dead and over 200 injured, many maimed for life. It was indeed the worst *structural* failure ever to occur in the United States. The plaintiffs' claims, also the largest ever in a structural failure case, amounted originally to more than three billion dollars. Donald Hall settled more than 90 percent of these claims out of a sense of duty and social responsibility.

Within a few hours of the accident rumors about the cause of the failure began to fly. As usual, the general contractor and his subcontractors were the first to be suspected of malfeasance and malpractice. Then technical opinions blossomed. Since the people on the two walkways were stomping in rhythm with the music, *obviously* the up-and-down vibrations of the walkways must have had *exactly* the same rhythm; technically, they were *in resonance* with the impacts of the stomping people, and, as *everybody knows*, continued resonance can quickly destroy even a sound structure (see p. 272). Then engineers and laypeople began suspecting the quality of the materials used in the walkways (*everybody knows* that weaker materials are cheaper than good materials) or the skills of the workers who welded and bolted them together *(everybody knows* that skilled workers demand higher salaries than *unskilled ones)*. For a relatively long time the only unsuspected members of the construction team were the architects and the design engineers.

The management company of the hotel was the first to take action. It asked the design team of the hotel to prepare the drawings for a second-floor walkway *supported by columns* and authorized its immediate construction. Simultaneously it entrusted to Weidlinger Associates a most thorough analysis and check of the entire structure of the hotel complex (except the walkways), from the rotating restaurant at the top of the tower to the spiral canti-levered stairs connecting the upper three floors of the function block with the atrium floor, to the foundations of the three components of the complex. Shortly thereafter, at the request of the Kansas City mayor, the federal government authorized the National Bureau of Standards to perform an official investigation with "the objec-tive of determining the most probable cause of the collapse." E. O. Pfrang and R. M. Marshall of the bureau, two well-known and highly respected engineers, performed an in-depth investigation, using theoretical calculations and experimental verification of the walk-ways components, and issued an official report in 1981. As is its custom, the bureau did not assign blame to any party but made it clear that the responsibility for the collapse could mainly be attributed to the structural engineers, who eventually lost their licenses in the state of Missouri.

How could this tragedy have occurred in the year 1981 in the most advanced technical country in the world and after two years of design and two of construction? In order to clarify this mystery, we must understand how the walkways were originally designed and how they were eventually built.

The two walkways on the west side of the atrium involved in the collapse (the third-floor walkway that was separately hung remained in place) consisted of four 30 ft (9 m) long spans on each side, consisting of two longitudinal wide-flange steel beams each 16 in. (400 mm) deep. The four 30 ft. (9 m) beams were connected by steel angles bolted to the upper flanges at the beams' ends, thus spanning the 120 ft. (36 m) atrium width (Fig. 15.2). The south ends of the walkways were welded to plates in the floors of the function block, and their north ends were supported on sliding bearings in the floors of the tower. The purpose of the sliding supports was to allow the beams to expand or contract with temperature changes without giving rise to thermal stresses (see p. 274).

Intermediate supports of the walkways at each end of the 30 ft. (9 m) beams consisted of transverse *box beams*, fabricated by butt welding along their entire length two 8 in. (200 mm) deep channels (Fig. 15.3). In the *original working drawings* (the last engineering drawings submitted to the contractor and the architects by the design engineers) each box beam had *single* holes at both ends of the flanges (Fig. 15.4), through each of which was threaded a single 1¼ in. (32 mm) steel rod that served as hanger for *both* the second-

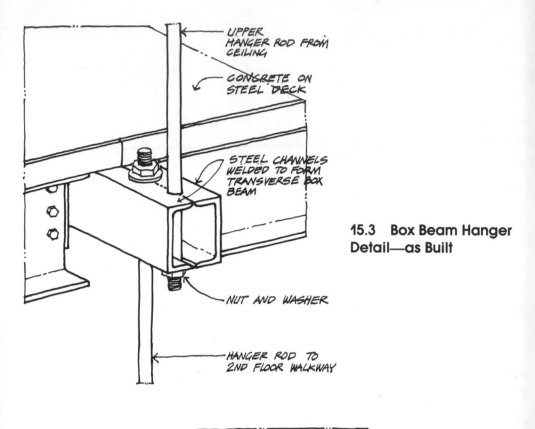

UPPER HANGER ROD FROM CEILING

CONCRETE ON STEEL DECK

STEEL CHANNELS WELDED TO FORM TRANSVERSE BOX BEAM

15.3   Box Beam Hanger Detail—as Built

NUT AND WASHER

HANGER ROD TO 2ND FLOOR WALKWAY

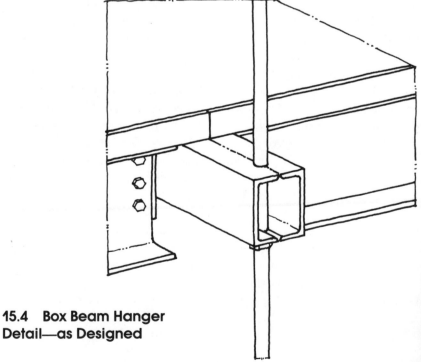

15.4   Box Beam Hanger Detail—as Designed

and fourth-floor walkways. In this design the load of *both* walk-ways was supported every thirty feet by means of nuts screwed into a *single* rod on each side of the walkways at the level of the second-floor *and* the fourth-floor box beams. Thus the single rods hung from the steel trusses of the atrium's roof supported the weights of *both* walkways, but the box beams of *each* walkway supported only the loads on *that single walkway.*

In the *shop drawings* (the final drawings submitted by the con-tractor to the design engineers and the architects) each end of the *fourth*-floor box beams had *two* holes through both flanges, one at 2 in. (50 mm) from the end and the other at 6 in. (150 mm) from the end (Fig. 15.3). Two *upper* hangers, ending at the fourth-floor level and consisting of 1¼ in. (32 mm) rods, went through the *outer* hole in each box beam of the fourth floor and supported the *fourth-floor walkway only* by means of nuts and washers at their *lower* end—i.e., *below* the box beams of the fourth-floor walkway. Two separate *lower* rod hangers, starting at the fourth-floor level, went through the *inner* hole of each fourth-floor box beam, supported by a nut and washer at their *upper* ends—i.e., *above* the fourth-floor box beam—and supported at their lower ends the second-floor walkway. This design was a change suggested by the contractor in the *shop* drawings and stamped "Approved" by the architects and "Reviewed" by the structural engineers. (Design engineers are advised by their attorneys never to stamp the contractor's shop drawings "Approved".) In the final contractor's design the loads of *both walkways* was transmitted to the roof trusses by the shorter upper rods, which passed through *only the fourth-floor box beams* and supported the second-floor walkway by two additional shorter rods hanging from the fourth-floor box beams. Thus in this design the fourth-floor transverse box beams supported the loads of *two* walkways, rather than the *one* of the original design.

At this point the reader will probably think: "By now I know why the tragedy occurred. The box beams of the fourth-floor walk-way were designed to carry the load of one walkway and instead had to carry twice that load. No wonder they failed!" That would not be wrong, but neither would that be completely right, as the in-depth investigation of the National Bureau of Standards proved to laypeople and engineers alike.

The job of Pfrang and Marshall might be thought relatively simple: to determine whether the rods and the box beams of the final design could resist the tension in the rods and the bending in the box beams from the hanging walkways. For this purpose they determined the *dead load* of the walkways by taking from engineering manuals the weight of each walkway component and adding them up. But they also weighed the components recovered from the collapse and found that the dead load was actually 8 percent higher than the computed load, because the deck of the walkways consisted of a corrugated steel deck and 3¼ in. (82 mm) of concrete, *plus* a cement topping not shown on the drawings but authorized in the *specifications* (the written document describing each component of the project accompanying the final engineering drawings). The *live load* was required by the Kansas City Building Code to be 100 lb. / sq. ft. (5 kN / m²) or a total of 72,000 lb. (3,200 kN) for *each* walkway. By mere chance a videotape of the tea dance competition was being made on that memorable day, and it showed that there were sixty-three people on the two walkways, mostly concentrated on the south half and east side of the second-floor walkway, from which they had a better view of the band and the dance contestants. The actual live load, 9,450 lb.* (420 kN), was thus a small fraction of the live load required by the code.

Pfrang and Marshall realized immediately that the weak elements in the chain of structural elements were the box beams of the fourth floor. But since the stress analysis of the complex beams could not be accurately obtained by theoretical calculations, they tested in the laboratory both brand-new duplicates of the box beams and some of the undamaged actual box beams. They also computed *and* tested the ultimate strength of the hanger rods. They could thus *prove* the real cause of the walkway collapse.

The six upper hanger rods, carrying the load of the walkways and thus supporting 24,000 lb. (1,066 kN) each, pulled up on the thin lower flanges of the fourth-floor box beams through a single nut and bolt connection. Under this load (*twice* the design load), the bolt first bent the lower flange of the box beams, then broke through the lower hole in it, pulled out of the hole in the upper flange, and became disconnected from the box beam (Fig. 15.5). This first happened at the midspan upper hanger rod; the remaining upper rods, incapable of taking over the load unsupported by the failed rod, pulled out of their holes, and both walkways fell down. The walkway system not only was underdesigned but also lacked redundancy (see p. 55), a most prudent reserve of strength

---

* 63 people @ 150 lb. each = 9,450 lb.

in structures in public places. The dangerous suggestion of the contractor, aimed at simplifying the construction of the walkways, was fatal because it went unnoticed by the design engineers.

We can do no better than report in abbreviated form the conclusions of the National Bureau of Standards report:

1. The walkways collapsed under loads *substantially less* than those specified by the Kansas City Building Code.

2. All the fourth-floor box beam-hanger connections were candidates for initiation of walkway collapse.

3. The box beam-hanger rod connections, the fourth-floor-to-

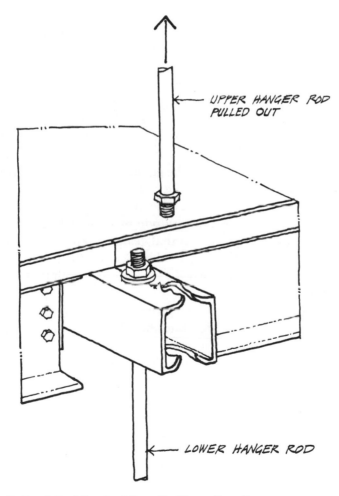

15.5   Pulled-Out Rod at Fourth-Floor Box Beam

ceiling hanger rods, and the third-floor-walkway hanger rods did not satisfy the design provisions of the Kansas City Building Code.

4. The box beam-hanger to rods connections under the original hanger rod detail (continuous rod) would not have satisfied the Kansas City Building Code.

5. Neither the quality of workmanship nor the materials used in the walkway system played a significant role in initiating the collapse.

The National Bureau of Standards report adds: "The ultimate capacity actually available using the original connection detail would have been approximately 60% of that expected of a connection designed in accordance with the specifications of the Kansas City Code." Since 60% = 0.60 is equal to 1 / 1.67, and 1.67 is an average coefficient of safety for steel structures, the above statement is equivalent to saying that under the *original* engineering design of the connections, which did *not* satisfy the code, the walkways *might not have collapsed* under the actual loads on them on July 17, 1981.

Who is to blame for the tragedy? The Missouri licensing board and the Missouri Court of Appeals found fault with the design engineers because they did not notice the essential difference between their original design and the design suggested by the contractor that they acknowledged reviewing. The National Bureau of Standards made it clear that even the original walkway design did not satisfy the Kansas City Building Code provisions but also stated, although indirectly, that the original design might not have caused a collapse under the minor live load present on the fatal day. From a human point of view, the original design, although illegal, might have avoided the tragedy.

Legally the principal and the project manager of the structural firm responsible for the design had their Missouri engineer's licenses revoked. The attorney who represented the state licensing board, Patrick McLarney, added, "It wasn't a matter of doing something wrong, they just never did it at all. Nobody ever did any calculations to figure out whether or not the particular connection that held the skywalks up would work. It got built without anybody ever figuring out if it would be strong enough. It just slipped through the cracks."

16

The Politics
of Destruction

To every thing there is a season,
and a time to every purpose under the
heaven.

Ecclesiastes 3:1

We build structures with the faith that they will last forever. As we have seen in the previous sections, the forces
of nature and human error often conspire to confound
our optimism and cause structural failures. But there
are causes yet to be explored arising from the pressure of population growth, our lack of respect for the past, or our belief that violence solves some problems. These include neglect, abandonment,
replacement, and war.

The Growth of Cities

The pressure of an ever-increasing population squeezes inward on
our cities, giving rise to higher and higher buildings. (Since 1850
there has been an explosive fivefold increase in the world's population to 5.3 billion.) As the land in the generally limited area of
our central cities becomes more valuable, yesterday's low-rise

building becomes uneconomical. In 1989, for instance, twenty-seven high-rise buildings were under construction in Manhattan alone, many replacing older, smaller structures.

The wrecker's ball demolishes in days what took years to build, without concern for historical interest, human convenience, or beauty. Often, for economic considerations or to speed up the process, explosives are used to accomplish the same results in hours. The Deauville Hotel in Atlantic City, New Jersey, was dynamited forty years after its construction, and the thirty-three buildings formerly housing twenty-nine hundred families and known as Pruitt-Igoe in St. Louis, Missouri, were demolished in 1973 after having stood for less than eighteen years, a symbol of a failed experiment in high-rise public housing.

Throughout history there are examples of the abandonment of structures for political reasons after they have served their useful purpose, when the civilization that supported them died out or moved away.

The towering ruins of the Krak des Chevaliers stands as a mute reminder of the Crusades. Built in the early thirteenth century as the fortress of the Knights of St. John in Tripoli (now Syria) and described by Muslims as a bone struck in the throat of the Saracens, it was finally captured in 1271 by Bibars, the sultan of Egypt, and, protected by its isolation and the dry desert atmosphere, has survived without further damage through the intervening centuries.

In the Yucatán Peninsula, when the stronger leadership from Mayapán wrested control of the Mayan peoples away from the priests of Chichén Itzá, their temples were abandoned in the fifteenth century. The deteriorating structures were captured by the crawling vines, rendering them almost invisible in the jungle.

The peaceful Minoans of Crete—their cities even lacked fortifications—suddenly disappeared a thousand years after their origins around 2500 B.C., leaving behind the Knossos temples and palaces that speak to us of a gentle Bronze Age civilization. Their structures were destroyed by an earthquake, possibly related to the violent eruption of Santorini, but later rebuilt and finally burned most likely by the more aggressive mainlanders from Greece.

The Zuñi and Hopi Indians of the southwestern United States concentrated their dwellings in flat-roofed, terraced structures built of stone or adobe. These multistoried pueblos typically had a single opening at the lowest level leading into a well-protected court

16.1 The Parthenon, Athens, Greece

as defense against hostile attack. Ladders that could readily be removed connected the various levels. Peopled by peaceful, sedentary tribes that farmed the land, the pueblos suffered from a shrinking population and cultural degeneration leading to their abandonment before the seventeenth-century colonization of the Southwest by the Spaniards.

Fortunately many of these structures have survived in spite of the attempt of man to destroy them as exemplified by the following tales of two cities.

The Survival of the Temple of Athena

The Parthenon, dedicated to Athena Parthenos (Athena the Virgin, the goddess of peace, wisdom, and the arts), and the greatest Greek temple in Doric style, stands on the hill of the Acropolis, high above Athens, as a symbol of the endurance of Greek civilization (Fig. 16.1). It was designed and built by the architect Ictinus and his collaborator Callicrates under the supervision of the sculptor Phidias between 447 B.C. and its inauguration in 438 B.C., during the years of peace, when Athens enjoyed democracy under Pericles, a brilliant statesman, a military commander, and a patron of the arts. The Parthenon's marble statue of Athena by Phidias, clad in gold draperies encrusted with ivory and glass, stood in the *cella* or *sacrarium* of the temple, a token to the building's loving vigilance over the city and its meaning to the Athenians who climbed the Acropolis as pilgrims to venerate their goddess.

Indeed, the Parthenon became the most admired and imitated temple of antiquity. The bas-reliefs of its *metope* (the marble tablets over the column-supported beams) and the high reliefs of its *pediments* (the triangles formed on the facades by the roof gables) were among the greatest sculptures of all time.

But sacred awe of the Parthenon did not last forever. One thousand years after it was built, the statue of Athena (now known to us only through Roman copies) was removed, and it disappeared forever in the fifth century A.D. The cause of this desecration was ironically another religion, as the temple was transformed into a church dedicated to St. Sophia, interestingly the Christian saint of wisdom. In the sixth century the Parthenon was transformed into a church dedicated to another virgin, the Mother of God. The roof and two rows of interior columns were removed, an apse was built at the East end and a door opened between the cella and the chamber behind it. These alterations involved the first damage to the sculptures, but worse damage was yet to come.

A thousand years later, in 1546, the Turks captured Athens, and the Parthenon became a mosque, luckily without ulterior structural alterations, but with the addition of an independent minaret. Then, during the seventeenth-century war between the Turks and the Venetian maritime republic, the Turks used the temple as a powder magazine, and the captain general of the Venetian fleet, Francesco Morosini, shelled it in 1687, blowing out the middle of the temple. As a testimony to his victory Morosini wanted to carry the chariot of Athena from the west pediment to Venice, but although he failed to lower the sculpture, he succeeded in damaging this most famous of the Parthenon high reliefs.

One expects destruction in war, but the next assault on the Parthenon was caused not by war but by love—the love of art—by an English art lover, Thomas Bruce, the seventh earl of Elgin. In 1801 he obtained a royal Turkish decree authorizing him to make casts and drawings of the Parthenon's sculptures, tear down adjoining buildings, *and* remove sculptures. Thus it was that in 1816 the Elgin Marbles were bought by the British government and transported

16.2   The Colosseum, Rome, Italy

to the British Museum in London, where they are still on exhibit and in a way safe (although at the time this is written the Greek government is fighting in the courts to have the sculptures returned to Athens).

At this writing (1991) the Parthenon is closed to visitors while efforts take place to stop the accelerating damage done to the marble by the industrially charged air of Athens, one of the most polluted cities in Europe. The reader who loves great architecture may well ask whether the Parthenon's life will be endangered forever, but we believe that at long last international interest in this magnificent twenty-five-hundred-year-old monument and our improved preservation technologies have a good chance of saving it for the joy of us all, provided war does not touch it once again.

Bread, Games and Faith

The Flavian Amphitheater, or Roman Colosseum, was a temple dedicated to a human god, the emperor, who kept the populace in submission by gifts of bread and games *(panem et circenses)* (Fig. 16.2). The bread was needed food, but the games were the bloody

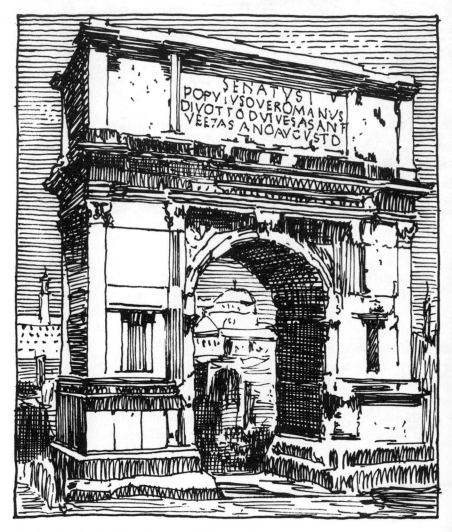

16.3   Arch of Titus, Rome, Italy

fights between trained gladiators, one of whose lives, when he was subdued by his adversary, was at the mercy of the emperor and the spectators, depending on whether they felt that he had fallen valiantly or weakly. If the emperor turned his thumb down, the vanquished gladiator was finished like a fallen bull in a bullfight; if the imperial thumb was up, he was saved for the next fight. In the first centuries A.D. the same public also enjoyed the maiming and devouring of the Christian martyrs by lions and tigers, massacres the memory of which were to save the Colosseum from total ruin thirteen hundred years after their discontinuance A.D. 404.

The Colosseum is the largest monument of Roman antiquity, an oval arena 617 by 512 ft. (185×154 m), with three floors of arched galleries and a fourth floor, pierced by square windows, that supported a retractable canvas awning to shade the crowd from Rome's brutal summer sun. It could seat fifty thousand spectators, a substantial number even by modern standards, and was begun A.D. 72 by Vespasian, the emperor famous for his taxation of public urinals, who overcame the objections of his courtiers by asserting that the money thus raised "would not stink" *(non olet)*. Vespasian's son Titus, victor of the war against the Hebrews, who was glorified by the most famous of Roman triumphal arches (Fig. 16.3), completed the Colosseum A.D. 80, celebrating the occasion with one hundred days of festivities and bloody games.

After discontinuance of the games the Colosseum suffered from neglect, vandalism, and numerous earthquakes until the middle of the eighteenth century. As Rome was reborn in the period between the fourteenth and seventeenth centuries by the triumphant expansion of Christianity, the largess of the popes, and the new atmosphere of the Renaissance, the Colosseum became the quarry whose stones built the Eternal City. Yet it was such a massive structure that only a fraction of its upper floors, probably shaken to the ground by earthquakes, has disappeared. Since its bits and pieces were used to build the facades of some of the most beautiful Renaissance *palazzi*, one may quibble that the Colosseum stones have not been really misused. For instance, the Palazzo Massimo alle Colonne (Fig. 16.4), the last creation (in 1536) of the master architect Baldassarre Peruzzi, with its unique rounded facade, pierced by an entrance flanked by Roman columns, is of such perfection as to let us forget where it comes from.

16.4   Palazzo Massimo alle Colonne, Rome, Italy

The destruction of the Colosseum would thus have continued unhindered had it not been for the decree of Pope Benedict XIV, seated on St. Peter's chair from 1740 to 1758, who pronounced it a sacred monument in honor of the Christian martyrs. In that gesture we have a rare example of human destruction stopped by a spiritual imperative of a respected leader.

War, the Destroyer of History

Humanity knew how to destroy before it learned to build; to this day people often destroy what others have built. This paradoxical behavior can be historically followed along an exponentially increasing curve of violence and destruction, reaching its inconceivable climax in our own time.

World War II, the most devastating of all wars, was fought for the high-minded purpose of saving European civilization from nazism, but reached an unsurpassed level of savagery on both sides. In a preview of the hecatomb to come, the Fascists annihilated the population of the Basque town of Guernica by aerial bombing in 1937, the first instance of this horror. In 1940 an eleven-hour aerial bombardment erased from the map of Great Britain the town of Coventry and its magnificent fourteenth-century Cathedral of St. Michael. A story circulating soon after the war, almost certainly apocryphal, is indicative of the unbound strength of purpose attributed to the British prime minister, Sir Winston Churchill. The courage and cunning of the Polish underground had succeeded in delivering a sample of the Enigma machine, the mechanical encoder of the Nazi high command, to Alan Turing, one of the greatest mathematicians of our time, who, with its help, succeeded in breaking the German ultrasecret code. According to the story, as a consequence of this incredible feat, the messages exchanged between Hitler and his high command reached Churchill's desk *before* they reached Hitler's! But Churchill, determined to reach his ultimate goal of destroying nazism at all costs, did not inform the Royal Air Force of the upcoming German raid on Coventry and let the town be destroyed, lest Hitler find out that his code had been broken by the enemy. Whether this story is true or not, the breaking of the German code reduced the sinking of the U.S. ships on the way to Great Britain from one out of two in the first year of American intervention to one out of five in the second. The bombing of Britain, although unsuccessful both physically and psychologically, continued from 1940 to 1945, as proof that destruction and death have never solved human societal problems.

At the insistence of Sir Winston, in the cold night of February 13, 1945, four months before the German unconditional surrender and with the Russian troops eighty miles away, Dresden was devastated by successive waves of 1,400 Flying Fortresses, followed on the morning of February 14 by another 1,350 planes dropping 650,000 incendiaries, the first "carpet bombing" in the history of modern warfare. The city that ranked as one of the most beautiful in the world, the showplace of German baroque and rococo architecture of the eighteenth and nineteenth centuries, and its superb cathedral were destroyed and 130,000 Germans died in the fire storm. The American writer Kurt Vonnegut, a prisoner of war held in a camp of one of the suburbs, wrote: "They flattened the whole damn town." The harbor city of Hamburg in northern Germany had already met the same destiny. It may be suggested that the Allies had been "compelled" to use violence by the violence of the Nazis, who systematically destroyed towns and cities in countries resisting their conquest.

By mid-1945 the United States was ready to use the most violent force of nature, nuclear energy, against the Japanese. Behind this last episode of World War II lies an amazing story of scientific dedication and engineering know-how, starting in 1938, when two German physicists, Otto Hahn and Fritz Strassmann, to their complete surprise, were able to show that as the result of bombarding atoms of various elements with slow-moving neutrons (atom particles without electric charge) sixteen new elements were produced, among them radium, which in turn, by further neutron bombardment, produced *transuranian elements*, elements above uranium in the table of elements. It was to be the glory of another German physicist, Lise Meitner, in collaboration with her nephew Otto Frisch, to explain that in this latter reaction the radium atom had been split into two atoms, whose weights, or masses, added up to *less* than the weight, or mass, of the original radium. Checked by Einstein's formula $E = mc^2$, the value of the energy E in this reaction should, *and did*, equal the loss of mass m times the square of the velocity of light c, 186,000 miles per second (298,000 km / sec). Even if in this experiment the loss of mass m was extremely small, the energy E was very large because of the enormous value of c, the velocity of light in a vacuum, shown by Einstein to be the largest velocity reachable in our universe.

On December 2, 1942, the Italian Nobel laureate Enrico Fermi and his collaborators succeeded in producing a chain reaction in which a nucleus of uranium 235 bombarded by slow neutrons (the fast neutrons are inefficient because many bounce back) emitted *more* neutrons than it absorbed, reaching explosive power in one-tenth of a second. This phenomenon of chain reaction through *nuclear fission* had opened the path to both unlimited energy for the good of humankind and the atom bomb.

On August 6, 1945, the *Enola Gay,* a U.S. B-29 bomber named after the mother of the pilot, dropped a uranium fission bomb, equivalent to 12,500 tons of TNT, on the Japanese city of Hiroshima, destroying 90 percent of it and killing in a flash 130,000 people and 40,000 more by radiation in the following years. Three days later a second bomb with a core of plutonium (another radioactive element) equivalent to 22,000 tons of TNT was dropped on Nagasaki, completely destroying one-third of the harbor city and killing 75,000 people instantly and 75,000 more in the following five years.

Fusion bombs, first suggested by Enrico Fermi and realized in 1952 by the Hungarian-born physicist Edward Teller, are bombs in which the explosive combination of deuterium and tritium (two elements called *hydrogen isotopes,* with the chemical properties of hydrogen but different atomic weights) produces a transformation of mass into energy as in fission. The largest modern *fusion,* or *hydrogen, bombs* are equivalent to *forty or more million tons of TNT,* an incomprehensible value of destructive power. Fifty thousand nuclear bombs, both fission and fusion types, have been built in the world; this is equivalent to distributing twenty tons of explosive TNT to each man, woman, and child on earth! Besides the United States, the USSR acquired nuclear bombs in 1949, Great Britain in 1952, France in 1960, China in 1964, and India in 1974. It is authoritatively believed that at present (1991) at least eight more nations have nuclear armaments and many more have the potential to acquire them in the near future.

Nuclear knowledge, by now available to all the governments on earth, has convinced the great powers that a nuclear world war would be a suicidal means of trying to settle international disputes. Thus, provided proliferation is stemmed and incidents are miraculously avoided, nuclear bombs may have made impossible the occurrence of world wars and opened a new era of peace and well-being for humanity. This vision of the *complementarity* of the nuclear bombs, of their danger *and* of their dictate of peace, first born in the mind of the great Danish physicist Niels Bohr in the early forties, may, we hope, become the goal of *all* governments for the greatest good of the human race.

May this happen soon.

17

The Structure
of the Law

If a carpenter undertake
to build a house and does it ill,
an action will lie against him

English common law
(fifteenth century)

Civilization is governed by principles of constraint and
consent known as the law. In primitive societies, disputes were settled by vendettas, which ended when a
life was taken to compensate for a lost life and equilibrium returned. This kind of private justice was the rule even in the
Old West, where the gun was the law.

The earliest regulations governing the adjudication of structural failures date from the time of the sixth king of Babylonia
(1792–50 B.C.) and are known as the Code of Hammurabi:

> If a builder build a house for a man and do not make its
> construction firm and the house which he has built collapse
> and cause the death of the owner of the house, that builder
> shall be put to death.

If it cause the death of the son of the owner of the house, they shall put to death a son of that builder.

If it cause the death of a slave of the owner of the house, he shall give to the owner of the house a slave of equal value.

If it destroy property, he shall restore whatever it destroyed, and because he did not make the house which he built firm and it collapsed, he shall rebuild the house which collapsed at his own expense.

If a builder build a house for a man and do not make its construction meet the requirements and a wall fall in, that builder shall strengthen the wall at his own expense.

These regulations fall under the category that the Greek philosopher Aristotle in 340 B.C. called the *natural* law or that derived from custom or precedent. Such rules of custom were the basis for the first Roman law, as set down in the Twelve Tables in 450 B.C.

Aristotle identified the second part of the law as that which is man-made or legislated. The most important event in the codification of laws was led by Justinian and completed in 535. He collected new and old laws and synthesized them into a 150,000-line code (Codex Constitutionum), defining the four areas of law: those governing the rights of people, the treatment of property and possessions, obligations under contract and tort (under which disputes concerning structural failures are dealt with), and succession.

Because of the extent of the Roman Empire, Roman law was the rule in much of the Western world except, as we shall see, in England. The Code Napoléon, developed in 1804 under the leadership of the French emperor, was derived from and represented a modernized version of Roman law. Because of the wide-ranging imperial conquests of Napoleon, his code became widely accepted throughout continental Europe.

Separated from the rest of Europe by the Channel, a barrier that helped maintain its identity, England developed its own approach to the law. The Magna Carta, written in 1215, established the foundation of English constitutional liberty. Since that time common law evolved, based first on custom (Aristotle's *natural law*) and later on precedent developed through decisions in prior cases. This common law crossed the Atlantic with the first settlers and became the basis of law in the United States.

How differently would the Malpasset disaster (p. 166), which was regulated under the Napoleonic code, have been treated under common law, under which responsibility for injury is covered by the 1868 ruling in Great Britain in the case of *Rylands v. Fletcher*, which decided "that the person who for his own purpose brings on his own land and collects and keeps there anything likely to be mischieveous, if it escapes must keep it in at his peril, and, if he does not do so, he is prima facie answerable for all the damage which is the natural consequence of its escape. And upon authority this we think is established to be the law whether the thing so brought be beasts or water or filth or stenches."

Nowadays in the United States most structural collapses eventually come before a legal tribunal to adjudicate responsibility. Engineers charged with conducting investigations to determine the technical causes of a failure are known as *forensic engineers* and require, besides a subtle knowledge of how structures behave, a sleuthing spirit that looks for both major and minor evidence of the causes of a failure. These investigations are often based on such barely noticeable symptoms or challengeable hypotheses that even honest, knowledgeable experts do not always agree on the cause or causes of a failure. This lack of agreement often leads to legal battles among experts in court cases that make their outcome as exciting at that of a murder case. After all, in both situations the basic question is, who is the culprit, and structural evidence is often, as the attorneys call it, circumstantial. The story of two courtroom encounters by Mario Salvadori will illustrate this point.

Did He Jump or Fall?*

It was 1945, and I had never before set foot in an American courtroom, not even as a juror. But the attorney in charge of the case for the Local Insurance Company, one of the largest in the United States, had thoroughly prepared me for it.

The insurance company lawyer—I will call him Mr. Wright—first came to my office, carrying the heavy attaché's case with the documentation for the trial, and asked me an unusual question: "Can you determine on the basis of accepted physical laws and mathematical calculations whether Mr. X, a man of given weight, shape, and height whose body was found eighteen feet [5.4 m] from the foot of a wall of a seventeen-story building, had fallen accidentally or had jumped from the penthouse terrace of the building?"

* All names of persons (except Mario Salvadori's), companies, locations, and dates in this and the following section are fictitious but reflect actual cases.

In my applied mechanics research I had frequently applied Newton's laws of dynamics and their mathematical equations to determine the motion of all kinds of bodies, but never to a human body. Why was Mr. Wright interested in such a question? "Because Mr. X had a *double indemnity clause* in his life insurance policy."

"And what is a double indemnity clause?"

"It is a clause stating that accidental death doubles the front value of the policy, but suicide doesn't." I thought for a few seconds, then said: "I believe that if you can give me the values of all the parameters of the problem, I can *try* to give you an answer, but I do not promise that I will succeed and much less that the answer will be in your favor."

"Fair enough," said Mr. Wright.

A few days later Mr. Wright, who had answered in writing all my queries, came to my office to coach me on the courtroom behavior of an expert witness. This was going to be a jury trial, and if I decided to participate, I should: (1) never lose composure, hard as the cross-examining attorney, a Mr. Crowley, might try to rile me up and undermine my qualifications as an engineer and a physicist; (2) talk to the members of the jury, *never* to the judge or the attorneys, and address myself as often as possible to the only member of the jury capable of understanding what I would be talking about, an engineer; (3) speak calmly, loudly, and clearly and sound authoritative. He also gave me details of the examinations of previous witnesses, including a deposition from Mr. X's housekeeper. I was never to mention these details in court, because they would be "hearsay" of no legal value, *objected* to by the cross-examining attorney and *sustained* by the judge, the Honorable Mr. Solani.

We agreed on a daily fee, and I began analyzing the "problem" in my head, although I was a bit queasy about its real nature. I had never looked at a human tragedy with the cold eyes of applied mechanics, but there was nothing I could do about its human aspects and, who knew, with a bit of luck I might be able to state on the basis of the evidence that Mr. X had fallen from that terrace and thus help his heirs. From the viewpoint of dynamics, the "problem" looked to me simple but interesting.

Half a day of library research showed me that a recently published complete solution of the problem was available in a physics magazine. I need only put numbers in the equations of this paper and compute the *maximum* distance from the foot of the wall Mr. X's body could have reached in an accidental fall, a so-called *free fall.* If the actual distance from the wall in Mr. X's fall—18 ft. (5.4 m)—was less than or at most equal to the free fall distance, Mr. X's death was an accident. If Mr. X's body was found a greater distance from the wall than the maximum free fall distance, he *must* have jumped. Unfortunately for his heirs, even giving Mr. X all the benefits of the doubt, the maximum free fall distance was only 12 ft. (3.6 m) (Fig. 17.1).

Several months later Mr. Wright summoned me to the New York State Supreme Court for the trial. The large room was crowded with people (I did not learn why until a year later). The Honorable Mr. Solani sat rather unmajestically relaxed on his throne, the twelve members of the jury, in two rows, on his left, and the witness chair on their right, at right angles to the rows of jurors. I climbed into the chair, my calculations in hand, and a clerk of the court approached me, set my left hand on a Bible, asked me to raise my right hand, and said loudly, "Do you solemnly swear to tell the truth, the whole truth, and nothing but the truth, so help you God?" The thought crossed my mind that in science the "truth" does not exist, since science does not prove but can only describe the ways of nature. I answered, "I do," anyway.

Mr. Wright stood in front of me, hands on the lapels of his jacket, looked for approval to His Honor, smiled at the jury, and then asked me to spell my name and state my address. "My name is Mario Salvadori (S-A-L-V-A-D-O-R-I). I live at Forty-five East Eighty-first Street in Manhattan." He proceeded to investigate my educational and professional background, and the preliminaries over, he slowly presented me with the "question": "Dr. Salvadori, assume that the body of a man with such and such physical features is found eighteen feet from the foot of a wall, et cetera, et cetera, can you tell the ladies and gentlemen of the jury whether the man fell or jumped to his death?"

Before I could open my mouth, Mr. Crowley, the attorney for Mr. X's first wife, jumped up from his chair and shouted to the judge: "Objection, Your Honor, this is a *hypothetical* question!"

"Objection sustained," said Judge Solani immediately.

I was asked to step down and left with Mr. Wright. I was thoroughly surprised. "That was pretty quick, Mr. Wright, and I presume it is the end of my testimony."

"Oh, no! His Honor needs time to study the ruling. I feel confident he will reverse his opinion on the question once he understands the basis of your testimony."

He knew his man: When the identical question was put to me

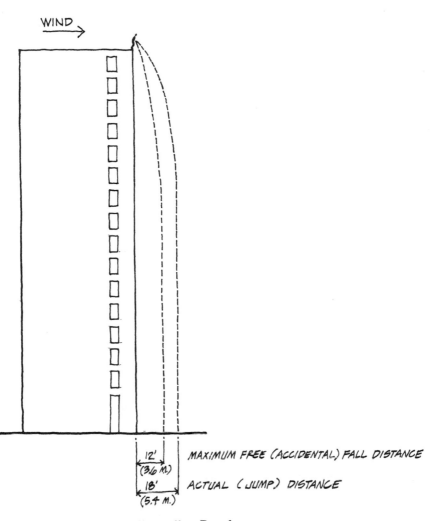

WIND →

12'
(3.6 M.)
MAXIMUM FREE (ACCIDENTAL) FALL DISTANCE

18'
(5.4 M.)
ACTUAL (JUMP) DISTANCE

17.1 Jump or Fall from the Roof

in Judge Solani's court a week later, His Honor denied Mr. Crowley's objection, and my examination started. It took less than an hour and was never interrupted by Mr. Crowley's objections. I addressed myself to the engineer on the jury, who couldn't help showing his assent to my statements by smiling and "yessing" them with his nods. The other jurors looked at me with frozen expressions on their faces. Obviously, as hard as I tried to put my answers in the simplest possible terms, I was talking above their heads. Luckily for me, at the end they seemed to understand well enough the gist of my conclusion. Mr. Wright relinquished me to his adversary with the words "Your witness!" Mr. Crowley started my cross-examination. I was totally unprepared for what was to follow and can present my dialogue with Mr. Crowley only in the form of a script for a play or a movie, not as a verbatim account but as the recollections of a memorable, even traumatic experience:

MR. C   *(sarcastically):* My, oh, my! Dr. Salvadori, you certainly are an engineer's engineer! You don't have just one doctorate, you have two! Would you kindly tell the members of the jury how many of these so-called doctorates are from an honest-to-goodness *American* university?

DR. S   None. I obtained both my degrees from the University of Rome in Italy before coming to the United States.

MR. C   Well now, Dr. Salvadori, would you kindly tell the members of the jury how much the Local Insurance Company is paying you to say that Mr. X committed suicide?

DR. S   *(indignantly):* Not one penny.

MR. C   Do you mean to tell His Honor and the jury that you are donating your services to the Local Insurance Company?

DR. S   Not at all. I mean to say that the Local Insurance Company is paying me a daily fee to find out *whether* Mr. X fell or jumped to his death. *[Big smile from the engineer.]*

MR. C   And would you mind telling the members of the jury what this daily fee amounts to?

DR. S   I'll be glad to. My fee is one hundred dollars for a day of seven hours.

MR. C   Not bad, Dr. Salvadori, not bad at all! Many of us have to work much harder to make less.

[DR. S   *remains silent because he doesn't think that making $12.50 an hour is so much.*]

MR. C   All right, all right. Now, Dr. Salvadori, what is the object I am holding vertically at the edge of this table?

DR. S   From this vantage point it looks like what is known in the English language as a pencil.

MR. C   I am now asking you, sir *[I had never been addressed so respectfully before]*, if I let go of the pencil, will it hit the floor with the point or the eraser end?

DR. S   I haven't the faintest idea.

MR. C   Ladies and gentlemen of the jury, this man *[I had been demoted from* "sir"*]*, who doesn't even know whether a pencil will hit the floor with the point or the eraser end, presumes to know *exactly* how far a human body, the body of a live man, will fall from the top of a building!

DR. S   Had you not interrupted me, Mr. Crowley, I would have told you, His Honor, and the jury that I haven't the faintest idea *now* but that if you gave me that pencil, paper, and time, I would tell you exactly how the pencil would fall. And, may I add, the pencil would fall the way I would determine *not* because I say it, but because the English physicist and mathematician Isaac Newton said so over two hundred fifty years ago." *[Biggest smile from the engineer and faint smiles from some members of the jury.]*

MR. C   *(temporarily beaten back, but still hoping to catch me):* Dr. Salvadori, did you by any chance see the local official U.S. Weather Bureau bulletin for May sixteenth of last year, the day Mr. X's body was found at the foot of the wall?

DR. S   Yes, I did.

MR. C   *(unpleasantly surprised but recovering):* Then you do know that on May sixteenth, 1944, a north wind was blowing here at a speed of twenty miles per hour [32 km/h], gusting at a speed of up to *thirty-five miles per hour* [56 km/h]!

DR. S   Yes, I do.

MR. C   But then don't you believe that a man's body *[and here I quote Mr. Crowley]*, a body *with a soul*, clad in light pajamas, in falling from a height of one hundred seventy-seven feet [53 m], could have been *ballooned out* of the wall, by a wind gust of a speed of thirty-five miles per hour [56 km/h]. Couldn't that be a much greater distance than your estimated twelve feet [3.6 m], let's say, as much as nineteen feet [5.7 m] from the wall?

DR. S   Mr. Crowley, did *you* read carefully that U.S. Weather Bureau bulletin for May sixteenth, 1944?

MR. C   Of course, I have.

DR. S   Then could you kindly tell the ladies and gentlemen of the jury the orientation of the wall we have been talking about?

MR. C   South, of course. The wall faces south.

DR. S   Then, Mr. Crowley, anytime you can show His Honor, the members of the jury, and me a *north wind* blowing *out* of a *south wall* at a speed of thirty-five miles per hour [56 km/h], I will agree with your ballooning hypothesis and concede the case. *[Even His Honor, who apparently had paid little attention to the proceedings so far, lifts his face from the desk and laughs, while all the member of the jury smile.]*

MR. C   *(lifting his arms in desperation):* Your witness.

I must confess that my last answer was not entirely accurate. On the lee side of a building there is a relatively minor void, created by the change in direction of the wind from blowing horizontally on the roof of the building to down the lee wall. This void could suck a falling body a small distance *toward* the wall. In measuring the maximum fall distance from the wall, I had taken into account the negligible impact of this minor suction, but on the spur of the moment I had decided not to mention it because I believed it might have confused most of the jury, while not influencing my result.

This had been a rather sordid affair. I had never, for one thing, been so badgered in public in my life, and I felt diminished, disgusted, and sad. But a distinguished-looking lady in her early forties approached me together with two teenagers, proffered her right hand, and said: "I am Mr. X's first wife, and these are our children. I wish to apologize to you for the behavior of our attorney; you deserved a more dignified treatment."

"I am sorry, madam," I answered, "but in good conscience I could not make a statement in your favor, much as I would have liked to."

"You were right," she said, and left.

I must now add that Mr. X's neighbors, who had been the first to discover his body, had called the second Mrs. X and accompanied her to the foot of the wall. They had testified that upon seeing the dead body of her husband, she had run back to the penthouse, with the excuse of phoning his brother, and had jumped to her own death from the same terrace. As testified to by their live-in housekeeper, the night of their suicide, the couple had quarreled into the wee hours of the morning. I deeply believe in Newton's laws but must confess that this information, unallowable in court, and the words to me of Mr. X's first wife wiped out any doubts I may have had about the accuracy of my calculations. I felt deeply relieved.

A year later a letter from the chief counsel for the Local Insurance Company gratefully acknowledged my services and informed me that the *Mrs. X v. Local Insurance Company* case had made legal history. After the unappealed judgment in my case, most double-indemnity policy payments were negotiated. Both parties liked this system: The insurance company avoided the cost of court proceedings and a possible insurance company-hating jury, and most plaintiffs were happy to take the money and run, thereby perhaps saving legal fees. No wonder the courtroom had been crowded.

Trials, especially trials dealing with a scientific issue, were rare indeed.

We are aware that this case had little or nothing to do with architectural structures (except for the height of the building and the wind suction) but could not help including it here because it shows in clear light that the legal defense of even a case based on Newton's principles of mechanics requires both good professional preparation and certain oratorical skills that most engineers and other technologists are not inclined to learn or cultivate. As in most fields, what counts in a court debate is the whole man rather than the specialist.

The Big Bang in Court

A famous New York attorney, head of a large law firm, advised his young colleagues: "When in court, if you are right, smile. If you are in doubt, shout. If you know you are wrong, pound on the attorneys' table." We would like to add that in the third circumstance some, although not the best, attorneys also try to undermine the expert's standing by sarcasm, innuendo, and misinterpretation of his statements and aim at wearing him down by such numerous repetitions of the same question that the expert may easily lose his "cool" or get so fed up and frustrated that he or she ends up by giving an incorrect or damaging answer. When the cross-examining attorney listens to the examination by the opposing attorney in front of a jury, he may add mocking or surprised facial grimaces and particularly effective body language to express tacitly his disdain or pity for the expert and, as suggested by the master, may punch the table and get into such squabbles with the opposing attorney that the judge can stop only by banging the gavel.

In the Forty-fifth Street explosion case (p. 83), the attorney for the defendants, the owners of the exploded building, knew that the photo lab tenants were directly or indirectly responsible for the catastrophe, both according to the New York City Building Code and to the laws of physics. Thus he had to convince the members of the jury that the building's owners were not, or at least not greatly, responsible. The defendants' attorney knew he could not hope to win the case. Juries usually find in favor of innocent victims and almost never for rich building owners, yet by lowering their responsibility, he could minimize the damages his clients would have to pay.

On the other end, the plaintiffs' attorney, for whom I was tes-
tifying, had only to prove to the jury that the explosion had occurred
because of violations of code rules and disregard of physical laws.
True, the best-educated member of the jury, the foreman, I was
told had only a high school diploma. It might not be easy for me
to explain the laws of physics to a group of twelve unsophisticated
people, but in my experience, "unsophisticated" does not mean
"dumb." Most often, it means the opposite: a person with an alert,
innate intelligence.

The proceedings started peacefully enough with my examination as the plaintiffs' expert. I was duly sworn, routinely asked to
spell my name and state my address. But no sooner had the plaintiffs' attorney started addressing me by the title of "Doctor" than
the defendants' attorney jumped up from his chair and in a skep-
tical tone of voice and the greatest courtesy said:

DA (DEFENDANTS' ATTORNEY):	Objection, Your Honor, the *man* in the chair, according to his own record, has two degrees *he* calls doctorates from the University of Rome in Italy. How do we know that they are equivalent to real, honest-to-goodness *American* Ph.D.'s? He should be addressed as Mister, not as Doctor.
PA (PLAINTIFFS' ATTORNEY):	Your Honor, this *gentleman* has two doctorates from one of the most prestigious universities in Europe, the University of Rome. He is also a tenured profes-sor at Columbia University, an Ivy League *Ameri-can* university. He has the right to be addressed as Doctor.

*[Judge ponders this legally difficult and unusual question as I wave
my right hand in his direction.]*

HH (HIS HONOR):	Yes? *[Doesn't want to sustain or deny the objection and avoids calling the expert either Mister or Doctor.]*
M. S. (MARIO SALVADORI):	Your Honor, Mr. Attorney, I apologize to you and the jury, but being a professor, I may be forgiven a moment of absentmindedness. I forgot to list in my curriculum vitae a degree of Doctor of Science from an American university.

*[The jury seems amused. I reflect that the defense attorney didn't do
his research thoroughly enough to find out that my American degree*

was honorary and may or may not be considered equivalent to a degree earned in two or more years of research. Anyway I tripped him and feel vindicated. I smile modestly.]

HH: All right, *Doctor. [to the PA]* Please, proceed.

[The defense attorney from now on does not interrupt the plaintiffs' attorney.]

When the attorney for the plaintiffs relinquished me with the words "Your witness," His Honor called a ten-minute recess, and the jury filed out of the room. As I was walking back and forth through the room, I casually went by the judge's bench, and he inquired about the American university that had granted me a doctorate. In hearing that it was a degree *honoris causa* from Columbia, he laughed heartily and mentioned that he was a graduate of that very university. A cordial conversation of a few minutes ensued. The jury returned to the room, and the defense attorney addressed me with a serious face and a menacing tone of voice:

DA   Doctor, I must inform you that I have caught you talking to His Honor during the absence of the jury and that this infraction of the law is a reason for a mistrial as good as any—

M. S. *(interrupting him in a humble and apologizing voice):* I am terribly sorry, Mr. Attorney, I have been in court only once before and I was not aware—

HH   *(firmly):* All right, all right. Just proceed.

DA   *(proud of his small victory, gleefully starts his cross-examination. Inquisitively):* Doctor, if I understand you correctly, your entire argument is based on a most controversial, purely abstract formula, a *mathematical* formula. The value of the result in this formula depends exclusively on the value of a coefficient *[turning to the jury]*, just a number. And you give this abstract number the incredibly low value zero-point-zero-seven so as to obtain an incredibly low value for the pressure capable of exploding the water tank. In simple words, you are trying to prove that the water tank was weak, defective. But you must know from your studies for *two* doctorates that many renowned scientists have derived much higher values for your number. Among them the *internationally famous* Dr. Theodor von Karman has derived for this number the widely accepted value zero-point-two-eight, and this makes the *true* pressure needed to burst the tank *four times larger!*

[M. S., as instructed by his attorney, passively awaits the defense attorney's question.]

DA   Doctor, how did *you* derive the value of this coefficient? Do you really believe that this tank buckled under the low value you *personally* and arbitrarily attribute to the water pressure?

M. S.   Your Honor, I am afraid this long question requires a long answer. May I proceed?

HH   Of course. We have plenty of time.

M. S.   To start with, Mr. Attorney, Dr. von Karman, who by the way studied in Budapest at a European university, was a very good friend of mine *[putting himself at the level of the great von Karman in the eyes of the jury]*, and I am familiar with his derivation of the value you mentioned for the buckling coefficient in the dome formula. I am sure you must be aware that in a second, more refined derivation of the coefficient's value, published jointly by Dr. Theodor von Karman and his associate Dr. H. S. Tsien, they lowered the previous value from zero-point-six-zero to zero-point-three-six-six.

[Defense attorney expresses surprise but does not speak.]

M. S.   The trouble with both derivations, Mr. Attorney, is that neither value of the buckling coefficient derived by Dr. von Karman agrees with the reality of experimental results. Now, as a mathematical physicist, I am a great believer in the value of theory but bow to experimental results. Theory may not take into account subtle but essential material behaviors and be incorrect, but careful experiments seldom ignore them. I emphasize this to explain that as I was in search of the most accurate value for the buckling coefficient, I ran three times, twice by research in the literature on buckling of domes and once by a telephone call, into the same *experimental* value of our coefficient, and it was zero-point-zero-seven.

[Defense attorney looks impatient with the long answer but does not object.]

M. S.   Your Honor, may I explain to the members of the jury where I found the experimental value of the buckling coefficient?

HH   Go ahead.

M. S.   I found out that the eminent Spanish engineer Eduardo Torroja had tested a scaled-down model of a large dome for a Swiss church. In the tests he filled with water a number of pails hanging from the dome model, thus submitting it to increasing loads, until it snapped through. From the value of the total load he derived the value of the buckling coefficient, and it was zero-point-zero-seven.

I then discovered that the eminent Dr. Paul Csonka, also of Budapest University, had designed and built a dome for a gym in Budapest. After three years of normal snowfalls, Budapest experienced an exceptionally heavy snowfall, and when the snow finally melted, Dr. Csonka found that his dome had buckled in waves. He then reasoned that a high snow load buckled the dome, while a normal snow load didn't. He derived the values of the coefficient for a normal and an exceptional snow load and thus obtained a lower and an upper value for the coefficient. The upper value was zero-point-zero-seven.

Finally, I called the engineering design office of the U.S. Steel Company and asked its chief engineer what value of the buckling coefficient it used for the design of steel domes of nuclear reactors. (I myself happened to be designing one such dome at the time.) His answer was: "The theoretical value is higher, but we use an experimental value of zero-point-zero-seven." On the basis of these three reliable pieces of information, I adopted the value zero-point-zero-seven.

[Most of the jurors look convinced; one seems confused.]

DA   Really, Doctor, are you comparing the behavior of your first two domes, which were made out of concrete, with the behavior of a steel dome?

M. S.   Yes, because they behave identically, except for a constant, called the *modulus of elasticity*, that takes into account the properties of the materials. The modulus of elasticity of steel is much larger than that of reinforced concrete.

DA   But the steel domes are much thinner than the concrete domes!

M. S.   And this is why the dome thickness appears in the buckling formula to take into account different thicknesses.

DA   But the domes you mentioned have nothing to do with the bottom head of a pressure tank. They span *[somewhat exaggerating]* hundreds of feet, and tank heads span at most two feet!

M. S.   This is why the radius of the dome also appears in the original formula for the buckling of domes, derived by the great Russian engineer Dr. Timoshenko.

It had not been that difficult to explain to the "poorly educated" members of the jury a number of fairly subtle technical arguments: that a simple constant can define the toughness of different materials depending on its numerical value, that all spherical domes behave in the same way under the same type of load, but that the value of the radius of a spherical dome takes care of the different values of the load needed to burst them; and that the value of the thickness of a dome is the third basic parameter influencing its behavior. An uneducated jury may behave more wisely than most of the members of the intelligentsia are willing to concede.

The plaintiffs won the case.

18

Conclusion:
Can We Prevent
Future Failures?

If a little knowledge is dangerous, where is
the man who has so much as to be out of
danger?

T. H. Huxley

The preceding cases of structural failure have shown the reader
a variety of fairly typical collapses that have occurred from
ancient times to the present. These cases have also emphasized the outstanding progress achieved in all aspects of
structural design during the last half century and should have suggested a number of provocative questions: Has all the theoretical
and technological progress of recent years reduced the danger of
structural failures and, particularly, of catastrophic collapses? What
about the future? Will we be able to eliminate many causes of
structural disasters as medicine has eliminated many sources of
worldwide infectious diseases?

These questions, important as they are, cannot be easily answered because structural failures flow from a large number of different causes, but we may obtain reasonable answers by reviewing different kinds of failures and their present remedies in a realistic manner, without forgetting the human error, the main cause of failures sometimes due to unavailable knowledge.

Only five basic factors influence every structural design and, hence, the safety of all built structures, and each may be totally or partly responsible for a failure. Let us investigate their impact on our safety. They are:

1. Structural theories
2. Calculation techniques
3. Material properties
4. Communication procedures
5. Economic factors

Structural Theories

The ancient world achieved amazing feats of structural virtuosity on the basis of a limited knowledge of structural theory. The largest dome of modern times has a span only five times that of the Pantheon, and our tallest building is only three times as tall as the Pyramid of Khufu or Cheops. On the other hand, our forefathers built their monuments on the basis of trial and error, a reliable but costly method, while we erect our buildings, most of the time, by more or less scientific methods and expect them to stand up almost forever. Hagia Sophia partially collapsed three times under the impact of relatively minor earthquakes; each time it was repaired, and it has now stood unscathed for centuries. The skyscrapers of San Francisco, on the other hand, bent but did not break under the formidable Loma Prieta tremor.

All basic structural theories used today may be traced back to Galileo (1564–1642) and Isaac Newton (1642–1727). The refinements of Newton's mechanics, which have allowed such amazing structural progress in the last fifty years, do not need the use of more recent and abstract theories of relativity proposed by Albert Einstein (1879–1955) or the quantum mechanics developed since the 1920s. Similarly, the mathematics of today's structural theory is essentially based on the calculus of Newton and G. W. Leibniz (1646–1716) and on differential equations that are a direct derivation from the calculus. It is only most recently that newer mathematical fields have begun to be applied to structural design, but they have not yet influenced engineering practice to any practical extent.

The most powerful recent methods of structural analysis do not even require the solution of differential equations (some of which cannot be solved exactly, anyway) because we can easily transform them into the solution of the good old algebraic equations of high school memory by the so-called *method of finite differences*. The method of *finite elements* applies the numerical method of finite differences in a physically meaningful way, allowing a relatively easy setting up and solution of problems considered unsolvable only a few decades ago. At least in structures, it would seem that the more complicated the problems become, the easier they are to solve!

Once in a while, and more frequently at the present time because of the use of complex structures and exceptionally strong materials, our mathematical formulations run into the feared *nonlinear differential equations* (equations involving the powers of an unknown function and or its derivatives), which most of the time cannot be solved exactly in a finite number of steps. But here methods of *successive approximations* come to our aid, reducing once again our calculations to the basic operations of arithmetic.

It has been predicted that even if more refined *physical* theories will be adopted to improve structural design, the solution of the corresponding mathematical problems should present no practical difficulties. As for the development of such physical theories, there is no doubt that they will rely on the results of atomic and nuclear physics and on those of modern chemistry and, hence, that they will require the most refined method of experimental research, besides highly theoretical investigations. This kind of progress is to be expected but probably will be the task of future generations.

Calculation Techniques

It is hard to believe that many structuralists active today started their careers using simple instruments like the slide rule, invented independently almost four hundred years ago by two Englishmen on the basis of the logs of John Napier (1550–1617). Of course, they also used trigonometric and log tables and, above all, pencil and paper. Today the hand calculator does the job of all these tools in a fraction of a second and at practically no cost.

But even if the hand calculator is a most useful everyday tool, in the last few years the personal computer has become the invaluable instrument of structural calculations. While only a few decades ago the number of algebraic equations one could dare solve by hand or by mechanical, hand-cranked calculators was ten or twenty, today the computer allows the solution in a few hours, and for a relatively small amount of money, of as many as fifty thousand to one hundred thousand equations. This amazing instrument also spits out in a few seconds the solution by successive approximations of complex equations appearing in the dynamics of structures, a field that had been only barely investigated in the recent past and is of the greatest importance, for example, in earthquake design.

One cannot overemphasize the contributions of the computer to structural design: It has allowed a quantum jump in the acquisition of realistic solutions to problems otherwise considered insolvable and, what is just as important, has given us *optimalization* methods and, hence, methods for minimizing costs. The solution of earthquake problems would be inconceivable without the use of the computer, which has thus also contributed to saving lives and money.

The continuous rapid improvement of the computer and its surprising reduction in price make it easy to predict that it will continue to increase our construction capability as well as the quality of our buildings. Whatever rate of progress we shall achieve in structural design, the computer will always be available to perform the needed complex calculations.

Material Properties

With the exception of wood, natural materials suffer from being strong only in tension, like vegetable fibers, or only in compression, like stone. The first artificial materials, like straw-reinforced mud *(adobe)* (Fig. 18.1) and straw-reinforced dried bricks, improved slightly on the strength and availability of natural materials. It wasn't until the inhabitants of the Euphrates-Tigris Basin invented kiln-burnt bricks and the Romans produced weather-resistant poz-

18.1   Great Mosque of Djenne, Mali

zolan concrete that numerous large structures could be built of man-made materials.

The invention of reinforced concrete by French engineers in the middle 1800s produced the first all-purpose artificial material, used today all over the world to build some of our tallest buildings, our largest roofs, and our most economical housing. Improvements in cement chemistry are bound to widen the use of this marvelously moldable material.

As noted, steel's increase in strength is all too often accompanied by an increase in brittleness. This brittleness will limit steel's strength much above that already reached. At the same time, modern ease of transportation has spread the availability of steel to new areas of the world, areas that lack local sources of iron ore or coal, like Japan, which today trades steel with the United States. Steel's rival in strength, aluminum, has been used in countries rich in the needed (common) ores, but its most expensive component, electric energy, makes problematic its wider manufacture. We can soon expect, instead, structural use of new materials like carbon-fiber and ceramic-matrix compounds, which have already been successful in airplane construction. At present (1991) carbon-fiber components, five times lighter and five times stronger than steel, are tentatively entering the structural and architectural field, and it is easy to forecast that their use will rapidly become popular as their costs fall.

It is not up to structuralists like us to suggest what the chemists and the materials engineers will invent in the near future, but the market for structural materials all over the world is so wide that the incentive for the invention of new, inexpensive, stronger, and safer materials is bound to continue increasing. A hint of things to come is given by the laminated materials composed of one-molecule layers of different chemicals that achieve extreme strengths without becoming fragile. Just as in the field of plastics, started by celluloid in 1869 and rapidly expanded by the invention of Bakelite in 1909, we must expect the availability of extraordinary new materials, each specifically aimed at particular types of structures.

Communication Procedures

Only yesterday the exchange of essential information among the members of the construction team depended almost exclusively on hand-produced, time-consuming, expensive, and hard-to-correct or change drawings. Today a system of complex printers and high tech software allows the computer to draw rapidly, correctly, and in the finest detail drawings that are also easily modified whenever necessary. CADD (computer-assisted design and drawing) systems can present graphically the results of the elaborate calculations for a fifty-story concrete building in a matter of hours for a small fraction of the cost of hand-drawn drawings, one more essential contribution of the computer to the structural field. Progress is so rapid in this recent technology that one may expect even more exciting developments in this field. Some, like the software that first draws on the screen the picture of a building and then moves it in any direction and rotates it about any axis so that it may be looked at from any perspective, are already available. We can thus check whether our design is also aesthetically pleasing and, by an additional program, whether it would cost too much. In the software field, particularly, the sky seems to be the limit.

Last but not least among today's communications problems is the organization of information transmission among the many members of the construction team, each a master in his or her own field of specialty but seldom as knowledgeable in other fields. An international meeting took place in New York City in 1989 to seek resolution of the problems arising from the interaction between engineers and architects, ignoring (because of organizational difficulties) those among designers, contractors, developers, and labor. Finally we must add to these the problems arising from the need for supervision of the less experienced members of an office staff by the senior partners when such offices may number hundreds of engineers and architects. In this field, too, the computer allows setting up tighter procedures and checks that, if adhered to, might reduce the dangers of this human source of error. When we realize the complexity of this problem, it is sometimes surprising that such a small number of failures occur!

Economic Factors

Since an engineer is said to be an idiot like any other idiot, but capable of doing for one dollar what any other could only do for two dollars, economic factors have always been of the greatest importance in structural design. For example, the ratio of labor to material costs, even recently very different in different parts of the world, requires the detailing of a high-rise building to be erected in Texas to be different from that required in New York. The use of steel, so all-pervading in the United States, is less common in Italy, where this metal costs twice as much as in our country. In the developing countries the lack of expert labor suggests the use of higher coefficients of safety than those in more technologically advanced countries, and one could go on with the list of influences of such economic factors. Even in the same location the labor situation at a particular time can influence, for example, the choice of structural materials, as was partly the case in the selection of concrete for the construction of the Columbia Broadcasting System Building in New York City in the 1960s, at a time when most of the local, specialized steel labor was employed in erecting the World Trade Center towers.

The present development of our technological societies certainly points to a very specific trend in construction: a reduction of labor costs resulting from the growing use of laborsaving devices, machinery, and schedules. This tendency may well introduce in the construction trades the speed and accuracy typical of other trades, to the advantage of economy and safety, since pressure of time and money is often the cause of structural failures.

Conclusion

We can now try to answer our original question: Will progress in the field of structures reduce the number of failures?

Our answer is still ambivalent because each of the changes for the better we have tentatively forecast for each of the factors influencing structural design acts simultaneously to reduce *and* to increase the dangers of failure.

Let us consider, for example, the influence of computer calculations. By now numerous programs are available for the solution of both common and unusual problems in structural design. They are particularly popular because they allow the average designer to perform calculations he or she would not be able to perform without their help and because they are written by outstanding structuralists and carefully tested over long periods of time and on many typical structures. The users, even when unfamiliar with the logic of a program, or incapable of understanding it, apply it to their own problems with unqualified assurance. Yet some of the most authoritative programs have been shown to contain errors or to be inapplicable to particular problems, while inexperienced users do not always check whether or not their outputs conform with the results suggested by engineering practice. At the present time legal debates are taking place to determine if in such cases the responsibility for the consequences of the errors falls on the structuralist using the program or on the programmer who wrote it. The issue is complicated, despite the clear caveats accompanying such programs that deny the programmer's responsibility for the consequences of its applications. Moreover, when hundreds upon hundreds of numbers are fed into the computer, it is not uncommon to discover that a few are incorrect. Thus blind faith in a program or in the accuracy of its input may lead to significantly erroneous results.

We have repeatedly emphasized that in the final analysis almost all structural failures may be attributed to human errors. But these may be of a varied nature: Some are due to knowledge as yet unavailable and are thus unavoidable; others may occur because of delayed communication of available knowledge; some are due to ignorance of recently acquired knowledge; and a few to misunderstanding of accepted knowledge, a rare few to outright ignorance, and finally, in exceptional occurrences, to incorrect procedures (mostly in construction). It has been estimated that one-third of all the structural failures in the United States in the last fifty years were due to outright human errors.

Ambition, one of the prime movers of human activity, may push us to erect new towers of Babel or to devise better design and construction methods. We must conclude that in the field of structure, as in any other field of human endeavor, technological improvements alone cannot guarantee a decrease of failures and may even increase it. Only a deeper consciousness of our human and social responsibilities can lead to the construction of safer buildings.

Appendices*

APPENDIX A

Loads

When all is said and done, most of the time structural failures flow from human error, always in concert with physical forces or *loads* acting on structures. If the earth did not attract, the wind did not blow, the earth's crust did not shake or settle unevenly, and temperature did not change, there would be no need for today's structure.

Some of the loads acting on structures are there for all of us to see, like the weight of the furniture on the floor of an apartment building, but others, like the pressure and the *suction* caused by the wind or the *thermal loads* caused by changes in temperature, are less obvious, although just as significant. Let us briefly explore together the world of loads.

The Dead Load

Regrettably the story of an apple falling on the head of a sleepy Isaac Newton is without historical foundation. Yet it is a good example of the forces the earth exerts on all bodies, the so-called *gravity loads*. As you learned in school, young Isaac *assumed* that two bodies attract each other with a force proportional to the product of their masses divided by the square of the distance from each other. He used this assumption to verify both the fall of the mythical apple and the motions of the planets. And it worked. Not bad for a nineteen-year-old student at Cambridge University, on leave at home because of the plague. Architectural structures consist of massive elements, like columns, beams, arches, and domes, and their own load, the so-called *dead load*, is most of the time the heaviest they must support. It depends on the volume of the element and the unit weight of its material.*

The evaluation of the dead load of a structure presents the engineer with a paradox: It cannot be computed until the structure is designed, but the structure cannot be designed until the dead load is computed and added to all the other loads. Only long practice will teach the engineer to make a good first guess of the size of a structural element, but you can be sure that the dead load will never be ignored because it is always there; it is a *permanent* load. Actually we include in the dead load the weight of whatever is always there, like the building partitions, which may be moved around but are always present, as well as the pipes, ducts, and the other components of the air-conditioning and plumbing systems.

Live Loads

There may be art for art's sake, but there cannot be architecture for architecture's sake. Every work of architecture is built for a purpose. And since in the real world there are forces, there cannot be architecture without structure.

The gravity loads the structure must support *in addition* to its own dead load are called *live loads* and include the weight of the furniture, people, goods, fixtures, snow, etc. Since live loads vary greatly from one building to another and since they may change from day to day, even hour to hour, the evaluation of all their possible combinations, while perhaps feasible, would be enormously time-consuming and uncertain. To avoid these difficulties, live loads are *mandated*—prescribed—for the structural engineer by *building codes* issued by the building departments of countries, states, counties, and cities. These codes list the *mandatory minimum* live loads for each type of building and each kind of load.† The *code loads*

---

* For example, a reinforced concrete floor of an apartment building may be 10 in. (250 mm) or 10 / 12 of a foot thick; thus each square foot of floor has a volume of 1 foot by 1 foot by 10 / 12 of a foot—that is, 10 / 12 cu. ft. ($0.25 \times 1 \times 1 = 0.25$ m^3). Since stone concrete weighs, on an average, 150 pcf (pounds per cubic foot) (25 kN / m^3), each square foot of floor weighs 10 / 12 cu. ft. times 150 or 125 psf (pounds per square foot) (6.25 kN / m^2).

† For example, the live load on a schoolroom floor in New York City must be no less than 40 psf (2 kN / m^2) and in a public space, like a corridor, 100 psf (5 kN / m^2).

are conventional loads that most often assume the live load to be spread uniformly over a floor or a roof; they are *uniform loads* and, in general, quite safe—i.e., larger than the expected actual loads. Yet it is important to be aware that the codes do not excuse the engineer from carefully evaluating live loads if these may be expected to exceed the loads prescribed by the code.

Structural failures are seldom due to the live loads, but . . .

During the construction of a reinforced concrete building in New York City, the design engineer received an unexpected telephone call from the supervising engineer on the site informing him that the floor of an office was deflecting, or bending down, more than expected. An immediate inspection revealed that the contractor had been temporarily storing in that room layer upon layer of 2 in. (50 mm) thick heavy travertine slabs, destined for the facade, thus loading the floor with over 300 psf (15 kN / m^2) instead of the specified code value of 40 psf (2 kN / m^2). Under the circumstances, if the floor had collapsed, the design engineer would not have been at fault, but if the travertine had been destined only temporarily to be stored in that room, he would have been guilty, even though the code did not demand such a high live load. In any case, this occurrence was a good test of that particular floor, and both the design engineer and the engineer on site were delighted with its behavior.

The evaluation of live loads, although tedious, is important. Luckily engineers now have at their disposal computer programs that make these calculations fast, accurate, and almost painless. They take into account all code requirements, including the reasonable code assumption that the chance is so minimal of *each* square foot of *each* floor of a building's being loaded with the code loads *at the same time* that *live load reductions* are permissible in the design of high-rise buildings, in accordance with formulas given in the codes.

Dynamic Loads

The loads considered so far are tacitly assumed to be applied *slowly* so as to reach their design values after the passage of a finite time, although this may be only seconds in certain cases. This is a reasonable assumption for the dead load since a building in construction takes months or years to reach its height, and for the live load of, say, snow, that takes hours to accumulate on a roof. Slowly growing loads are called *static loads* or said to *act statically*. Other loads, like those caused by winds and earthquakes, grow rapidly or even suddenly; they are called *dynamic loads* or said to *act dynamically*. They are the cause of many disastrous structural failures and high losses of life.

The difference between a static and a dynamic load may be grasped by a simple demonstration. Gently place a brick, or a book, on the platter of a kitchen scale and determine its weight, say, 5 lb. (11 kg). Then *hold* the brick *in contact* with the scale platter but without resting it on the platter. Now let go, *drop* the brick on the platter, and observe the largest weight shown by the scale hand, which will oscillate a few times and then go back to 5 lb. (11 kg); it will probably be about 10 lb. (22 kg) or *twice* the static load of the brick. You have just discovered that a weight applied *dynamically* can be equivalent to twice its static weight. Loads applied suddenly (like the blow of a hammer on a nail) are called *impact loads* and can be equivalent to many times their static values; they can be very dangerous unless their dynamic effects are taken into account.

A force does not have to be an impact to have dynamic effects; it is enough that it increase quickly to its final value. But how quick is quick? Is one second fast? Are two seconds slow? The effect of a force changing in value depends not only on how fast it changes but on the structure it is applied to. This is so because each structure has a characteristic time of vibration, called its *fundamental period* or simply its *period*, and each force will have its own *static* or *dynamic* effects on the structure depending on one thing: Does the force reach its maximum value in a time *longer* or *shorter* than the structure's period? We all are familiar with the period of a pendulum; it is the time the pendulum bob takes to make a round trip oscillating from an extreme right to an extreme left position *and back* to the extreme right. A tall building oscillates in the wind like an upside-down pendulum. When a wind gust pushes the top of the building one foot to the right in the lee direction, the top of the building oscillates for a while between one foot to the right and one foot to the left of its original position. If it takes four seconds to go through one such full oscillation, the period of the building is said to be four seconds and the wind gust will have static or dynamic effects on that building depending on whether it grows to its maximum value in more than four seconds, say, ten seconds, or less, say, half a second.*

Varying forces may have a different type of dynamic effect if they are repeatedly applied *in rhythm* with the period of the structure. Such forces are said to be *in resonance* with the structure and called *resonant forces*. These rhythmic forces are particularly dangerous, even if their initial value is small and their effects are initially minor, because with *repeated* rhythmic application the effects *accumulate* and can reach large values. Pushing

---

* The explosive power of a nuclear bomb, equivalent to many millions of tons of TNT, is due to the growth of the explosion pressure of the air to the maximum value in microseconds (millionths of a second). The destruction of Hiroshima and Nagasaki was the result of explosions equivalent to only twelve thousand and thirteen thousand tons of TNT, respectively, but with an explosion time of about twenty microseconds.

a child in a swing demonstrates resonant effects. If you give the swing a little push each time it comes back toward you, the child will swing higher and higher—that is, the oscillations will grow larger and larger. Your little pushes are *in resonance* with the period of the swing and produce effects much larger than did your initial little push. Similarly, if wind gusts were *in resonance* with the period of a building (luckily a rare occurrence), they could induce increasing swings of the top of the building and eventually even collapse the building.

The oscillations of a tall building must sometimes be damped to avoid the inconvenience of airsickness to the occupants. This has recently been done by the use of a gadget first introduced to dampen machinery oscillations, called a *tuned dynamic damper*. The damper action is based on the Newtonian concept of *inertia:* that a mass tends to stay put (or move at a constant velocity) unless acted upon by a force. A tuned damper consists of a large mass, often of concrete weighing many tons, set on a thin layer of oil at the top of the building and connected to its outer walls by steel springs and shock absorbers. (Fig. A1a). When the building starts oscillat-

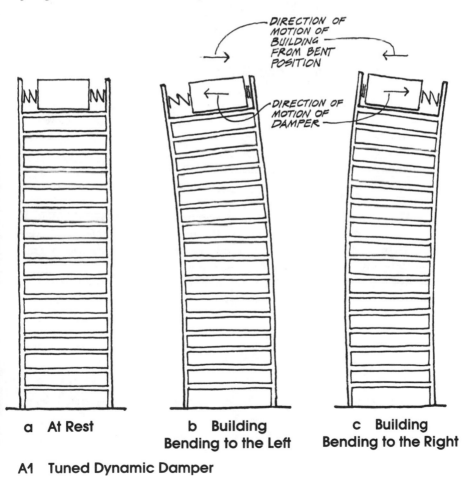

DIRECTION OF MOTION OF BUILDING FROM BENT POSITION

DIRECTION OF MOTION OF DAMPER

| a   At Rest | b   Building Bending to the Left | c   Building Bending to the Right |

A1   Tuned Dynamic Damper

ing, the damper tends to stay put because of its large inertia and allows the building to slide *under* it on the oil layer. When this happens, the springs on one side of the damper become longer and *pull* the building back (Figs. A1b and A1c), while those on the opposite side become shorter and *push* it back to its original position. It may be proved that to obtain this desirable result, the horizontal oscillations of the damper mass under the action of the springs must have the same period as that of the building's—i.e., the damper must be *tuned* to the building; hence its name.

We must finally mention that even perfectly constant forces that are neither impact nor resonant may also have dynamic effects similar to those of resonance when interacting with certain types of structures. For example, a steady wind hitting a tall cylindrical smokestack generates *alternate* lateral forces on it. These are generated by the air particles rounding the smokestack and moving alternatively away from its right and left side in small eddies, called *von Karman vortices* (from the name of the Hungarian physicist Theodor von Karman, who first studied this phenomenon). Such small *aerodynamic forces* cause increasing lateral swings of the smokestack and may eventually collapse it.*

Earthquake, Thermal, and Settlement Loads

Violent motions of the earth's crust, the quaking of the earth, shake buildings and generate high dynamic loads in their structures. Such events have caused destruction and death ever since human beings gathered in villages, towns, and cities. Luckily, improved knowledge of seismicity and of dynamic structural behavior may soon allow us to predict earthquake occurrences. Even now we know how to build structures capable of withstanding even strong earthquakes.

Loads caused by changes in temperature, *thermal loads*, and those resulting from uneven settlements of the ground, *settlement loads*, are particularly insidious because they are not visible, like those caused by gravity, and may be most damaging if neglected.

We learn in school that when temperature increases, bodies expand and that they contract when temperature decreases. (Water is the only material on earth that *expands*, into ice, when frozen.) Consider, for example, a steel bridge 300 ft. (30 m) long erected in winter at an average temperature of 45°F (8°C). In summer, when the air temperature may rise to 100°F

---

* A constant force does not have a period and hence *cannot* be resonant with the period of a structure, but steady aerodynamic forces may generate resonant vortices.

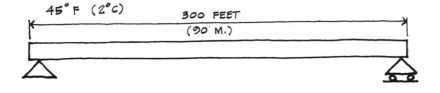

45° F (2°C)   300 FEET
                     (90 M.)

a Original Length

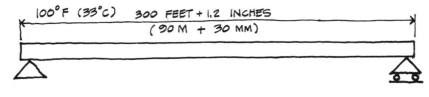

100°F (33°C)   300 FEET + 1.2 INCHES
                (90 M + 30 MM)

b Free Expansion

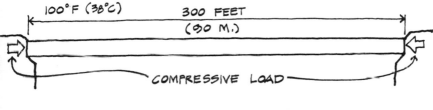

100°F (38°C)   300 FEET
                     (90 M.)

COMPRESSIVE LOAD

c Restrained Expansion

A2 Thermal Expansion of Bridge

(38°C), the length of the bridge will increase (Fig. A2b). It may be shown that *if free to expand*, the bridge would lengthen by only 1.2 in. (30 mm). But if both end supports of the bridge were designed to *prevent* this thermal expansion, they would push the bridge back to its original length, and the thermal compression of the bridge structure would diminish its capacity to carry traffic loads that cause compression in the bridge by 22 percent (Fig. A2c). Obviously the bridge must be allowed to lengthen by means of one *roller support* (Fig. A2a).

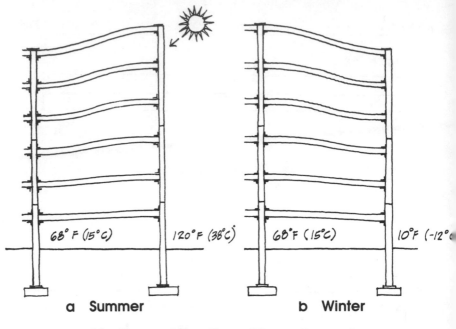

| 68° F (15°C) | 120°F (38°C) | 68°F (15°C) | 10°F (-12°C |

a Summer   b Winter

A3 Thermal Bending of Frame Beams in:

Similarly, if the outer columns of an *air-conditioned* building become warmer and elongate, the beams connecting them to the inner columns will be bent, as shown in Fig. A3, and the corresponding *bending stresses* must be considered in the design. Similar conditions arise when the foundations of the building settle unevenly into the ground as the result of uneven soil properties, as shown in Fig. A4, in which the three footings on the right sink more than those on the left.

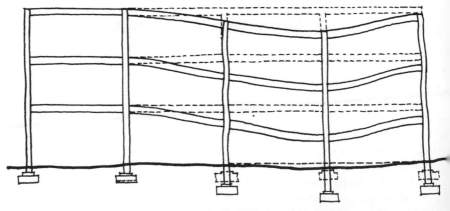

A4 Uneven Settlement of Building Foundation, Causing Bending of Beams

APPENDIX B

Stress and Strain

We have stated, and will illustrate, that the forces acting on a structure can only pull or push on its elements. To speak of these forces in engineering parlance, structural elements can only be put in *tension* or in *compression* by *tensile* (pulling) or *compressive* (pushing) forces.

You may *feel* tension and compression in the muscles of your arm by pulling or pushing on the handle of a closed door or by pulling or pushing with one hand on the other. When you stand, your legs are compressed by your weight; when you hang by your hands from an exercise bar, your entire body, except your head and neck, feels tensed. If you pull on a rubber band, thus stressing it in tension, it becomes longer, while if you push on a rubber sponge, it becomes shorter. Lengthening and shortening, the *strains* in the material, characterize tension and compression in any structural member, but structural materials are much stiffer than rubber bands and sponges, and their elongations and shortenings are seldom visible to the naked eye.*

---

* A reinforced concrete column, 1 ft. (300 mm) square and 12 ft. (3.6 m) high, carrying a load of 70 tons (64 t) becomes only 5 / 100 in. (1.3 mm) shorter.

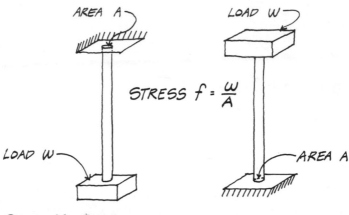

$$STRESS\ f = \frac{W}{A}$$

a   **Caused by Tension**   b   **Caused by Compression**

B1   Stress

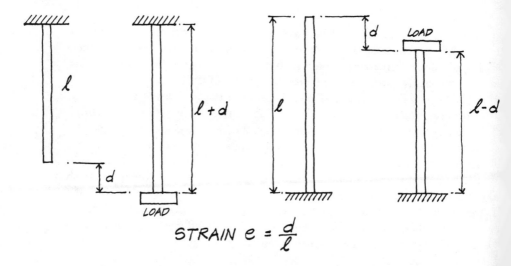

$$STRAIN\ e = \frac{d}{l}$$

a   **Caused by Tension**   b   **Caused by Compression**

B2   Strain

All structural materials are strong in either tension or compression, and one—steel—is equally strong in both. Because wood is also strong in both tension and compression (although not equally), it has been used in construction since the beginning of civilization. Stone, by contrast, is strong in compression but weak in tension; it can be used in columns and arches, which develop almost exclusively compression, but not in beams, which must resist both forces. Concrete is also weak in tension, and this is why French engineers suggested in the 1850s that steel bars be embedded in areas of concrete beams and other structural elements where loads could develop tension. They thus invented *reinforced concrete*, which today is the most economical and widely used structural material the world over. (You may be guessing—and you'd be right—that if reinforcing bars are not placed correctly in the concrete, or are not sufficiently strong to resist the tension, or get corroded by rust, a reinforced concrete structure may collapse.)

A material's strength in tension or compression is determined by testing how much load *each unit area* can resist before breaking (Fig. B1). Such unit load, measured in pounds per square inch, or psi (N / mm^2), is called the *ultimate strength* of the material. (It may be 4,000 to 15,000 psi [28 to 69 N / mm^2] for concrete in compression and as much as 300,000 psi [690 N / mm^2] for steel in tension.) Engineers are very conservative, as they should be to avoid failures. They will not allow a structural material to "work" at more than a fraction of its ultimate strength. When dealing with static loads, they adopt *safety factors* on the order of 2—that is, they use *working stresses* about one-half of the ultimate strength. When considering dynamic loads, they may require coefficients of safety as high as 4 or even larger. The greater the uncertainty about the material's strength, the values of the loads, or the behavior of the structural system, the higher the coefficient of safety. One may call it a factor of prudence or, if one likes, of ignorance.

The strain e of a material (a pure number) under a stress f is measured by dividing its elongation d (lengthening or shortening) by its lengths l (Fig. B2).* The two quantities f and e describe the two essential structural properties of a material. Their ratio $E = f / e$, called the *modulus of elasticity*, is typical of each material; its value describes uniquely its toughness under load.

---

* If the weight of an elevator cab pulling on a steel cable 200 ft. (2,400 in., 61 m) long lengthens it by 2 in. (51 mm), the strain e in the cable is 2 divided by 2,400, or 8.3 thousands of an inch per inch (0.0083 m / m). With a stress f in the cable of 120,000 psi (276 N / mm^2), the elastic modulus of the cable is E = 120,000 / 0.00083 = 240 million psi (32.5 kN / mm^2).

APPENDIX C

Structural Materials

We all are familiar with the most widely used structural materials, for they are natural, like wood and stone, or man-made like bricks, concrete, and steel, the strongest of them all.

In addition to the property of strength, a structural material under load must exhibit two behaviors called *elasticity* and *plasticity*. The first requires that when a load is removed from a structural element, the element returns to its original unloaded shape (Fig. C1). The need for this requirement is fairly obvious: If, upon unloading, the element remained deformed, the next time it is loaded an *additional* deformation would appear, and after a number of loadings and unloadings the element would be so deformed as to be unusable (Fig. C2).

Most structural materials not only behave *elastically* as demanded by the requirement we have just discussed but also deflect under load *in proportion* to the load and are said to be *linearly elastic*. This means, for example, that if a child stands at the end of a diving board and causes it to deflect

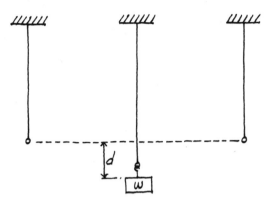

C1   Elastic Behavior of Bar

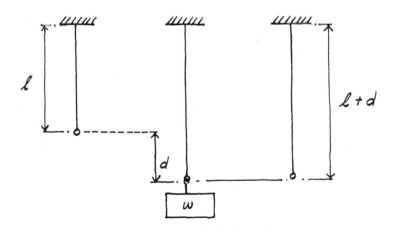

C2   Permanent Deformation of Bar

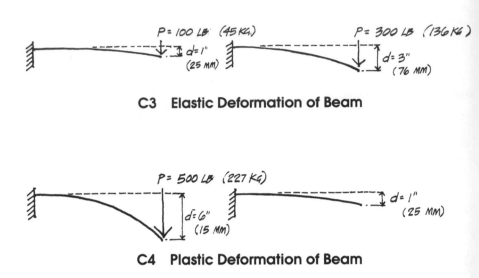

C3   Elastic Deformation of Beam

C4   Plastic Deformation of Beam

down, a person weighing three times as much and standing on the board will cause the end to move down three times as much (Fig. C3). This property is essential since if the deflection is *larger* than the proportional deflection you expect from linearly elastic behavior, you know that the material is *overstressed*. Your concern will be confirmed by the fact that when the diving board becomes unloaded, the deflection will not vanish and a *permanent deformation* will curve the board down. In this case, we say that the board behaved *inelastically*, or *plastically* (Fig. C4).

When a material behaves elastically, the stress is also proportional to the deformation (elongation or shortening) of a unit length of material, which we call the *strain* (Fig. B2). We can just say, as we do in psychology, that a structure is strained when it is stressed, one more facet of the analogy between structures and humans.

You may believe that materials with a large *elastic limit* are always preferable to those with a low limit. But this is not so. Glass, for example, behaves elastically up to the breaking point—it is called *brittle*—and is dangerous because it does not give notice that it is reaching its ultimate strength. Instead, materials that exhibit a permanent deformation after a certain load is reached (called the *yield point*) and are said to have a *plastic behavior* above the yield point are preferable because a permanent deformation is the loudest alarm a material can give that it is ready to fail and should not be subjected to additional loads.

APPENDIX D

Structural Systems

We build structural systems by putting together structural elements made out of structural materials. This is a lot of fun, like playing with building blocks and Lego or Erector sets or making sand castles on the beach. Nothing is more rewarding than watching a structure go up, particularly if you are a knowledgeable kibitzer. The other side of the coin, to investigate why some fall down, is a job requiring the intuition of a Sherlock Holmes and the inquisitive interest of a child.

Human creativity has invented an incredible variety of structures using a few basic physical principles, a small choice of materials, and a limitless set of shapes, but what makes building a fascinating task, and the investigation of failures an alluring job, is that structures have a grand purpose: to help humans live better lives by guaranteeing, within limits, their comfort and safety.

Natural laws basic to structural design are simple, and so are the behaviors of structural elements: They can develop only tension or compression. Thus it is surprisingly easy to understand the behavior of structural systems. Moreover, there are very few of them.

Stability and Equilibrium

The first requirement of any architectural structure is to stay put, not to move, or, as engineers say, to be *stable*.

One fine evening in 1960 the owners of a group of lovely houses built at the *top* of a steep slope overlooking the Pacific Ocean on the outskirts of San Francisco, upon coming home, found their houses at the *foot* of the slope, without their accustomed view. Unfortunately their abodes had been built on a clayish soil, solid when dry but slippery when wet, and the torrential rains of the last few days had transformed the slope into a greased skid.

Indeed, a structure may be unstable without breaking up. In the 1964 earthquake in Nigata, Japan, a multistoried apartment tower was turned on its side without damaging its reinforced concrete structure; but with floors as walls and walls as floors (Fig 6.6).

A structure not only must be stable—that is, not be subjected to large displacements—but, except for the tiny changes in the shapes of its parts caused by the forces acting on it, must not move at all; it must be in *equilibrium*.* This requirement implies, of course, that *each element* of a whole structure must also be in equilibrium so that the structure will stay together.

We owe to Newton's genius the laws that govern equilibrium, and they could not be simpler. Set a book on the desk, and push it left with your right hand. It will move left. Now push it right with your left hand. It will move right. Now push it simultaneously left with your right hand and right with your left hand, pushing equally hard with both hands. The book will not move; it is in equilibrium *in the left-right direction*. To make sure the book will not move in the forward-backward direction, either don't push it at all or push it equally with both hands in the forward and backward directions. How come the book does not move either up or down? It is certainly pulled *down* by gravity (and this is why it does not move up), but it is supported by the desk that must *push up* on it with a force equal to its weight. (You can check this by putting the book on a kitchen scale that will push it up with its spring or by lifting it in the palm of your hand, *feeling* how you must push up on the book to keep it in equilibrium.)

By guaranteeing equilibrium in the three *perpendicular* directions we have labeled "left-right," "forward-backward," and "up-down," have we guaranteed that the book will not move at all—that is, that it is in *total*

---

* "Equilibrium" is a Latin word meaning "equal weights" or "in balance" and shows that the Romans had a correct intuition about the requirements of equilibrium.

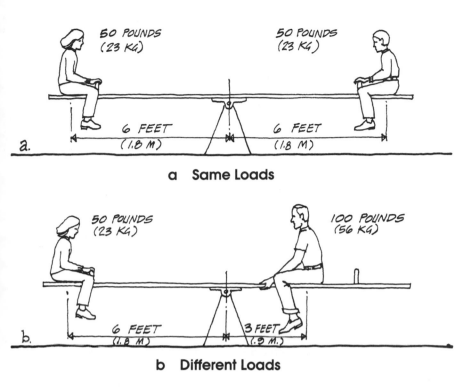

a   Same Loads

b   Different Loads

D1   Seesaw in Equilibrium

equilibrium?* Alas, no. There is still oscillation. When you enjoy a rocking chair, you are really staying on the same spot—i.e., you are in equilibrium in three directions, but you *are* still moving because the rocking chair *rocks* (oscillates), more or less like a seesaw.

The rules for preventing rocking or *rotational* motion, also established by Newton, can be demonstrated with the help of a seesaw. Go to the park and note that the seesaw is pinned to its support so that it certainly is in translational equilibrium in our three perpendicular directions but that it is still free to rotate around the pin. Let's assume that the seesaw is 12 ft. (3.6 m) long and pinned at its center (Fig. D1). If we sit two children of equal weight, say, 50 lb. (23 kg), at its ends, the seesaw does not move; it remains horizontal. But if one of the children shifts toward the pin, the seesaw rotates: The child who moved goes up, and the other goes down. We have lost *rotational equilibrium.* Now let's assume that a heavier child, say, weighing 100 lb. (46 kg), wants to get on the seesaw but keep it in

* Any three directions at right angles to each other would do to check equilibrium in *translation* (from the Latin verb *translare* meaning "to move along a line"), but this does not guarantee *total* equilibrium.

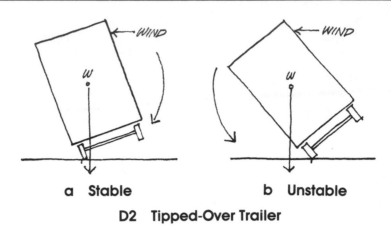

a   **Stable**   b   **Unstable**

D2   Tipped-Over Trailer

equilibrium. By trial and error he will find out that since the 50 lb. (23 kg) child sits 6 ft. (1.8 m) from the pin, he (the 100 lb. [46 kg] child) must sit 3 ft. (0.9 m) from the pin. And you do not need to be a Newton to realize that the seesaw is then in rotational equilibrium about the axis of the pin because:

50 lb. times 6 ft. = 100 lb. times 3 ft. = 300 ft.-lb.
(23 kg times 1.8 m = 46 kg times 0.9 m = 41.4 kg-m)

The horizontal distance of a vertical force from a point (and more generally the perpendicular distance of a force from a point) is called the *lever arm* of the force, and Newton's law of rotational equilibrium states that on opposite sides of the point (in our case, the pivot), the products of the forces and their perpendicular lever arms must be equal, so as to have opposite but equal tendencies to rotate an object. In engineering the product of a force times its perpendicular *lever arm* is called the *moment* of the force, and Newton's requirement for *total* rotational equilibrium is simply that the forces applied to a structure must have equal and opposite moments about three perpendicular axes.* You may call this *the seesaw law* if you like. It can be used, for example, to show why hurricane winds wreak havoc on trailer camps and trailer towns. If a strong wind hits a lightweight trailer, it tends to overturn it by pushing and rotating it onto its side along the opposite lower edge of the trailer (Fig. D2). On the other

---

* We apologize for introducing here so many words with meanings different from those you are familiar with, like "stress," "strain," "instability," and "moment," but they will come in handy in what follows.

hand, the weight tends to make it rotate back around the same edge in the opposite direction. If, as is often the case, the moment of the wind is larger than that of the trailer's own weight, the trailer overturns. Heavy buildings with a concrete or a steel structure are seldom overturned by the moment of the wind, but some high rises must be anchored into the soil to avoid such danger.

Structural Elements

Ever since humans invented agriculture and husbandry (nineteen thousand years ago) and settled in communities, an infinite variety of structures have been put together by means of only four structural elements— the bar or cable, the strut, the arch, and the beam—and their extensions in two dimensions—the tent, the wall, the dome, and the slab. Let us briefly learn how each of these elements performs its function.

A *straight* element in pure tension is called a *tension bar* or simply a *bar* and is used in many industrial buildings and roof designs (Figs. D3a and b). Bars are made out of wood or metal, mostly steel, and may be inclined at any angle. The *cable* may be *curved* under its own weight (as in telephone wires) or be straight when pulled in pure tension (as in an elevator cable). Whether made out of steel and used in our suspension bridges, or out of vegetable fiber rope, as used by the Incas in theirs, cables can develop tension only because they are so thin with respect to their length that they bend under minimum compressive loads (Fig. D3c).

A cable is a stable structure when used as a vertical hanger pulled by a single load but is unstable when hanging from two points and carrying moving or variable loads because as the loads change position or value, the cable must change shape in order to be able to carry them *only* by means of tension (Fig. D3d). Cable instability limits the use of cables in architectural structures despite the enormous strength of modern steel cables. These consist of *strands* twisted around a fiber or steel *core* and made of straight wires "hardened" to their ultimate strength (of up to 300,000 psi [2068 N / mm²]) by pulling them through *drawplates* with smaller and smaller holes (Fig. D3e). Cables are the most essential element of large structures like suspension bridges, suspended roofs, balloons, and tents.

A straight element under pure compression is called a *strut* (Fig. D3a) and is used mostly in bridges and roofs. When used vertically, a strut is called a *column*. The column has the basic function of transferring loads to earth. Marble columns have supported the roofs of Greek temples for over twenty-five centuries, and steel columns support today's tallest building, the Sears Building in Chicago (1,450 ft. [435 m] tall).

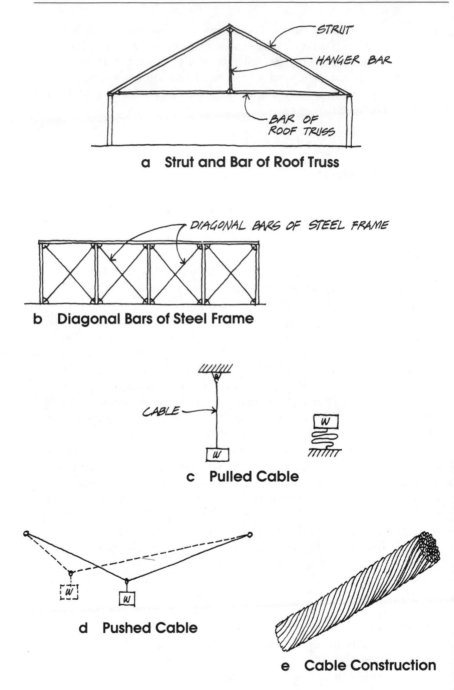

a   Strut and Bar of Roof Truss

b   Diagonal Bars of Steel Frame

c   Pulled Cable

d   Pushed Cable

e   Cable Construction

D3   Structural Elements

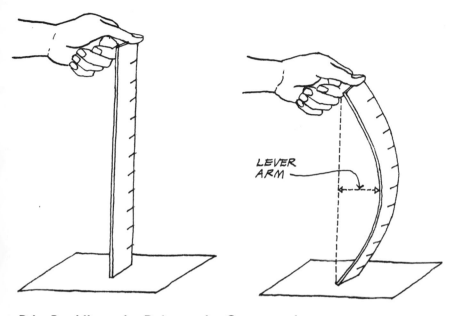

LEVER
ARM

D4   Buckling of a Ruler under Compression

It may be thought that since compression shortens and tension lengthens, the behavior of a strut is the "opposite" of that of a bar, but this is not so. The more you pull a bar, the straighter it becomes (Fig. D3c), but if you compress a strut too hard, something unexpected takes place. As first proved mathematically by the Swiss mathematician Leonhard Euler (1707–83), a *thin* strut submitted to an axial compressive load will not remain straight but bend out *suddenly*, or *buckle*, at a specific value of the compressive load, called its *critical* or *Euler value* (Fig. D4). It is worth mentioning that Euler really had found a solution "in search of a problem" because in his time columns were made out of rather weak materials and were chunky; in practice they did not buckle. Today buckling is considered a very dangerous structural phenomenon because our strong materials allow us to design thin elements in compression (columns, struts, arches, and domes) that buckle *without giving notice*.

If an ax is pushed into a piece of wood, it splits it by *pushing* out the wood fibers. By the same kind of action a *wedge-shaped* stone pushes out on two adjacent wedged pieces of stone with the force of its own weight and the loads on it. This is why an *arch* can be built with materials strong in compression by means of wedge-shaped stones, called *voussoirs;* it works in compression and stands up, provided its ends are prevented from moving outward by stones anchored in the soil, called *abutments* (Fig. D5). Each of the two halves of an arch is incapable of standing up by itself, but if a top voussoir, or *keystone,* is inserted between them, "two weaknesses become a strength," as Leonardo da Vinci (1452–1519) wrote in his Madrid Folio I, and the arch stands up. An arch buttressed by abutments is thus a curved element capable of spanning a horizontal distance developing compression along a curve. The Romans used semicircular stone arches, spanning up to 100 ft. (30 m), in the bridges of their fifty thousand miles (31,000 km) of roads from London to Baghdad. Modern arch bridges with spans of 1,300 ft. (390 m) have been built of reinforced concrete and with spans of 1,700 ft. (510 m) of steel. Since the inward push, or *thrust,* of the abutments on the arch is essential to arch action, weak abutments are the most common cause of arch bridge failures.

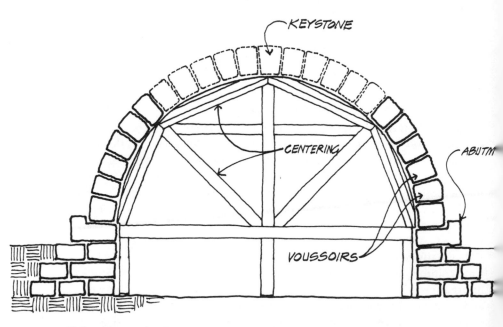

D5   Stone Arch

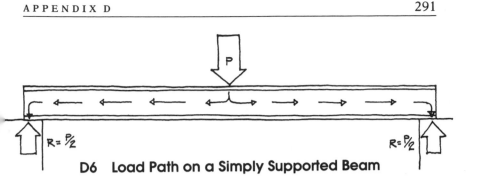

D6   Load Path on a Simply Supported Beam

A *beam* is a straight, usually horizontal element capable of transferring vertical loads to its supports *horizontally* (Fig. D6). Beam action can be demonstrated by means of a long foam rubber sponge (of the kind used to clean blackboards) on which are drawn equally spaced vertical line segments and a horizontal line halfway between its top and bottom, called the *neutral axis* of the beam (Fig. D7a). If such a beam is set on two end supports and loaded at midspan, it deflects in a curved shape, and the distance between the vertical line segments shrinks at the top and lengthens at the bottom (Figs. D7b and c). Since lengthening is *always* due to tension, and shortening to compression, the rubber model shows that a beam on two supports, or *simply supported*, develops tension below its neutral axis and compression above it; it is said to work in *bending*.

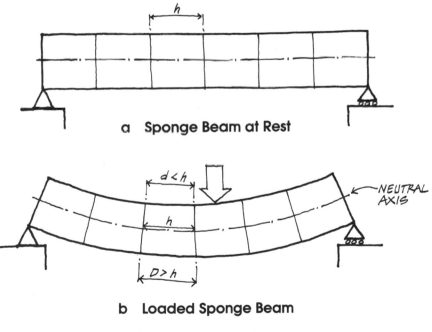

a   **Sponge Beam at Rest**

b   **Loaded Sponge Beam**

D7   Beam Curvature

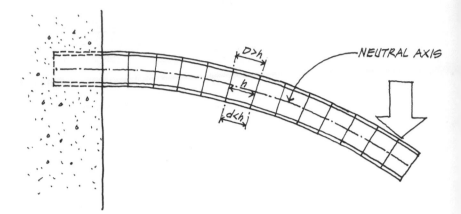

D8   Cantilever Beam

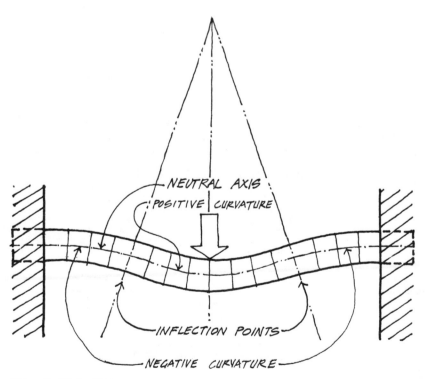

D9   Built-in Beam

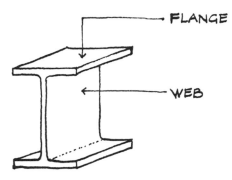

D10   I Beam

A beam built into a wall at one end and free at the other, a *cantilever* beam, develops tension above and compression below the neutral axis (Fig. D8) A beam built into walls at both ends, a *built-in* beam, develops tension and compression as shown in Fig. D9.

The beam material in the neighborhood of the neutral axis develops minor stresses because the neutral axis is neither lengthened nor shortened. Thus it is underutilized, and it is advantageous to move some of this material toward the top and bottom of the beam. This results in efficient steel beams called *I beam* or *wide-flange beams* (Fig. D10), consisting of two *flanges* connected by a thin *web*, which are used both as beams and as columns (strong in buckling) in steel-framed buildings.

The (mostly *downward*-acting) beam loads are equilibrated by the *upward*-acting *beam reactions*, according to Newton's law of translational equilibrium (Fig. D6). These opposite actions give rise to a tendency of adjoining vertical beam sections to slide or *shear*, one with respect to the other, deforming rectangular slices of the beam into parallelograms (Fig. D11). This condition, usually most strongly felt near the supports, gives rise to equal and opposite vertical forces called *shears*, which additionally tend to rotate the parallelograms. To counteract this tendency, equal and opposite horizontal shears must act on the horizontal faces of the paral-

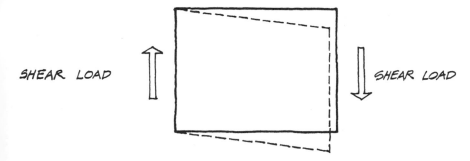

D11   Shear Load on Beam

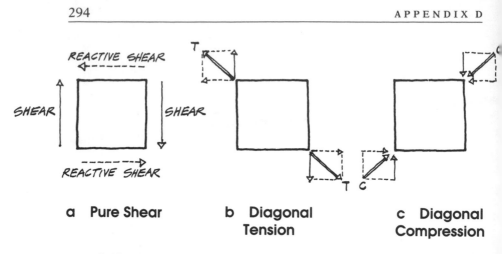

a **Pure Shear**   b **Diagonal**   c **Diagonal**
                             Tension   **Compression**

D12   Shear Equivalent to Tension and Compression

lelograms, according to Newton's moment law of rotational equilibrium
(Fig. D12a). Certain authors consider shears a third type of stress, in addition to tension and compression, but as shown in Figs. D12b and D12c, by
combining horizontal and vertical shears, one realizes that they are equivalent to tensions and compressions in opposite diagonal directions. This
equivalency is demonstrated physically by underreinforced concrete beams
that crack in tension, as shown in Fig. D13, or by the thin webs of steel
wide-flange beams that become wavy (they buckle) under compression, as
shown in Fig. D14.

D13a   Tension Cracks in Concrete Beam

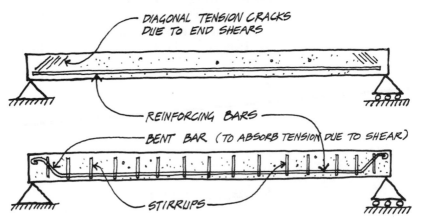

D13b   Reinforcing to Resist Shear in Concrete Beam

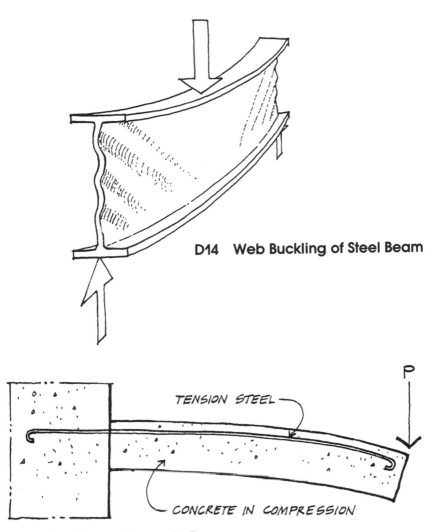

D14   Web Buckling of Steel Beam

TENSION STEEL

P

CONCRETE IN COMPRESSION

D15   Cantilever Concrete Beam

Beams can be built of materials, like steel and wood, capable of resistance to both tension and compression. Beams of reinforced concrete must have steel reinforcing bars located wherever tension may develop under load. In a cantilever concrete beam, steel must be located in areas of tension, as shown in Fig. D15, in accordance with Fig. D8.

Under loads that often change directions from upward to downward and back again, as may happen in bridges under moving traffic, beam stresses may change from tension to compression and back to tension, when the loads change the beam curvature from downward to upward, and vice versa. When these changes occur millions of times, as in machine elements, steel elements may break under low stresses because of a phenomenon called *fatigue*.

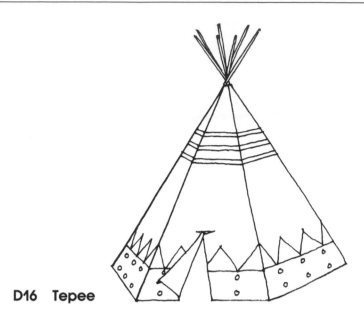

D16   Tepee

A *tent* is the tensile extension in two dimensions of the cable. Tents have been used for thousands of years by nomadic tribes (Fig. D16) and have become popular once again to cover large areas through the use of modern plastic fabrics, steel cables, and steel struts (Fig. D30).

The *wall* is the flat two-dimensional extension of the column and is used in modern construction both in small buildings to carry gravity loads and in tall buildings to resist wind and earthquake forces. They are made of bricks in the first case and of reinforced concrete in the second case.

The *dome* is the extension in three dimensions by rotation of a vertical thin arch about a vertical axis through its top. Its continuous surface may be considered to consist of a series of the rotated arches set next to each other and *glued* together. If the dome material can develop tension, as, for example, in a reinforced concrete dome in which horizontal steel *hoops* are set around the dome, the thin arches are prevented from opening up by the tensile hoops and do not need external abutments (Fig. D17a), although domes are usually also braced by a bottom tension ring (Fig. D17b). Some of the largest roofs of antiquity were built in the shape of majestic domes, the most majestic spanning 140 ft. (42 m) over the Pantheon in Rome.

The *slab* is the flat extension in two directions of the beam. Usually of reinforced concrete, a slab acts like a series of rectangular cross section beams set next to each other and glued together. Concrete slabs are used all over the world to build floors in all types of buildings (even those with steel columns and beams) and act as "two-dimensional beams" bending in one or two directions depending on how they are supported (Fig. D18).

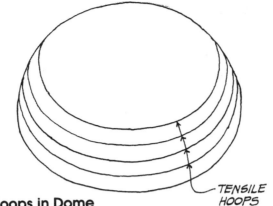

a   Tensile Hoops in Dome

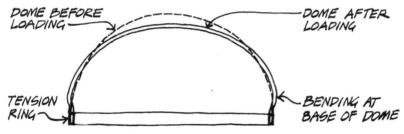

b   Tension Ring at Base of Dome

D17   Dome

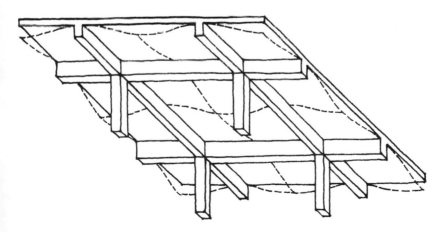

D18   Beam-Supported Floor Slab

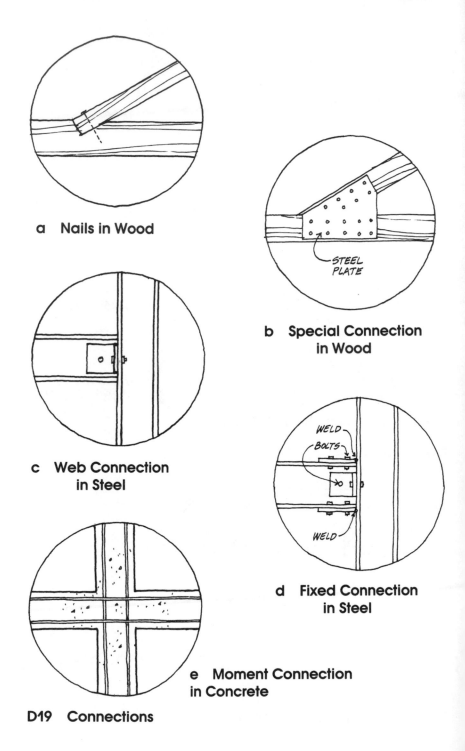

a   Nails in Wood

b   Special Connection
in Wood

STEEL
PLATE

c   Web Connection
in Steel

WELD
BOLTS

WELD

d   Fixed Connection
in Steel

e   Moment Connection
in Concrete

D19   Connections

Connections

Structural systems are put together by joining structural elements. In wood construction, connections are realized either by means of nails (Fig. D19a) or by special connectors (Fig. D19b). In steel construction, two basically different types of joints are used, depending on whether one wishes to allow or prevent the relative rotation of the elements being joined. Joints permitting the relative rotation of adjoining elements are called *hinges*, while those preventing it are said to be *rigid* or *moment-resisting* joints. In steel elements, hinges, also called *shear joints*, are usually obtained by connecting only the web of a steel beam to the supporting columns (Fig. D19c). *Moment connections* are obtained by connecting both the web and the flanges (Fig. D19d). In reinforced concrete the connections are built by pouring the concrete into forms. The continuity of the reinforcing bars across the joints of adjoining elements (Fig. D19e) and the bond between the concrete of adjoining elements make most reinforced concrete structures behave monolithically.

The behavior of structures joined by shear connections is totally different from that of structures joined by moment-resisting connections. Moment-resisting joints give the structure monolithicity and greater resistance to lateral forces, like wind and earthquake, but increase the values of stresses caused by changes in temperature and soil settlements. Shear joints weaken structural resistance to lateral loads while reducing the values of thermal and settlement stresses.

Trusses

Since tension and compression are the two basic types of stress developed by structural elements and since materials like wood and steel can resist them both, one may naturally ask: Is it possible to put together a structure in which every element develops *only* tension or compression and no bending? The answer is that such structures have been put together since early times; are used today in bridges, roofs, and wind-resisting frames; and are called *trusses*. Trusses are obtained (theoretically) by joining tension bars and compression struts by means of *hinged joints*. The variety of such structures is obviously great, but all consist of combinations of the same type of rigid element, a *hinged triangle*, the simplest rigid shape a structure can have. Fig. D20 shows two of these combinations used in truss bridges.

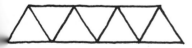

a   **Warren Truss**   b   **Pratt Truss**

D20   Truss Bridges

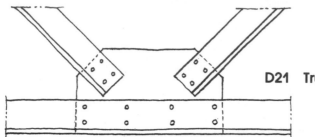

D21 Truss Joint in Steel

We must emphasize that particularly in the 1800s, bridge hinges were built by threading big bolts through holes at the end of the bars to be jointed. In order to allow free rotation of the joined elements, such joints should have been lubricated at frequent intervals, a difficult and costly operation. In practice the joints suffered from corrosion (rust) and the hinges became "frozen" after a relatively short time, thus transforming them from hinged to moment-resisting joints. Today the bars and struts of a truss are rigidly joined together and designed as *moment-resisting* (Fig. D21) rather than hinged, but in most trusses the bending or beam stresses are much smaller than the axial (tensile or compressive) stresses.

Space Frames

A commonly used structural system, one useful in roofing large areas, is the *space frame*, essentially a three-dimensional combination of parallel trusses with diagonal elements connecting the joints of the upper chords of each truss with the joints of the lower chord of the adjoining trusses (Fig. D22). Because of the inclined elements connecting the trusses, space frames act monolithically in two directions and most often roof rectangular areas. Space frames of steel are airy, light, and elegant and can economically span distances of over 300 ft. (90 m).

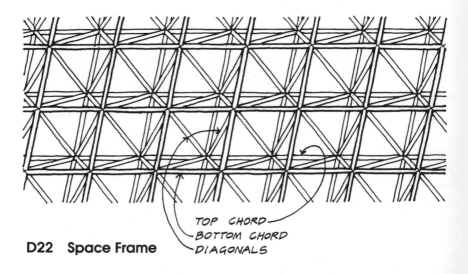

TOP CHORD
BOTTOM CHORD
DIAGONALS

D22 Space Frame

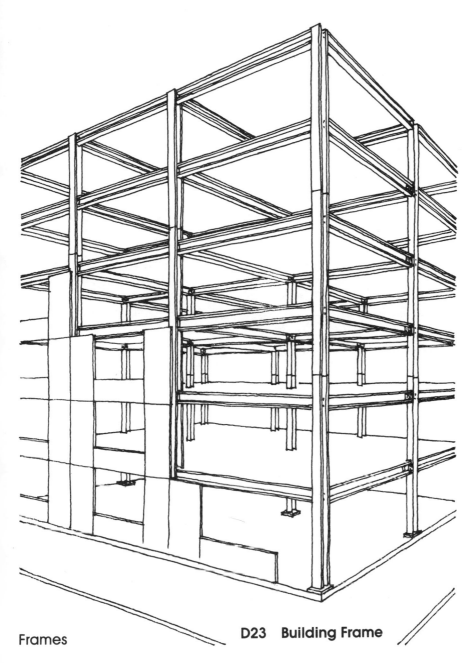

Frames **D23 Building Frame**

Most of the buildings in the world are structured today by three-dimensional *frames*, consisting of floor slabs supported by beams, beams supported by columns, columns supported by foundations, and foundations sitting on the earth. The beams and columns, usually set at the corners of a rectangular grid, are made out of steel or reinforced concrete; the floor slabs, most of the time, of reinforced concrete. Before they are enclosed by the *skin*, the frames of tall structures look like gigantic jungle gyms (Fig. D23).

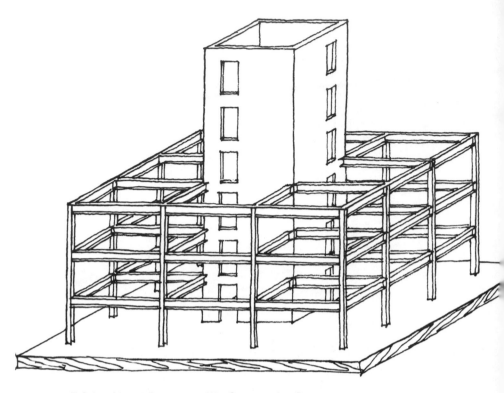

D24   Steel Frame with Concrete Core

Because moment-resisting connections are more costly than shear connections, many modern high-rise buildings have *hinged* frames carrying the gravity loads and a central *core* of reinforced concrete walls, resisting the lateral forces of wind and earthquakes (Fig. D24). The hinged frames lean on the core for support against lateral forces and would collapse like a house of cards were it not for the bending resistance of the core, which acts like a stiff, tall, thin tower.

In some buildings the resistance against lateral loads is obtained by means of tall, thin walls, called *shear walls*, set within the building or constituting part of the outer skin. The shear walls are oriented in two directions at right angle to each other so as to be capable of resisting lateral forces coming from any direction (Fig. D25).

Before the invention of artificial structural materials, rudimentary frames were built with walls of stone, bricks, or adobe—dried mud strong in compression, reinforced with straw strong in tension (Fig. 18.1)—and floors of wood planks supported by wooden beams. The weakness of the connections between the floor slabs and the walls made these buildings incapable of resisting strong lateral forces and liable to collapse during hurricanes and earthquakes. Today similar inexpensive buildings are made with concrete or brick walls (up to twenty-five stories high) and reinforced concrete slabs, with better connections between these two elements and greater safety against lateral loads. This type of construction, called *bearing wall* construction because the weight of the floors bears on the walls, gets additional resistance to lateral loads from the walls acting as shear walls.

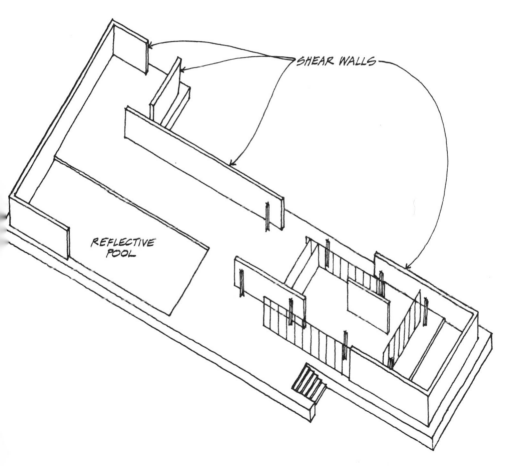

D25   Shear Walls in Mies van der Rohe's Barcelona, Spain, Pavilion

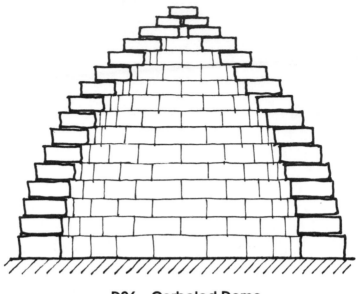

D26   Corbeled Dome

Domes

Hemispherical *corbeled domes* were built of stone since Greek antiquity to
cover circular areas of small diameter (Fig. D26). In such domes the stones
of each layer are cantilevered beyond those of the layer under it, and the
domes do not exert outward thrusts. The first monumental dome, the Roman
Pantheon, was built in 27 B.C., destroyed, and rebuilt out of concrete under
the emperor Hadrian in the second century A.D. (Fig. 3.1). It is 142 ft. (43
m) in diameter, a span surpassed only thirteen centuries later by the double high-rise dome of the Florence cathedral. The Pantheon's dome has
the shape of a half sphere with a circular opening at the top, rimmed by a
strong brick ring that acts as the keystone for all the vertical arches that
may be thought to be contained in the dome surface. What substantially
differentiates dome action from arch action is the dome's capacity of
developing hoop forces along its horizontal parallels. Under the dead load

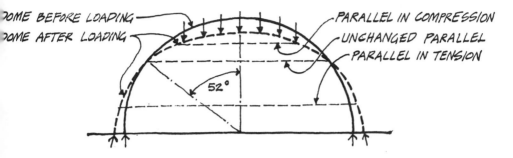

D27   Deformation of Dome by Vertical Loads

and most other distributed loads, the parallels are in compression in the upper part of the dome and in tension in its lower part (Fig. D27). Hence the imaginary arches in the dome are prevented from buckling by the hoop forces, and the dome can support larger loads over longer spans with minor deflections, provided tensile stresses can be resisted in its lower part.

Modern domes of reinforced concrete span distances of up to 700 ft. (210 m) and domes like the Superdome in New Orleans, with a curved lattice of steel beams, up to 680 ft. (204 m) (Fig. D28). Only balloon domes of plastic fabrics supported by air pressure and cable domes cover larger areas.

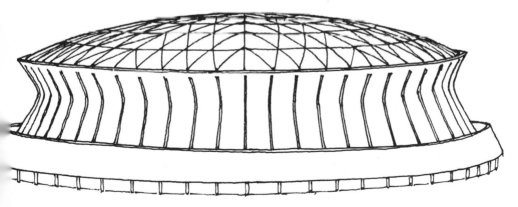

D28   Superdome, New Orleans, Louisiana

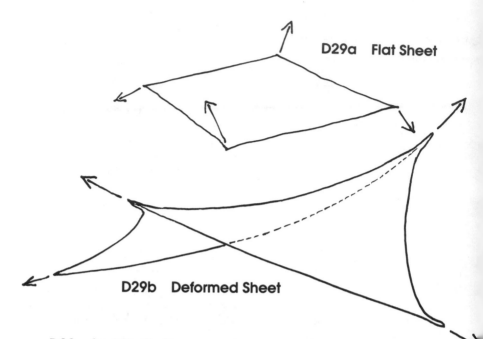

D29a Flat Sheet

D29b Deformed Sheet

D29 Saddle Surface

Other curved surfaces, like partial cylinders and *hyperbolic paraboloids* in the shape of saddles (Fig. D29), are also used as roofs over large areas. The ideal material for dome and other curved roofs, called *thin shells*, is reinforced concrete, which can develop both tension and compression and be poured over curved form work of wood or of inflated fabric balloons, first used for domes by the Italian architect Dante Bini (see p. 38). While the ratio of span to thickness in a chicken egg is 30, reinforced concrete domes have been built with ratios of up to 300, ten times *thinner* than an egg.

Tensile Structures

Since time immemorial nomadic tribes have protected themselves from the weather with *tents*, consisting of skin or fabrics given curved shapes by compressed wooden struts and tied to the ground by ropes. The development of plastic fabrics, exceptionally strong, weather-resistant, and supported over large spans by steel cables attached to steel or reinforced concrete struts, has permitted the roofing of stadiums and other open buildings by modern tents of a variety of exciting shapes. The largest area covered by a tent system to date is that of the Haj Terminal in Jidda, Saudi Arabia, 4.6 million sq. ft. or 105 acres (460,000 m²) in area and based on the design of the American engineer Fazlur Khan (Fig. D30).

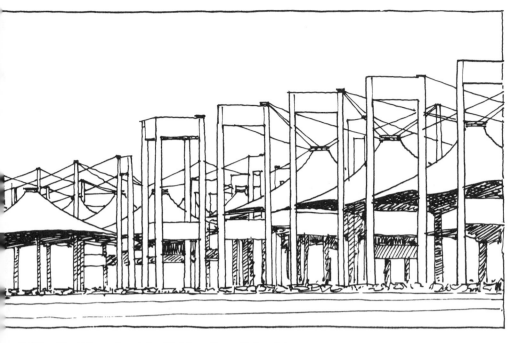

D30 Haj Terminal in Jidda, Saudi Arabia

Large roofs in the shape of inverted shallow domes or dishes, called *tensile roofs*, are built by suspending from a circular or an elliptical compressed ring of concrete, supported by columns or walls, radial steel cables meeting at a *lower* tensile steel ring at the center of the curved area. The cables support roofing of reinforced concrete slabs a few inches thick (Fig. D31). One such roof, invented by the Uruguayan engineer Lionel Viera, covers a stadium of 300 ft. (90 m) diameter in Montevideo, Uruguay, and a similar one was used to roof Madison Square Garden in New York City.

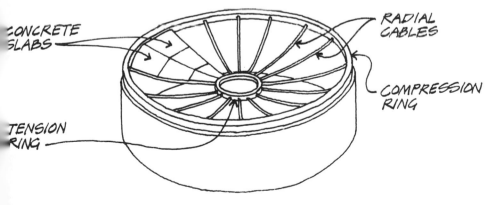

CONCRETE
SLABS

RADIAL
CABLES

COMPRESSION
RING

TENSION
RING

D31 Dished Roof of Montevideo Arena, Uruguay

To avoid having to dispose of the rain falling on the Viera roofs by pipes inside the building or by pumping it outside, tensile roofs have been built with two sets of cables, connected at the center of a circular area one to a lower and the other to an upper tension ring, separated by a vertical hub; the other ends of both sets of cables are anchored on a peripheral compression ring (Fig. D32). Such a roof, designed for the Utica, New York, Arena by Lev Zetlin, acts exactly like a bicycle wheel, with the cables as spokes and the compressed concrete ring as rim. Such extremely light roofs are particularly sensitive to high-speed wind velocities.

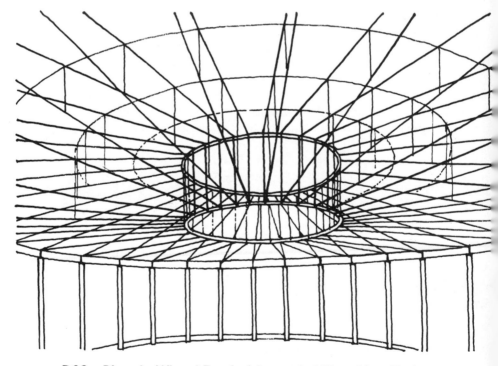

D32   Bicycle Wheel Roof of Arena in Utica, New York

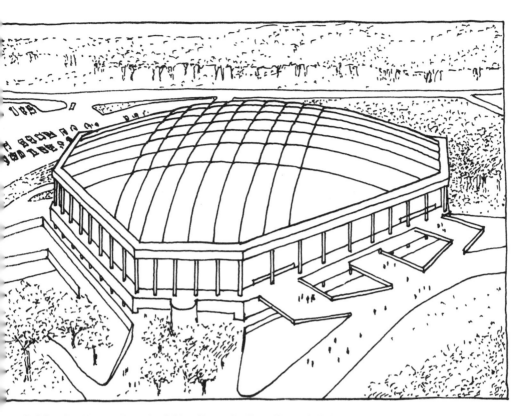

D33　Balloon Roof of Stadium in Pontiac, Michigan

Balloon roofs are used to cover both small tennis courts and the largest stadiums in the world. Proposed in Great Britain in a 1914 patent, they were first erected in Osaka, Japan, and then in the United States by the American engineer David Geiger. The largest such stadium in Pontiac, Michigan, shelters up to eighty-four thousand spectators (Fig. D33). Balloon roofs consist of large plastic membranes, stiffened by steel cables, that are curved in the shape of tensile arches by low air pressure (a few pounds per square foot) that keeps the membranes up. One may say that they are the only structures supported by columns of air. The low air pressure needed to keep the balloons up is provided by electric fans, activated by generators in case of an electric energy failure. Numerous balloon roofs have been built all over the world after the manufacturing of strong plastic membranes was perfected in the 1950s.

The few partial failures of balloon roofs that have occurred so far are due to hurricane winds, exceptional snow loads, thermal changes, and failure of the fans pumping in air to hold up the roof. The need to rely for stability on mechanical devices, like fans, and the possibility of their malfunctioning led to the development by David Geiger of *tensegrity domes*.

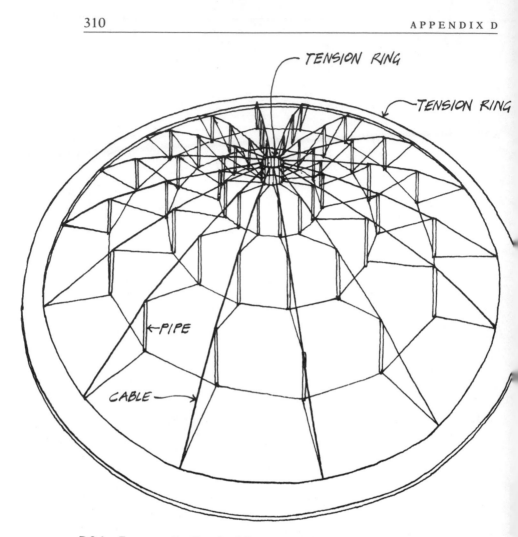

D34   Tensegrity Roof of Suncoast Dome, St. Petersburg, Florida

Tensegrity domes, patented in 1962 by Buckminster Fuller and based on the same concept as the sculptures of Kenneth Snelson, are among the few really new structural systems recently built so far (1992) to cover large areas. Only three have been built over circular stadiums (two in Korea and one in St. Petersburg, Florida), all designed by the late creative engineer David Geiger, who also designed them over noncircular areas. Tensegrity domes consist essentially of radial trusses, with upper and lower chords as well as diagonals of tensed steel cables, and pipe verticals of steel spreading the cables (Fig. D34). The joints of the lower chords are connected by tensed circular cables, and to maintain the radial trusses in a vertical position, as well as to serve as roofing for the area, a fabric cover is stretched over the top chords. The most delicate operation in the erection of tensegrity domes is the tensing of the multiple cable elements. The first elliptical dome 770 by 610 ft. (231×183 m) built with a tensegrity structure of hyperbolic paraboloid elements, designed by Matthys Levy in 1990, covers the Olympic Stadium in Atlanta, Georgia (Fig. D35).

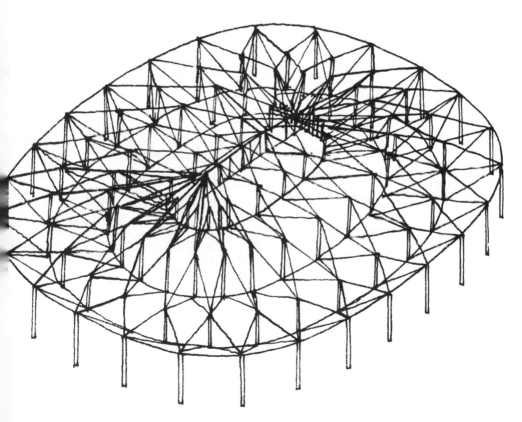

D35   Hypar Tensegrity Roof of Georgia Dome, Atlanta, Georgia

Suspension bridges, the longest bridges in the world, should not be classified as pure tensile structures because although their main elements, the cables, the *suspenders* connecting the roadway to the cables, and the inclined *stays* connecting it to the towers act in tension, the towers work in compression, and the roadway is stabilized by bending trusses, needed to counteract the instability of the cables (Fig. D36).

The longest suspension bridge span to date is that of the Akashi-Kaikyo Bridge in Japan, 6,800 ft. (2040 m) long. Cable *stayed bridges*, such as the recently completed Sunshine Skyway in Florida (Fig. D37), are elegant structures well adapted to shorter spans of up to 2,000 ft. (600 m).

D36   Suspension Bridge; George Washington Bridge, New York

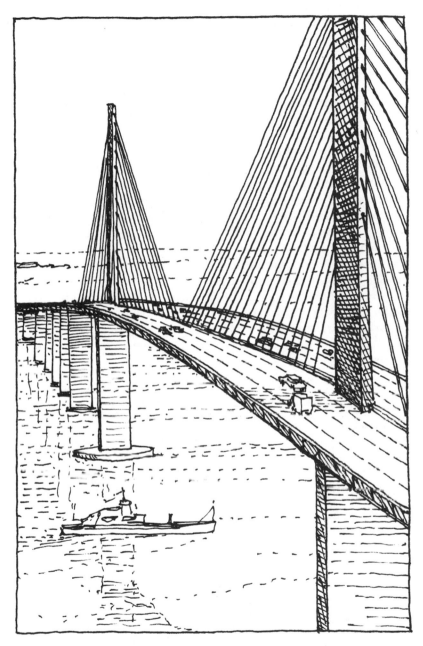

D37 Cable Stayed Bridge, Sunshine Skyway, South of St. Petersburg, Florida

Foundations

All loads on buildings, including the preponderant dead load, must be supported on earth (at least until the day we find economical ways of suspending them in midair by electromagnetic forces). If the earth's surface, as most of us subconsciously expect it to be, were evenly strong and stable, and all soils equally consistent and resistant to compression, the design and construction of *foundations* would be an easy task. Unfortunately soils have *different* and *variable* consistencies so that even it the absence of earthquakes they move.

A variety of procedures has been invented to remedy the deficient consistency of soils, which may vary on the same site even at points a few feet apart. The most common is the use of wood, concrete, or steel piles, capable of supporting a building either by developing friction against the soil or by reaching a strong layer, sometimes one hundred or more feet below the surface (Fig. 10.2). Soils can also be consolidated by vibrating them or by chemical means, as was done under the towers of the World Trade Center in New York City.

Such is the importance of determining exactly the variation of soil consistency at a site that structural engineers consult *geotechnical engineers* before building the foundations of any important building set on doubtful soil. This is particularly important when a soil's consistency varies from point to point of the same site, because *differential settlements* of the foundations may induce unacceptable high stresses in a structure, just as thermal changes do.

Index

Page numbers in *italics* refer to illustrations.